The Texas Monthly GUIDEBOOKS

WEST TEXAS
AND THE
BIG BEND

ERIC O'KEEFE

Gulf Publishing Company
Houston, Texas

D0932991

txr

Gulf Publishing Company
Book Division
P. O. Box 2608 □ Houston, Texas 77252-2608

10 9 8 7 6 5 4 3 2 1

Library of Congress Cataloging-in-Publication Data

O'Keefe, Eric.
    The Texas monthly guidebooks : West Texas and the
Big Bend / by Eric O'Keefe.
        p.   cm. — (The Texas monthly guidebooks)
    Includes index.
    ISBN 0-87719-250-2
    1. Texas, West—Guidebooks.   2. Big Bend Region
(Tex.) — Guidebooks.   I. Title.   II. Title: West Texas and
the Big Bend.   III. Series.
F384.3.038   1995
917.6404'63—dc20   94-36958
                                                        CIP

Texas Monthly is a registered trademark of Mediatex Communications Corp.

Printed in the United States of America

For Paul Forchheimer,
a friend to West Texans,
West Texas, and its many visitors.

Contents

Acknowledgments

Traveling West Texas is always a pleasure when your hosts include Frank and Martha Pollard of San Angelo, Dick and Jody Holland of Midland, the Alwans of El Paso, the Thompsons and the Morrows at Bloys Encampment, and Julia O'Keefe of Alpine. In addition to his hospitality, John Poindexter extended the use of his library along the banks of Cibolo Creek.

Representatives from cities, towns, chambers, and visitor bureaus throughout West Texas who facilitated this assignment include Nancy Perini in Abilene, Scott Owings in Amarillo, Kim Dillon in Del Rio, Tom Caradonio and Mary Lou Gallegos in El Paso, John Robert Prude in Fort Davis, Karen Piña in Lubbock, Suzy McElmurry in Midland, Linda Sweatt in Odessa, Marion Bottomley in San Angelo, and Bill Ivey in Terlingua.

Staffers at Texas Parks & Wildlife who routinely exceeded expectations include Jim Carrico and David Alloway at the Big Bend Ranch State Natural Area, Mike Pittman at Black Gap Wildlife Management Area, Rusty Sargent at Caprock Canyons State Park, Kelly Bryan at Davis Mountains State Park, Jack Kilpatric at Elephant Mountain Wildlife Management Area, Warren Watson at Hueco Tanks State Historical Park, and Mike Crevier, Bob Singleton, Georg Zappler, and Amelia Greene at TP&W Headquarters in Austin.

On a federal level, representatives who were similarly accessible and helpful include Dennis Vasquez at Big Bend National Park, Bob Crisman at Carlsbad Caverns National Park, Jerry Yarbrough at Fort Davis National Historic Site, Rich McCamant at Guadalupe Mountains National Park, Don Clapp at Muleshoe National Wildlife Refuge, and John Mangemeli at White Sands National Monument.

A few final contributors merit mention: former Governor Ann W. Richards for providing the foreword for this guidebook; Robert Rafferty, for providing the Del Rio portion of the manuscript, and B.J. Lowe, Toni King, and Katie Daily at Gulf Publishing Company for shepherding this work to press; Bill and Sarah Bourbon, for reviewing the Big Bend portion of the manuscript and sharing their many seasons in Brewster County with my readers; the Tony Freeman family, for ably guiding me to and through Palo Duro Canyon State Park; Park Kerr, for spearheading a memorable gastronomic blitz of El Paso and Juarez; Rowdy McBride, for sharing his considerable expertise on legal procedures south of the border; Richard McGee, for including yours truly among his *pro bono* clients; Joe Nick Patoski, whose many articles on West Texas served as reference and encouragement throughout this project; Victoria Thompson, for insisting that Presidio not be overlooked and for guiding me down its dusty streets; and Janie Wright, for overlooking all those overdue books at the Alpine Public Library.

Foreword

Texas is a place where we develop a love affair with the outdoors early and stay committed for a lifetime. When I think of West Texas, I think of camping and canoe trips and those precious moments when I get the chance to get down to the river and back to a place that puts the frustrations of life into perspective. From the brilliant red cliffs of Big Bend National Park to the vastness of the Panhandle Plains, traveling out West is sort of a Texas right of passage.

Yet the West Texas frontier brings to mind much more than natural beauty. It is the everlasting stage of Texas history. From the revolutionary battles of a fledgling Republic to the swirling song and dance of Indian ceremony, West Texas has served as the backdrop for the events that defined our heritage and shaped our lives. West Texas remains a place of wonder and adventure, where legends and heroes are larger than life and Texas history is as vivid as the stars in a midnight sky.

With the *Texas Monthly Guidebook to West Texas and the Big Bend* as your guide, you'll experience the beauty of West Texas in grand style. Eric O'Keefe has done an outstanding job collecting the sights and stories that make West Texas the heart and soul of God's country.

Ann W. Richards
Governor of Texas
(Jan. 1991–Jan. 1995)

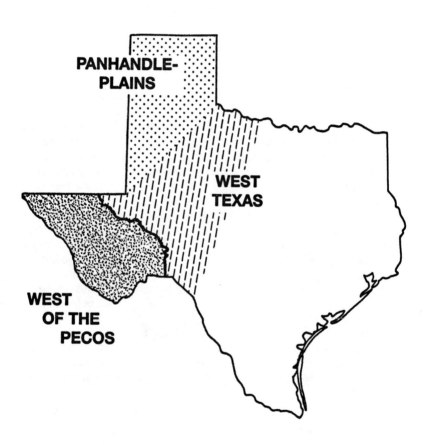

PANHANDLE-
PLAINS

WEST
TEXAS

WEST
OF THE
PECOS

Introduction

Just once during your visit to West Texas, follow these simple directions and you'll learn more about this country than any guidebook offers. One evening just after sunset, pull safely off whatever byway you're traveling and cut the engine. Step outside. It'll take a moment for your ears and eyes to adjust.

If you're like most people, you'll quickly find yourself hoping that you didn't lock yourself out of the car and praying that it starts once you get back in because most of us aren't fit to be out here on our own.

It's too big. It's too rugged. It's *that* authentic. Just a century ago, buffalo roamed, cavalry patrolled, and renegades haunted this last frontier. The few towns in West Texas, most just a decade old, were American attempts to settle country that Spain and Mexico gave up on centuries ago. Thousands of square miles north of the Río Grande remained unsettled, even unexplored, dating back to the 1500s. The best lands had been home to North America's great horsemen—the Comanche. Up in the hills, the Apache lived—high in the Guadalupe, Davis, and Chisos Mountains. The conquistadores had a name for the rest of the land: *despoblado*—unpeopled. The term described barren flats, rugged canyons, and distant mesas prone to flash floods and plagued by lethal reptiles and spiny cacti.

Tear up a few highways, board up a few towns, roll up the barbed wire, and you're back in the country Cabeza de Vaca crossed nearly five centuries ago. The millions of acres that stretch from the Río Grande to New Mexico and Oklahoma are full of national and state parks as well as ranches and farms where city lights and city ways won't take but visitors are always welcome.

LISTINGS

West Texas is comprised of a wide array of geological, biological, political, and historical regions. In the organization of this guidebook, three well-known ones are utilized: West of the Pecos, the Panhandle-Plains, and West Texas. Only one region, the Trans-Pecos, is so distinct that few will find fault with its limits: the Mexican border to the south and west, the New Mexican border to the north, and the Pecos River to the east. The second one, the Panhandle-Plains, has clear boundaries along its northern and western reaches: Oklahoma and New Mexico. Along its southern and eastern edges, however, several criteria limit its range such as the Permian Basin and the Rolling Plains. The third grouping is referred to as West Texas. A more specific term is inappropriate because this region includes portions of the Edwards Plateau, the Chihuahuan Desert, the Rolling Plains, and the Permian Basin. Point of fact: The simplest way to categorize all three groups is by their area codes—915 and 806.

Immediately following a brief introduction to each region begins an alphabetical listing of cities and the larger parks. All descriptions start with the county name, the most recent population figures, and the area code. All these major listings include some or all of the following criteria:

Tourist Services

Most are not-for-profit organizations whose mission includes assisting visitors either planning trips or just in town. Examples include the National Park Service and local chambers of commerce or visitor bureaus. When appropriate, for-profit guides or shuttle services are also included.

Guidebooks and Publications

In addition to local visitor guides, magazines and newspapers published weekly or less frequently are listed. Less likely to clutter your mailbox, they often cater to out-of-town readers.

Bird's-Eye View

Sometimes it's the top of the county courthouse (Marfa), sometimes it's a view from a prominent city park (El Paso); it might even be the top of Texas (Guadalupe Mountains National Park).

Museums

In the major metropolitan areas, count on museums to operate according to posted schedules. Many smaller historical societies don't have the personnel or funding to cover all shifts or, in some cases, even regular shifts. If you are making a special trip to a specific small-town museum, call in advance. They'll appreciate the courtesy and you'll be happy to see someone there.

Historic Places

Ruins, ranch houses, abandoned mining operations, and other historic sites are included under this heading. For a listing of Texas historical roadside markers, pick up a copy of *Why Stop?* by Betty Dooley Awbrey and Claude Dooley (Houston: Gulf Publishing Co.).

Other Points of Interest

Look for zoos, observatories, planetaria, research centers, and most state parks under the Other Points of Interest headings.

Sports and Activities

A generous helping of participant and spectator sports and activities are included. Many are free.

Colleges and Universities

Every institution of higher education surveyed welcomes visitors even if just for a guided tour. Almost all of them sponsor activities open to the public, ranging from NCAA football games featuring nationally ranked teams to rodeos, concerts, art shows, and seminars. Many have facilities covered elsewhere in the book, like museums and galleries.

Performing Arts

A partial listing includes world-class musicals like *TEXAS* (performed each summer in Palo Duro Canyon State Park), concerts, dramas, operas, and dance. The telephone number listed offers the best opportunity to nail down specific times, dates, and prices.

Shopping

The objective is to offer products or services that you either don't find at home or don't find this cheap. Many of the shops and *tien-*

das make up for their poor or downright shabby decor by offering the real McCoy: *ristras* from nearby fields or rare rock samples right off the ranch. Major shopping centers are included in case you end up far from home without one of life's many accessories.

Side Trips

You won't bump into these places in the city, town, or park being featured. They're often out of state, usually out-of-the-way, and always well worth the time.

Annual Events

Listings range from nationally known events like the Terlingua Chili Cook-Off or the John Hancock Bowl to the not so well-known. With few exceptions, all are well established and regularly held. Each event lists a contact phone number. Often it rings at the local chamber or the visitor bureau. Use it—times, dates, fees, entertainers, and venues are all subject to change. Quite often the person giving you information can also offer updates on hotels and availability.

Restaurants

The purpose of this guide is to spread the word about good places you haven't been to before, i.e., chains and franchises are not included. What is included are local favorites, restaurants of note, and any other establishment that delivered what was promised or better. Bad food, poor service, and irregular hours were the principal factors in any omissions. The pricing guide for dining is a simple one: cheap, moderate, and pricey dinner entrées:

$ = Under $7.50, $$ = Under $15, $$$ = $15+ plus tax & tip

Using this scheme, add your choice of beverage as well as taxes and tip to estimate your dinner tab (or lunch if dinner is not served).

At the end of most listings as well as in the **CLUBS AND BARS** section is a reference to the alcohol served. **"Bar"** refers to a full liquor license (which means hard liquor as well as beer and wine). The **"beer and wine"** designation excludes mixed drinks.

The following abbreviations are listed after the pricing symbol and indicate which, if any, credit cards are accepted.

AE	American Express	**MC**	Master Card
D	Discover	**V**	Visa
DC	Diners Club	**Cr**	All major credit cards accepted

Accommodations

Covering hotels, motels, bed-and-breakfasts, and youth hostels, the pricing guidelines below are for rack rates, i.e., a standard room without any discounts, and are based on double occupancy.

$ = Under $40, $$ = $40-$75, $$$ = $75-$100 $$$$, = Over $100

The exorbitant combination of city, county, state, and hotel and motel occupancy taxes (up to 14 percent) may also be listed and is added to your bill.

No discounts or surcharges are factored in. Plenty exist. Some of the more obvious ones are membership in organizations like AARP or AAA, attendance at special events, a business-related stay, and off-season rates (when occupancy levels tend to slump).

Almost all of the toll free numbers listed are to central reservations centers, not to the properties themselves. Personnel at the property are better versed in pricing changes, more likely to offer discounts, and much more accountable when you arrive (always get a name).

Wheelchair Accessibility Symbols

Most public buildings and many private ones maintain reserved parking, and an increasing number offer handicapped facilities with no more than two steps to a wide entrance. Symbols used are:

No symbol: Inconvenient or no access.
W: Wheelchair accessible but not to areas like restrooms.
W+: All major areas including restrooms are accessible.
W+ but not all areas: Accessible and with restroom facilities, however, some areas are inaccessible.

GETTING AROUND

Driving in West Texas

Call the Texas Department of Transportation's Travel Information Center at 800-452-9292 for information on road conditions, weather delays, construction schedules, even foliage updates. Its phone lines are open seven days a week from 8 a.m. to 9 p.m. Interstate speed limits have a legal ceiling of 65 mph and are usually 55 mph in urban areas. After jetting across Far West Texas, New Mexico, or Chihuahua, take care in El Paso along Interstate 10. The posted speed limit is 55 mph, and the curving concrete canyons are a notorious speed trap with numerous blind curves to shield EPPD's radar guns. On all other thoroughfares, either the posted limit or 55 mph is standard, i.e., U.S. and state highways as well as FM and RR designations (Farm-to-Market and Ranch Road, respectively).

Don't be surprised to encounter Border Patrol check points as you leave areas like El Paso, the Big Bend, and Del Rio. As a rule the most courteous of federal officers, Border Patrol agents are looking for illegal aliens and/or contraband and usually ask for a verbal declaration of citizenship and perhaps where you've been or your final destination. Compared to Customs, they'll seem like the Welcome Wagon.

Thank Lyndon Johnson for the many roadside stops you'll encounter during your drive across West Texas. As the Lone Star State's director for the National Youth Administration in the 1930s, he kept thousands of Texans at work during the Depression building the nation's largest system of roadside parks. Many have vending machines, restrooms, and phones; others are quite spartan and offer just picnic tables and a trash bin.

Going into Mexico

Keep in mind that all regulations are subject to change, particularly to and from Mexico. For Americans and Canadians, no permits or passports are required to cross over and back. Deeper forays into Mexico require a tourist card (free), which can be picked up at the port of entry or at a Mexican consulate in the United States. Border cities like Juarez are best enjoyed for short trips to sightsee and shop or to dine and dance. Most merchants and restaurateurs welcome U.S. dollars. If you do have pesos, remember that a new peso began circulating in January 1993. Drop three zeros from old pesos.

To reenter, a verbal declaration of citizenship or the presentation of an alien registration card is typically all that is required. The American government allows U.S. residents to bring back without duty items for personal or household use with a value up to $400.00 (retail) every 31 days. In addition, U.S. residents may bring from Mexico into the U.S. once every 31 days up to one quart of liquor per person 21 or older and/or one carton of cigarettes or 100 cigars (not Cuban). The U.S. Department of Agriculture has strict guidelines on bringing fruits, vegetables, plants, bulbs, seeds, and cuttings back to the States. Don't forget the State of Texas, whose Alcoholic Beverage Commission levies a minor charge on any alcohol brought back from Mexico.

West of the Pecos

Despoblado. It means unpopulated, and it describes the region west of the Pecos and north of the Río Grande as accurately in the 1990s as when conquistadores arrived in the sixteenth century. This massive territory shapes the lives of its citizens and the tours of its visitors in every respect. Here's an example: Like kids everywhere, junior high and high school students in south Brewster County take a bus to school. The only difference is out here they ride 75 miles each way. That's every morning and every afternoon. Keep distances of that sort in mind during any visit West of the Pecos. Convenient it is not. Try spectacular, historic, *despoblado.*

Governments local, national, and international have designated the arid Trans-Pecos and its mix of mountains, deserts, waterways, and caverns a treasure for all mankind. Once you arrive (an accomplishment in itself), you'll begin to see how the parts fit together: an enormous expanse of Chihuahuan Desert atop geologic formations 30 million years old, 300 million years old, even Precambrian. Rocky Mountain rivers set this country apart from neighboring terrain and distinguish it from other American deserts like the Mojave, the Sonoran, and the Great Basin. Surrounding it all, the Río Grande and the Pecos rivers (with some help from Mexico's Río Conchos) turn some of America's most inhospitable country into some of its most dramatic.

1

WEST OF THE PECOS

ALPINE

BREWSTER COUNTY SEAT   ★   5,637   ★   (915)

Alpine has been a way station for conquistadores, Comanches, and, most recently, thousands of Sul Ross State University students. Ranching and the railroad gave birth to Alpine over a century ago (1883) and are key elements of an economy that also relies on the university and tourism. One of the best ways to arrive in the Big Bend and the only stop that AMTRAK's Sunset Limited and Texas Eagle make between Del Río and El Paso is in Alpine (800-872-7245). Daily flights to Alpine out of Dallas/Fort Worth are scheduled on Lone Star Airlines (800-877-3932).

TOURIST SERVICES

ALPINE CHAMBER OF COMMERCE
West Highway 90 and Third • 915-837-2326
P.O. Box 209 • Alpine • 79831 • Monday–Saturday 9–5

Alpine serves as the crossroads and refueling stop for many visitors to the Big Bend and has numerous restaurants in addition to the area's largest bed base. Information on accommodations, attractions, and transportation services is available here.

FIRST NATIONAL BANK IN ALPINE
Intersection of Highway 118 N. and Highway 90 W. • 837-3375

This is the only ATM serving Brewster, Jeff Davis, and Presidio counties, an area 20% larger than Maryland and twice as big as Connecticut. Participating systems include Cirrus, Pulse, Plus, Discover, Service Card, and Texas Cash.

BIRD'S-EYE VIEW

SKIES OF TEXAS
FAA Certified Air Charter Service • 837-2290

If you really want a look around, all the driving in the world won't beat an hour-long charter via the Skies of Texas. Pilot George Merriman flies to Lajitas, the Big Bend, and far into Mexico in a Beechcraft Bonanza (four-seater) or a Baron (six-seater). Additional services include pick-up and/or drop-off at airports and airstrips large and small around the country and in Mexico.

MUSEUMS

MUSEUM OF THE BIG BEND
Lawrence Hall • Sul Ross State University Campus • 837-8143
Tuesday–Saturday 9–5 • Sunday 1–5 • Closed Monday
Free • W

This museum chronicles millions of years of natural history and the thousands of years that man has traversed and inhabited the Big Bend. The contributions of American Indian, Spanish, Mexican, and Anglo-American cultures are examined including numerous artifacts and mementos (many from pioneering Big Bend families). Exhibits include prehistoric dinosaur fossils, an authentic stagecoach and carriage, and the Kids Discovery Center. If you pass through during March, stop by to view the Trappings of Texas exhibit which is presented in conjunction with the Texas Cowboy Poetry Gathering.

SPORTS AND ACTIVITIES

Baseball

KOKERNOT FIELD
Loop Road • 837-8226 • (SRSU Athletic Department) • W

If you time your visit right, the Sul Ross State University Lobos or the Alpine High Fighting Bucks will be taking practice or playing a game at this, America's finest small-town baseball field. Built after World War II at a cost of $1,250,000 by local rancher and team owner Herbert Kokernot, Jr., this park has no equal. Its field compares with and often exceeds major league dimensions. The centerfield wall, known as the Green Monster, is 430 feet from the batter's box to the longest home run in the Lone Star State. The wrought iron lanterns, the manicured infield, and the red base paths, originally Georgia clay, bespeak a tradition of play that includes legendary names like Norm Cash, Jim Fregosi, Satchel Paige, and Gaylord Perry.

Hunting

For starters, consider both Black Gap Wildlife Management Area (see **BIG BEND NATIONAL PARK**) and Elephant Mountain Wildlife Management Area (see **SIDE TRIPS**). Both of these tracts are owned and administered by the State of Texas specifically for breeding and maintenance of indigenous species like del Carmen white-tailed and mule deer, javelina, quail, and dove.

Most other hunts are on private property. The Alpine Chamber of Commerce at 837-3638 has general information about prices, seasons, and availability. More specific questions can be directed to local guides like Rocky McBride at 837-3134 or Rowdy McBride at 837-2047.

Rodeo

Alpine is the home of National Intercollegiate Rodeo, and Sul Ross hosts a rodeo the first weekend in October for the Southwest Region featuring teams from Texas and New Mexico (see **ANNU-AL EVENTS**). Several others to consider are the World Championship Jackass Roping and Ranch Rodeo in Marathon, the Old Timers Rodeo in Marfa, and the Prude Ranch Rodeos in Fort Davis.

COLLEGES AND UNIVERSITIES

SUL ROSS STATE UNIVERSITY
E. Highway 90 • 837-8011 • W+ but not all areas

Celebrating its 75th Anniversary Jubilee, Sul Ross serves an enormous expanse of Far West Texas and also draws students from across Texas, nationwide, and internationally. Founded to train teachers in 1917, the teacher education program is the university's largest. Given the outstanding research opportunities throughout the Trans-Pecos, biology, geology, and the Range Animal Science program enjoy excellent reputations. With the rise of the *maquiladora* and the ongoing interest in the North American Free Trade Agreement, the SRSU MBA program has strengthened its reputation in international trade. Like Range Animal Science, the MBA has developed ties with the University of Chihuahua, and students from both universities take studies across the border.

The Theater of the Big Bend is well into its third decade, the Thouvenel String Quartet performs each semester, and concerts, performances, and pageants are regularly scheduled. The Archives of the Big Bend catalogs much of the history of the region—and the state. In intercollegiate athletics Sul Ross has had several notable campaigns including a Tangerine Bowl berth as well as an NAIA baseball crown. The greatest claim to fame has been the SRSU Rodeo Club. Much as Notre Dame and USC are farm clubs for the ranks of professional football, Sul Ross has had more than its share of alumni on the pro rodeo circuit, including El Paso native Tuff Hedeman. In addition to being a three-time world champion, Hedeman surpassed the $1 million mark in career bullriding earnings and is easily the all-time money winner in that category.

PERFORMING ARTS

THEATRE OF THE BIG BEND
Outdoor Theatre by Kokernot Lodge
Thursday–Sunday from early July to 2nd weekend in August
Admission: $3.50 (musical), $2.50 (play); $1.50 children • W
For over 25 years, this repertory company has brought Broadway to West Texas. Sponsored by the Sul Ross State University Fine Arts and Communications Department, each summer's program alternates nightly with a musical and a drama. Recent performances include *Arsenic and Old Lace, Cinderella, Gypsy, Little Shop of Horrors, Once Upon a Mattress, Pippin, Reckless,* and *Tintypes.*

SHOPPING

APACHE TRADING POST
1½ miles west of Alpine on Highway 90 • 837-5149
Monday–Saturday 9–6 • Sunday 1–6 • W
This log cabin just west of Alpine is a must for visitors to the Big Bend. Purchase topographic, geologic, and hiking maps of Big Bend National Park, Big Bend Ranch State Natural Area, and the Davis Mountain region, as well as books and videos on local history, natural sciences, and the Marfa Lights, which are viewed about 15 minutes farther west on Highway 90. Other items include rocks and crystals, Indian jewelry, rugs, and pottery.

ARTS AND CRAFTS MALL OF THE BIG BEND
101 W. Holland right across from AMTRAK • 837-7486
Monday–Saturday 10–6 • D • MC V • W
Stop in and you'll understand why some AMTRAK passengers have missed their trains while browsing. Over 100 different artists, artisans, craftsmen, and other exhibitors have booths, counters, corners, even nooks with their wares. At the high end of the price scale are antiques, sterling, china, and cowboy memorabilia. Also running into the thousands are amethysts, geodes, and quartz clusters as well as player pianos and rolltop desks. On the less expensive side are books, antique bottles, brainteasers, brands, hand-blown crystal, gourmet food products, paintings, photos, pottery, and even a year-round Christmas booth.

BIG BEND SADDLERY
E. Highway 90 • 837-5551 or 800-634-4502 • 837-7278 (fax)
Monday–Friday 8–5:30 • Saturday 8–5
The lion's share of business comes from the local ranching community. Saddles and tack along with authentic cowboy accessories like hats and jackets have kept the doors open since 1905. Specialty items range from handtooled leather goods like belts, notebooks, and checkbooks to handcrafted silver bracelets and earrings.

J. DAVIS STUDIO/PORTABLE ART
510 W. Holland • 837-3812 • Monday–Friday 10–5
Inlaid stoneware vessels with a Far West Texas influence are John Davis's forte. The advantages of stopping by his studio and seeing his wares locally are numerous: lower prices than what you'll pay at Joan Cawley's Gallery in Santa Fe, a broader selection, and the opportunity to view his wife's Portable Art. Robin Brown's hand-dyed and block-printed fashions are available nationally at the Smithsonian Museum Shop, Nordstrom's, and Jane Smith's in Aspen and Santa Fe. Just blocks from her factory, you can buy Portable Art by Robin Brown for all ages, sizes, and sexes.

OCOTILLO ENTERPRISES
205 N. Fifth St. • 837-5353 or 800-642-0427
Monday–Saturday 9–6 • Sunday 10–6
Owner Judith Brueske wrote a 50-page study on the Marfa Lights that is a bestseller locally. Pick up a copy at her shop and browse through books on area and regional travel, cultural, natural, and historical topics, westerns, books for kids, and an extensive selection of periodicals.

SIDE TRIPS

ELEPHANT MOUNTAIN WILDLIFE MANAGEMENT AREA
26 miles south of Alpine on Highway 118 • **364-2228**
Scheduled tours only; call in advance • Hunting by permit • W
The old Neville Ranch is now one of several sites in West Texas where bighorn sheep have been reintroduced by Texas Parks & Wildlife. Starting in February 1987 with ten rams and ten ewes and with a later addition of three young rams, the herd is now up in the mid-forties. The best way, the only way, to view this species at Elephant Mountain is by calling in advance and getting listed on one of the regularly scheduled tours for Texas Conservation Passport holders. The tours are two to four hours long; bring your

own supplies like binoculars, camera, and lunch. Elephant Mountain also offers hunting for dove, quail, deer, and javelina. For more information on species, permits, and seasons, contact the Austin office of Texas Parks & Wildlife toll free at 800-792-1112.

WOODWARD RANCH
Take Highway 118 18 miles south of Alpine • 364-2271
Daily 8 a.m. till dark • Full RV hookups • Camping • W
Mention the Woodward Ranch to any serious rock collector, and "red plume agate" is the response. Naturally occurring mineral formations have drawn rock hounds to Brewster County from around the world. Agates of all kinds, including red plume and flower garden, can be hunted, discovered, graded, weighed, and purchased at 50¢ a pound (if you do the hunting) or right off the shelf at the rock shop for prices that approach $200 for museum-quality pieces. Others include calcite, garnet, obsidian, selenite, and plenty of turquoise. Precious stones, including blue opal with purple fire and labradorite, are also found on the ranch. The rock shop also books tours to a variety of different mines in nearby Mexico: Boquillas and the Puerto Rico silver mine (including a candelilla wax camp tour) or San Carlos and its gorgeous agate mine featuring purple moss agate and sagenite.

Mountain bikers can ride on-road and off-road, birders can stalk beside two running streams, and picnickers have thousands of acres to choose from. RV hookups and camping sites are available.

ANNUAL EVENTS

March

TEXAS COWBOY POETRY GATHERING
Sul Ross State University • 837-8011
First full weekend of the month
This gathering was established to help preserve and promote the heritage of the American West. It kicks off Friday with open sessions, iron-bending demonstrations, and the well-attended Chuckwagon Supper complete with coffee, cobbler, and impromptu presentations. Remember, you'll be out past sundown and the mountains around you are more than a mile high, so bring a warm jacket and some blankets. Saturday features the Gear Auction at the Museum of the Big Bend and the bulk of the sessions on the Sul Ross State University campus. The annual Gathering Dance is held at the Alpine Civic Center on Saturday night. Presented simultaneously is the Trappings of Texas exhibit at the Museum of the Big Bend featuring examples of western craftsmanship.

April

GEM & MINERAL SHOW
Alpine Civic Center • 837-3301 (City Office)
Third weekend of the month • Admission and field trip fees
Every April, aficionados gather at the Alpine Civic Center to browse, buy and sell, and barter with demonstrating dealers. Mineral and fossil samples, gemstone faceting, and wire wrapping are some of the many exhibits. Field trips to private ranches and into Mexico are scheduled the weeks before and after the show and require pre-registration.

July

PAISANO BAPTIST ENCAMPMENT
10 miles west of Alpine on Highway 90 • 837-3074
Begins on fourth Sunday of July • Free (donations accepted)
Just before World War I, several prominent West Texans gathered beneath Paisano Mountain and founded this renowned Baptist encampment. Most were familiar with the non-denominational Skillman Grove Camp Meeting (see **Bloys Camp Meeting** in **FORT DAVIS**) and favored a Baptist encampment that would augment, not compete, with the older camp meeting. Since the early 1920s, Paisano has evolved into a West Texas tradition and serves as a testament to the vision of Brother L.R. Millican, a man whose considerable talents included preaching, cattle raising, and co-founding Hudspeth County. Paisano makes a point of offering something for the whole family. Newborns and infants are cared for in the nursery, a day camp is held for youngsters, and young adults enjoy a full youth program. Count on strong attendance at the daily services and at all meals, where everyone enjoys authentic cowboy cooking prepared under the direction of the 06 Ranch since 1922. Limited housing and 48 RV hookups are available.

October

SUL ROSS NATIONAL INTERCOLLEGIATE RODEO
SRSU Rodeo Arena just off East Highway 90 • 837-8200
First weekend of October • Adults $3, children $1 • W+
Alpine is the birth place of the National Intercollegiate Rodeo Association (NIRA). For half a century, the Sul Ross Rodeo Club and a large portion of the community have teamed up to host this event in the hope of getting a bid to Bozeman, Montana, and the NIRA Championships. Sul Ross has won more than its share of individual and team championships in Bozeman, and many of the participants go on to the pro rodeo circuit.

RESTAURANTS

($ = Under $7.50, $$ = Under $15, $$$ = $15+ plus tax & tip)

THE CINNABAR
207 W. Holland Ave. at the Holland Hotel • 837-3455
Monday–Saturday lunch and dinner • Sunday brunch and
dinner • $–$$ • MC V • W
Both the upbeat musical selection and the bright, new, eclectic decor signal changes at the Cinnabar. The well-rounded menu includes *quesadillas*, a cobb salad, and a spicy Caesar for starters. Entrées range from traditional—buttermilk battered chicken-fried steak, green chicken enchiladas, and 14-ounce ribeyes and T-bones—to exceptional—honey barbecued quail, grilled salmon, and a mixed fettucini with grilled vegetables and roasted tomato sauce. The wine list favors Texas selections but offers several better Californians. Cocktail and après at the well-stocked bar.

CORNER HOUSE CAFE
801 E. Ave. E • 837-7161 • Tuesday–Saturday
Breakfast and lunch • $
One of Alpine's most popular eateries. See separate listing under **BED & BREAKFASTS** below.

DOWNTOWN BROWN'S
203 N. Fifth • 837-2694 • Daily
Lunch and dinner (until midnight) • $ • MC V
The same inexpensive menu is featured for lunch and dinner. Appetizers include *quesadillas* and *nachos* (order them with the Works). The most popular entrée is the special of the day ($). Vegetarians can feast on grilled veggies while meat lovers enjoy BBQ and grilled brisket, chicken, and ribs. Plenty of sandwich choices, too. More than a dozen bottles of wine ($$), wine by the glass, and the Big Bend's largest selection of domestic and imported beers. On weekends, the beer garden features live music ranging from rhythm and blues to reggae or rock & roll. Occasional comedy gigs are booked. Beer and wine.

GALLEGO'S MEXICAN FOOD RESTAURANT
1102 E. Holland Ave. (Highway 90 E.) • 837-2416
Monday–Saturday • Lunch and dinner • $ • MC V • W
Formerly the old Green Cafe on Avenue G, Gallego's is even more popular in its present location across from the Sul Ross campus. Most locals believe that the menu has only one item—the luncheon buffet ($). Served from 11:30 to 1:30, it includes *flautas*,

tamales, chile rellenos, red cheese *enchiladas,* salad, *tostadas,* and plenty of beans and rice. Beer and *sangria.*

GOLDEN CHINA

104 N. Phelps three blocks west of SRSU on Hwy 90
837-3878 • Daily • Lunch and dinner • Sunday buffet • $–$$
MC V • W

High praise for the chef's shrimp special and the spicy pork. The drunken chicken (not on the menu) makes a great appetizer. Best bet for lunch is the inexpensive buffet. Allowances are made for patrons who aren't keen on Chinese food; several American entrées are included on the menu. No MSG. Beer and plum wine.

LITTLE MEXICO CAFE

204 W. Murphy Ave. a block south of AMTRAK station
837-2855 • Monday–Saturday • Lunch and dinner • $
Discount for seniors and college students

Several generations of Valenzualas are portrayed in photos along the walls of this one-room Mexican restaurant. The present generation, Lourdes and Sandra, run one of Alpine's most popular restaurants. Frequently ordered favorites range from the Mexican plate to the deluxe *campechanas* (best attempted as a half order). The Chaparral Burger is a meal in itself, and goes best with guacamole instead of ketchup. Beer.

LONGHORN CATTLE COMPANY

801 N. 5th (Highway 118 northbound) • 837-3692
Daily • Lunch and dinner • $–$$ • AE MC V • W

For over a decade, the Longhorn has been the Big Bend's best steak house. All the standards are ably served up—chicken-fried steak, a 12-ounce New York strip, beef or chicken fajitas, and the best salad bar in these parts. Don't overlook the catfish, the baked fish, or the marinated chicken breast. If you're in town on Sunday, more than likely you'll be enjoying the extensive and inexpensive buffet. Beer and wine.

PONDEROSA INN RESTAURANT

E. Highway 90 • 837-3321
Breakfast, lunch, and dinner • $ • W

The Ponderosa is back on track since chef Lewis Gordon returned to the kitchen. Locals are partial to the luncheon specials: fried chicken on Monday, chicken-fried steak on Wednesday, and chicken & dumplings each Thursday. An early morning visit is worthwhile just for the Breakfast Burrito. This monster is stuffed with potatoes, chorizo, beans, and cheese.

CLUBS AND BARS

THE CINNABAR

207 W. Holland Ave. • 837-3455
 See separate listing under **RESTAURANTS**. Bar.

CRYSTAL BAR

410 E. Holland Ave. • 837-2819
Daily 2–12 except Saturday night until 1 a.m.
 Right across the street from Furr's stands a nondescript build-
ing graced by a Stylle Read mural of a horseman, his mount, and
Cathedral Mountain. Inside, grimy gimme caps and gas station
signs set the tone. Stop by in the late afternoon for a game of 42
or darts with the locals. After sundown the youngsters show up.
Occasional bands and an able jukebox. Beer and wine.

DOWNTOWN BROWN'S

203 N. Fifth • 837-2694
Nightly until midnight except Saturday till 1 a.m.
 See separate listing under **RESTAURANTS**. Beer and wine.

ACCOMMODATIONS

($ = Under $40, $$ = $40–$75, $$$ = $75–$100, $$$$ = Over $100)

DAYS INN

E. Highway 90 • 837-3417 or 800 DAYS INN • $
 A single-story motel located just east of Alpine along Highway
90, the Days Inn has 40 smoking and non-smoking rooms all with
room phones (free local calls) and cable TV (HBO). The popular
Ponderosa Restaurant is right in the middle of the property by the
outdoor unheated pool. Free parking. Pets OK.

HIGHLAND INN

1404 E. Highway 90 • 837-5811 • $–$$
 This two-story motel is located directly across Highway 90
from Sul Ross State University and has 44 units including suites
and non-smoking rooms with cable TV and room phones (free
local calls). Amenities include a hotel restaurant, an outdoor
spring-fed pool, and free parking. Please register pets. AAA,
AARP, corporate, government, and military rates available.

HOLLAND HOTEL
207 W. Holland • 837-3455 • $$

A restored 1920s classic, the three-story Holland sits across from the AMTRAK station on the far side of eastbound Highway 90. Each room comes with kitchenette, cable TV, phones (free local calls), and coffee makers. Amenities include a hotel restaurant and bar—the Cinnabar—with room service. Call ahead for a courtesy shuttle to or from Alpine's airport. No pets.

Bed & Breakfasts

CORNER HOUSE CAFE and BED & BREAKFAST
801 E. Ave. E • 837-7161 • $

At the intersection of Highway 90 West and Highway 118 stands a two-story, beige brick house whose cafe and rooms are a West Texas favorite. Owner Jim Glendinning commissioned Ralph Peters, who built the house in 1937, to help renovate the property (1993), which has two bedrooms including one upstairs with a private bath. A full breakfast is served featuring a choice of muesli, fruit, oatmeal, sausage, bacon, and eggs (including omelettes). The cafe is well patronized and emphasizes wholesome, natural, and tasty food. Plenty of locals, including Sul Ross faculty and students, stop by for daily specials, coffees, and teas.

BALMORHEA

REEVES COUNTY   ★   765   ★   (915)

Situated beside a lonely stretch of Interstate 10, verdant Balmorhea is an ideal break on any trans-Texas trip. Every day, over 26 million gallons of spring water from beneath the Davis Mountains course through Balmorhea State Park and the town, and out into thousands of acres of cultivated farmland. Soak up some yourself; it's hours in almost every direction to the next stop.

POINTS OF INTEREST

BALMORHEA LAKE

Two miles south of town • **375-2308 (Balmorhea Lake Store) $2 daily per person over 14** • **W but not all areas**

If you want to swim, head to Balmorhea State Park. The lake is strictly for fishing: bigmouth, littlemouth, black and striped bass, carp, catfish, and crappie. If you haven't bought your fishing license, you'll spend another $13. RV hookups are available, and late night arrivals pay the next day.

BALMORHEA STATE PARK

Highway 17 four miles southwest of Balmorhea • **375-2370 Pool open year-round** • **Concessions available from Memorial Day through Labor Day** • **Admission: $5 per vehicle** • **W**

Balmorhea is as close to a beach as West Texas offers. The surface of the pool covers almost two acres, its depth exceeds twenty feet, and it holds over three million gallons of water. Spring fed, the water is crystal clear and refreshing: San Solomon Spring maintains a constant temperature range of 72 to 76 degrees. A concession stand opens from Memorial Day weekend through Labor Day and serves burgers, Cokes, and chips. Inner tube rentals are made on a first-come, first-served basis. Lifeguards patrol during the summer months; during the rest of the year guests sign a liability release before suiting up. Other summer extras are the twice monthly birding tours at the park and at nearby Phantom Cave Springs (call for dates and fees) and crystal-clear scuba diving.

ACCOMMODATIONS

($ = Under $40, $$ = $40–$75, $$$ = $75–$100, $$$$ = Over $100)

SAN SOLOMON COURTS

Balmorhea State Recreation Area • **375-2370** • **$–$$**

There are 18 adobe units at the State Recreation Area; all are within walking distance of the pool. Each has central heat and air and a TV, and some come with kitchenettes. Bring your own cooking utensils. Campsites are available with electricity ($10 per night) and without ($7 per night).

BIG BEND NATIONAL PARK

BREWSTER COUNTY ★ (915)

Unlike many Texas boasts, the Big Bend will never be referred to as the biggest, the tallest, or the greatest. To many, it's in the running for the most out-of-the-way. About three hundred thousand visit it each year. That's not even one-tenth the visitation at Grand Canyon National Park. Yet while a visitor to the Seventh Wonder of the World spends on average seven minutes actually looking at that great gorge, a three-day stay is the norm for Big Bend. Celebrating its golden anniversary in 1994, Big Bend stands at the intersection of desert, river, and mountain, a mix of plant and animal, heat and breeze, where northern Mexico ecosystems blend with the southern extension of the Rockies. Within the park's boundaries are found such a unique diversity of life forms that the United Nations has designated Big Bend National Park an International Biosphere Reserve. From a low point along the Río Grande of 1,800 feet (550 meters) above sea level, the elevation rises almost a mile to the top of Emory Peak, 7,800 feet (2,400 meters). Away from the river, saltcedars and reed grass give way to cactus and creosote bush. Higher up, the Chisos Mountains offer shade and protection to plants, animals, and man, and though prickly pears persist, so do maidenhair ferns and aspens.

This section of the *Texas Monthly Guidebook to West Texas and the Big Bend* is meant to get you on your way. You will find enough guidance to see many of the contrasting life forms, however, the intent is not to be a primary source but to facilitate and enhance your trip. Big Bend National Park has hundreds of sights. Some of the better known ones are listed below. Specialized guidebooks are available on all aspects of the park including birds and wildlife, plants, geology, and history. Naturalists, guides, and other specialists are available to guide you down the Río Grande, up in the Chisos Mountains, or out in Dagger Flat. Some charge a fee, others work for the National Park Service, and many just volunteer. Under **TOURIST SERVICES** are listed some of their names, and throughout this section are listed many books, publications, and other resources. Make use of them each time you're lucky enough to come back.

Access

There is no public transportation to or through the park. Alpine (about 100 miles north) offers regularly scheduled air service out of Dallas via Lone Star Airlines (800-877-3932), train service on Amtrak's Sunset Limited or Texas Eagle (800-872-7245), and bus service via Greyhound (800-231-2222). Auto and four wheel drive rentals are available at the Alpine Airport (915-837-3009). The major carriers, including American (800-433-7300), Continental (800-525-0280), Delta (800-221-1212), and Southwest (800-435-9792), come as close as Midland (200 miles) or El Paso (300 miles). Car rentals are available from the major agencies at both airports. Another option is Big Bend Shuttles (915-371-2523), which offers airport transfers from Alpine, Midland, and El Paso.

Alpine is also the closest city to the western edge of the park via Highway 118 and offers the quickest access for those driving in from the west. Travelers departing El Paso, Carlsbad Caverns, or Guadalupe Mountains national parks can detour south at Marfa on Highway 67 to enjoy *el Camino del Río* (the River Road—FM 170), which follows the Río Grande from Presidio through the Big Bend Ranch State Natural Area to Lajitas and ultimately to Big Bend National Park. Visitors driving in on Interstate 10 from Houston or San Antonio travel to Fort Stockton and then south on U.S. 385 through Marathon to the park. This route is quicker than driving west via Del Río on Highway 90 to Marathon and then south on U.S. 385 to the park's north entrance. All routes including the interstate are infested with deer. Take particular care on Highway 385 south of Fort Stockton and Highway 90 around Sanderson and Marathon.

The closest airstrips are at Lajitas (4,777-foot, paved), the Terlingua Ranch (4,800-foot, gravel) and Alpine (6,000-foot, paved). The following distances to the park are based on the shortest routes to park headquarters. Adjust drive time for speed limits, time of day through major cities, and slower night driving to avoid cattle and wildlife close to the park.

TOURIST SERVICES

Park entrance fee: $5 per vehicle or $2 per person not in car

There are several ways to enjoy the park: on your own, through the programs, facilities, employees, and volunteers of the National Park Service or the Big Bend Natural History Association, and with the services of a guide. The Big Bend Natural History Association, a non-profit organization, serves to support and augment the Park Service particularly with regard to educating visitors.

BIG BEND NATIONAL PARK

Distances From Big Bend National Park Headquarters

Starting Point	Distance miles/kilometers
Alpine	100 miles/161 kms
Big Bend Ranch (Warnock Center)	41 miles/66 kms
Big Bend Ranch (Fort Leaton)	100 miles/161 kms
Carlsbad Caverns NP	307 miles/495 kms
Dallas	559 miles/902 kms
Del Rio	253 miles/408 kms
El Paso Airport	323 miles/521 kms
Fort Stockton	127 miles/205 kms
Guadalupe Mountains NP	265 miles/428 kms
Houston	603 miles/973 kms
Lubbock	360 miles/580 kms
Midland Airport	232 miles/374 kms
San Antonio	406 miles/655 kms
Van Horn	200 miles/323 kms

Local guides include a talented assortment of individuals with varied backgrounds, educational levels, specialties, and fees. Most live west of the park in Study Butte, Terlingua, or Lajitas and are available to enhance your trip to the Big Bend area.

SUPERINTENDENT, BIG BEND NATIONAL PARK

Big Bend National Park • 79834 • 477-2251

The majority of park visitors pass through Persimmon Gap on US 385 south of Marathon. The Persimmon Gap Visitor Center serves as an appropriate introduction to the park and the National Park Service; it has the most up-to-date displays, materials, and news on campground occupancy. The National Park Service staffs this and four other ranger stations including one high in the mountains at the Chisos Basin, another down in the flats at Castolon, one at Río Grande Village, and the centrally located headquarters at Panther Junction. Look for schedules of park naturalist programs, including nature walks, workshops, and slide shows, at no charge posted throughout the park. A word of caution: The park service does not operate any emergency wrecker service. The two service stations located in the park—Panther Junction (gasoline, diesel, oil, and minor repairs) and Río Grande Village (gasoline and oil)—are private concessions. **For wrecker service in the park, call 477-2291.**

BIG BEND NATURAL HISTORY ASSOCIATION
P.O. Box 68 • Big Bend National Park • 79834 • 477-2236

A wealth of information—books, maps, and seminars—is available through this private, non-profit organization which provides visitors to Big Bend National Park a more comprehensive understanding than government funding allows. The well-informed staffers, the self-guided trail booklets, and the award-winning *Big Bend Paisano* are all examples of how the Big Bend Natural History Association makes the park more accessible to visitors. Call or write for their lengthy catalog of books, guides, audio/visual materials, and schedule of seminars. For phone orders, Mastercard and Visa are accepted and 2nd Day Air is available.

Private Guides

The following guides include former park rangers, university instructors, and naturalists with varying educational backgrounds. Though some run river trips, rafting companies are listed under the **River Trips** section of **SPORTS AND ACTIVITIES.** These guides freelance and are not employed by either the National Park Service or the Department of Parks & Wildlife. Expect to pay about $100 per day per group. Some charge more, and a few charge per person.

Bill Bourbon (371-2202) is a former park ranger who worked at Big Bend and Carlsbad Caverns national parks. He specializes in the natural history of the area including geology, botany, birding, and wildlife. He also can arrange vertebrate paleontology tours and excavations (dinosaurs, mosasaurs, and fishes). Jan Forte (371-2523) leads nature treks and can offer specialized tours including Indian pictographs. Sam Richardson (371-2548) was an art instructor in Austin before he migrated to the Big Bend. Consequently, his services as a naturalist for smaller groups and as a tour director for larger ones is enlivened with sketches, graphics, and other visuals. Barbara Standhardt (424-3422) earned a Ph.D. in paleontology and also offers nature hikes for novices and experts. Jim and Barbara Hines at Big Bend Birding Expeditions (371-2356) offer guided bird-watching tours.

GUIDEBOOKS AND PUBLICATIONS

BIG BEND: THE OFFICIAL NATIONAL PARK HANDBOOK

It's no surprise that the park bookstores have trouble keeping up with the demand for this well written and superbly photographed 128-page paperback ($5.95). It's the best general overview available on the Big Bend. Key sections include the most important aspects of the park, like biology, geology, and history, as well as lucid summaries by park experts on birding, hiking, running the river, and other activities.

THE BIG BEND PAISANO

Big Bend Natural History Association & National Park Service
P.O. Box 68 • Big Bend National Park • 79834 • 477-2236
Published four times annually, this award-winning publication is free at the park, or send four dollars for a year's subscription. Each twelve-page issue packs a load of pertinent information on park updates, trail openings and closures, notes on natural science, and Big Bend history.

BIRD'S-EYE VIEW

THE LOST MINE TRAIL

Trailhead starts at Panther Pass on the Basin Road
The views along this route are superb regardless of whether you take a 30-minute hike or go the full 4.8 miles (round trip). Park your car at the trailhead, spend a quarter for the self-guiding booklet, and hit the trail. It starts at 5,600 feet and goes up to 6,850 feet. Views of Casa Grande, the Sierra del Carmens, and Juniper and Pine canyons make it unforgettable. Best of all, the walk back is downhill (unlike the Window Trail).

HISTORIC PLACES

The streams and springs as well as the Río Grande itself nourished the plentiful game that attracted Paleo-Indians thousands of years ago to the Big Bend. It wasn't until the 16th century that the wanderings of Cabeza de Vaca brought a European through the Big Bend (1535), and it was almost two more centuries (1727) before subjugating the Native Americans emerged on Spain's political agenda. Much history has transpired since the Big Bend was ruled by Spanish and Mexican governors. Several historic structures, listed below, stand from those times.

CASTOLON

Via Ross Maxwell Drive (paved road)
Tremors from the Mexican Revolution were felt along the Río Grande, and the U.S. Cavalry responded by establishing a tiny cavalry post at Castolon. Barracks, officers' quarters, and other

structures were completed by 1920 but never used for military purposes. Today, the barracks houses a trading post and the officers' quarters serve park personnel. Remnants of the Big Bend's only cotton gin stand outside the trading post.

GLENN SPRING

Almost nine miles from the north end of Glenn Spring Rd. (improved) • Check with park personnel for road conditions and exact directions.

A steady supply of water made Glenn Spring an important stop on the Comanche Trail and for early settlers including H.E. Glenn, a Big Bend pioneer and Indian fatality. During World War I, Glenn Spring grew to its height and also made national headlines. In 1914, a candelilla wax camp began operation. Soon, American troops were posted along the Mexican border at points including Castolon and Glenn Spring. In 1916, a nine-man contingent from the Fourteenth Cavalry was attacked by Mexican renegades on May 5th (Cinco de Mayo). Three soldiers, one civilian, and an unknown number of attackers were killed. Several other attacks were staged simultaneously, and the *bandidos* were trailed into Mexico by the Eighth Cavalry.

MARISCAL MINE

Almost 20 miles from the east end of River Road • Accessible by high clearance or four-wheel-drive vehicles only • Check with park personnel for road conditions and exact directions.

The Big Bend area abounds in mineral deposits. The Presidio Mine near Shafter (on the far side of the Big Bend Ranch State Natural Area) produced more silver and gold than any mine in Texas history. Multinationals like DuPont and Dow ran fluorspar operations in Mexico just east of the park. And the Chisos Mine near Terlingua was a national leader in cinnabar (quicksilver) production. The Mariscal Mine also produced cinnabar and was the only commercial mine within the bounds of what is now the park. The mining facilities have been designated a National Register Historic District. In addition to dilapidated commercial buildings and rock houses, the most visible remnants are a Scott furnace and a concrete condenser.

OTHER POINTS OF INTEREST

HOT SPRINGS

From near the Río Grande Village, drive two miles down the improved dirt road to the Hot Springs parking lot. Park and then hike a quarter of a mile to the springs.

J. O. Langford left Alpine in 1909 looking for better health and bringing his wife and daughter, Lovie, to these hot springs. The abandoned buildings that stand today hardly convey their story, but Langford committed it to paper in *Big Bend: A Homesteader's Story* (University of Texas Press), co-authored by Fred Gipson. The springs spew over 250,000 gallons of 105-degree water daily, and you don't have to pay the dime he charged to enjoy them.

SANTA ELENA CANYON

Via Ross Maxwell Drive

If you don't have the opportunity to float the canyon (see **SPORTS AND ACTIVITIES**), be sure to either stop at the parking lot to enjoy the vista or hike the two-mile self-guided trail into the canyon's mouth. At 1,500 feet high, the sheer walls are not quickly forgotten. Neither is the silence. The first part of the hike crosses Terlingua Creek (occasionally muddy). Concrete stairs switchback into the canyon before descending to the river.

THE WINDOW

Chisos Basin • W

The Window is the sole drainage for the Basin and regularly offers unforgettable sunsets in addition to a pleasant hike which is paved and wheelchair accessible. It can be reached on foot via the Window Trail (2.8 miles). To hike down to the smooth pouroff, pick up a copy of the park service brochure on the Window Trail at the Chisos Ranger Station. Don't forget that it's all uphill on the way back. An excellent way to enjoy the view is the short Window View Trail (three-tenths of a mile round trip) which begins at the Chisos Basin Trailhead and leads to bench seats for prime sunset views.

SPORTS AND ACTIVITIES

Birding

Because of its location on the north-south flyway and its position along the dividing line between Eastern and Western species,

Big Bend offers more species of birds than any other national park. At last count, nearly 450 species had been identified including the only U.S. sightings of the Colima Warbler. More than 75 percent of these fly through, and the remaining 100 or so actually nest.

The top birding spot is the Río Grande Village with the Basin a close second. Springtime is best. To avoid the imposing mountains immediately east of the park (the Sierra del Carmens), northbound lowland and mountain birds fly along the southern flank of the del Carmens right through the Big Bend, with most continuing through. During their fall migration, many of these same birds take the opposite tack and veer east of the del Carmens, thereby avoiding the park and leaving a smaller group to pass through the park.

Driving Tours

Two excellent (and inexpensive) guides have been produced by the Big Bend Natural History Association in conjunction with the National Park Service for on-road and off-road touring: *A Road Guide to Paved and Improved Dirt Roads of Big Bend National Park* and *A Road Guide to Backcountry Dirt Roads of Big Bend National Park*. A complete list of routes, points of interest, and guidelines is provided. It's best to register at a ranger station and check your vehicle before any off-road trips. Keep in mind that the maximum driving speed in the park is 45 mph (72 kph), and that park rangers are authorized to give tickets. Point of fact: If ticketed, you either pay the fine or appear before a U.S. magistrate. There's no way out. An excellent first tour is the 30-mile Ross Maxwell Scenic Drive (paved). This route includes views of the Basin (framed by the Window) and Mule Ears Peaks and stops at historic Castolon and the Santa Elena Canyon overlook and Nature Trail.

Fishing

No fishing license or permit is required within the National Park. Over thirty species have been recorded including carp, freshwater drum, gizzard shad, and longnose gar. Catfish is most common, and a large yellow is the park record at 100 pounds.

Hiking/Backpacking/Camping

Though Texans have historically chosen New Mexico and Colorado for hiking and backpacking, a dedicated cadre has been making the ten-hour pilgrimage from Houston or Dallas to enjoy the Big Bend's 150 miles of trails and an unequalled amount of roadless terrain. Another attraction is the dramatic change in elevation: from less than 2,000 feet above sea level along the Río Grande to almost 8,000 feet on top of Emory Peak.

Only overnight trips require a backcountry permit (free of charge and available at any ranger station). Get a copy of the Big Bend Natural History Association's *Hiker's Guide to the Trails of Big Bend National Park* ($1.25). This 28-page booklet includes 36 hikes of all distances and in all parts of the park. Some require sneakers, others call for full backpacking regalia. As you survey the different choices, keep one thought in mind: *stay out of the Basin during the spring.* Spring break and Easter are perfect examples of the 80/20 Rule: Twenty percent of the park's trails get eighty percent of the hikers. Wait until fall and early winter to hike the Chisos. An additional reason is that some of the most rewarding hikes—the southeast Rim, for instance—are forbidden from February 1 until July 15 to protect nesting peregrine falcons. During the high season (springtime) get more out of your visit by choosing a less trafficked portion of the park. Spring is the best time for desert hiking: Avoid the heat and enjoy the foliage. When things slow down and you can really enjoy the Basin, drop 50¢ and pick up *Chisos Mountains Trails Map* (Big Bend Natural History Association), which lists trails, distances, campsites, and tips for travel in the mountains.

Horseback Riding

The park service will likely determine the future of a trailriding concession in 1995. Until that decision is made, only personally owned horses may be used within the park. There is plenty of fine print on bringing your own mount to the park, including cleanup, restricted paths, and sanitation. Contact park headquarters and ask for the park's *Regulations and Information Regarding Use of Personal Horses* (915-477-2251). Another option is to leave Trigger at home and make use of one of the off-park riding companies.

SPRING CREEK RANCH

17 miles north of Persimmon Gap on US 385 • **376-2260**

Fresh from 18 years at the Chisos Remuda, Lynn and Cathey Carter have set up their own outfit off US 385 between Marathon and the park's north entrance. They offer overnighters, multiday rides, and music by their son Craig's popular Spur of the Moment Band.

TURQUOISE TRAILRIDES
Study Butte • 371-2212

Just west of the park in Study Butte, these wranglers offer hourly, half-day, and full-day trips, and overnighters. The most popular excursions are to a pre-Columbian Indian camp and the combo trips in conjunction with local rafting companies.

Mountain Biking/Cycling

Off-road bikes are much more common than touring bikes in the Big Bend. More touring is done in Jeff Davis County in and around the Scenic Loop (see **FORT DAVIS**). All of the park's paved and primitive roads are open to cyclers, but none of the trails are. Possible itineraries can be studied using the two guidebooks recommended for driving tours and available from the Big Bend Natural History Association: *A Road Guide to Paved and Improved Dirt Roads of Big Bend National Park* and *A Road Guide to Backcountry Dirt Roads of Big Bend National Park*. Recommended rides include the River Road (west to east) and Old Ore Road. Good news for everyone, especially accident-prone mountain bikers, is the approval of a Rural Health Clinic affiliated with and run by the Big Bend Regional Medical Center for South Brewster County. The alternative is a painful 100-mile drive to Alpine.

River Rafting

There's a lot more to the park than piñon pines and dusty roads. A great way to escape the blazing heat as well as see an entirely different portion of the Big Bend is to ride the river. A 1978 Act of Congress designated the southern 118 miles of the national park— literally, the Big Bend—and an additional stretch downstream the **Río Grande Wild and Scenic River** (201 total miles).

The most common float trips in order of length and with approximate times are Black Rock Canyon (one-half day), Colorado Canyon (full day with lunch stop), Santa Elena Canyon (at least one and up to three days), Mariscal Canyon (at least one and up to three days), Boquillas Canyon (three days), and the Lower Canyons (a week). There are three ways to ride the river:

- bring your own equipment
- rent equipment at Study Butte, Terlingua, or Lajitas
- hire a guide service

By far the most common way to run the river is with one of the local guide services. The ones listed below are all licensed and fully insured, take care of shuttles to and from the trip, handle backcountry permitting (a requirement for all river runners), and depending on the length of the trip offer snacks, refreshments, meals, entertainment, even seminars. All offer similar packages for roughly the same cost, and each has creative programs featuring artists, entertainers, and chefs:

Big Bend River Tours (800-545-4240)

Far Flung Adventures (800-359-4138)

Outback Expeditions (800-343-1640)

If you plan on running the river on your own, still call one of the tour companies. All are outgoing and willing to tell you how the river is running and other details that only a local knows. A backcountry use permit is required for any river excursion. Backcountry use permits are free and are available at all Big Bend National Park Visitor Centers—Persimmon Gap, Panther Junction, Río Grande Village—as well as at the self-permit stations at Lajitas and the Stillwell Store en route to the Lower Canyons put-in at Heath Canyon across from La Linda. If you're going to float the Lower Canyons, Heath Canyon is the last put-in (though you can start as far upstream as you wish). The most common take-out is Dryden Crossing, 83 miles downstream. Advice gleaned from knowledgeable guides and the booklets listed below will certainly enhance any Lower Canyon trip.

Once you've secured a permit, if you have equipment, then you're off. If you need to rent rafting equipment, contact Río Grande Outfitters (371-2424) in Terlingua. Equipment runs about $15 per person per day, and the staff can help with routes and itineraries, put-ins and take-outs. Contact the Big Bend Shuttle Service (371-2523) to arrange to be dropped off, met, or maybe just to have your vehicles shuttled to your final take-out.

For serious river rats, a series of four guides to the Río Grande has been produced by the Big Bend Natural History Association in conjunction with the National Park Service. The series is entitled *River Guide to the Río Grande*. *General Information* includes regulations, safety, and ethics, and the others are for different stretches of the river: *Colorado Canyon through Santa Elena Canyon, Mariscal Canyon through Boquillas Canyon,* and *The Lower Canyons.* All are available through the Big Bend Natural History Association.

Rock Climbing

Think again. The igneous rock throughout the entire Big Bend/Davis Mountains region makes for treacherous climbing at best. The only suitable climbing in the region is at Hueco Tanks (see **EL PASO**).

SHOPPING

NATIONAL PARK CONCESSIONS

Basin• 9–5:30 or till 8:45 p.m. in summer
Castolon • 10–1 and 1:30–6
Panther Junction • 8–6
Río Grande Village • 9–6 June–Feb.; 9–8 March–May

Each store stocks essentials you were sure you brought. The Río Grande Village Store caters to the RV campground and offers a coin laundry and showers in addition to groceries and general merchandise. The Basin store has the widest selection, including meats, fruits, canned goods, and hiking supplies.

STUDY BUTTE STORE

Study Butte • 371-2231
Daily 7 a.m.–10 p.m. • Cr

For over half a century, the Study Butte Store has been the mercantile headquarters of the Big Bend. Ages ago, the store's clientele was cinnabar miners. Now the trade is locals and tourists. A sampling of the inventory includes cold beer, shotgun shells, aspirin, antacids, band aids, Dramamine, fresh produce, meats, canned vegetables and other groceries, videos, and pesticides. For motorists, there are jumper cables, gas, diesel, motor oil, transmission fluid, and fuel cans.

SIDE TRIPS

BOQUILLAS CANYON & BOQUILLAS, COAHUILA, MEXICO

Park at Boquillas Canyon parking lot for the trail to the canyon. Park at the Boquillas Crossing parking area for Boquillas, Mexico. The canyon walk is entirely on the U.S. side and gets off to a boring beginning. The rewards come twenty minutes into the hike, and the canyon itself is memorable. Budget at least 45 minutes each way. To go over to Mexico, walk to the river's edge and the ferryman will fetch you. He charges a couple of dollars per person round trip. After you cross, either walk or ride a burro to town (additional charge). Crossing over to this little *pueblito* is park tradition, and no visit to Boquillas is complete without stopping in on the Falcon family for *burritos*, a Coke, or a cold beer.

BLACK GAP WILDLIFE MANAGEMENT AREA

Take US 385 just north from Persimmon Gap and go east on FM 2627 15 miles • **376-2216**

Scheduled tours only; call in advance • **Hunting by permit only**

If you're not familiar with wildlife management areas, this is the state's largest. Unlike state parks, which are administered by the Public Lands Division of Texas Parks & Wildlife, wildlife management areas fall principally under the control of the Fisheries and Wildlife Division. Over 100,000 acres at Black Gap are devoted to developing and maintaining mule deer, javelina, dove, and quail (among others). With substantial Río Grande frontage, it's not surprising that the fishing is excellent and uncrowded. If hunting or fishing is not part of your plans, call in advance to be listed on a scheduled tour, available only to Texas Conservation Passport holders. About ten tours are offered annually. They take a full day and the longer one requires two. Bring everything with you: lunch, drinks, sunscreen, cameras, film, toilet paper. Other than hunting and fishing permits, nothing is sold at the wildlife management area, and once the tour leaves headquarters the only restroom available is the great wide open. These tours are an opportunity to visit parts of Texas that few folks have ever heard of and even less will ever see. If your timing is off and no tours are available, consider the Maravillas Canyon Tour offered at Stillwell's (see **Hallie's Hall of Fame Museum** below).

Because the primary mission of a wildlife management area is wildlife research and demonstration, this area does not offer the kinds of interpretive centers, amenities, or other facilities that visitors (nonhunters and nonfishers) might expect. Woe to those who journey out to the headquarters who have not called, are not listed for a tour, or are not registered to hunt or fish. Given the remote setting of Black Gap, this is more than a minor inconvenience. Even worse is to simply hike or camp on your own (state officials consider this trespassing). Hunting or fishing without registering or possessing an annual permit is a more serious criminal offense. For information about hunting seasons, the differing permits, and registration, as well as weather and conditions, contact Black Gap Wildlife Management Area Headquarters at 376-2216.

HALLIE'S HALL OF FAME MUSEUM

At US 385 just north of Persimmon Gap, go east on FM 2627 six miles • **Big Bend Route Box 430** • **Alpine** • **79830** • **376-2244**

Open daily • **No admission fee (donations accepted)**

Pioneer rancher Hallie Stillwell arrived in the Big Bend in 1910 via covered wagon and shows no sign of leaving. Museum architect (and great-nephew) David Busey has ably rendered Hallie's original abode, a small corner of the present museum, as well as designed a welcoming facility filled with family and historical treasures. Hallie's story, and that of her pioneering ranch family, has drawn admirers from across Texas as well as nationwide. Letters and photos from Texas governors ranging from John Connally to Ann Richards are interspersed with notes from notable Texans such as Walter Cronkite. The varied memorabilia include some of Hallie's many crowns as Queen of the Terlingua Chili Cook-Off (where she has reigned without challenge since 1967) to pistols, saddle guns, rifles, and shotguns that Hallie and her kin have used since the early days. Also on display are antique farm and ranch equipment and the remnants of a candelilla wax camp which the Stillwell Ranch operated during the drought in the early 1950s.

The Stillwell Trailer Park has complete hookups for RVs as well as camping sites, a washateria, showers, a grocery store, and gasoline. If you're interested in a first-rate tour of the Northern Chihuahuan Desert, sign up for the **Maravillas Canyon Tour** at the store. Your destination is the scenic canyon; your chariot is four-wheel drive. En route you'll view Indian pictographs, unusual geological formations, and desert flora and fauna. Bring your lunch, some binoculars, and a camera, and be prepared to get going early. The tour runs a considerate five hours, requires little hiking, and wraps up before the heat of the day. The cost is $30 per adult and $15 per child.

HEATH CANYON GUEST RANCH

Take US 385 just north from Persimmon Gap and go east on FM 2627 28 miles • **P.O. Box 386** • **Marathon** • **79842**
915-376-2235 • **$** • **Checks accepted**

Twenty-three miles past Hallie's Hall of Fame, where the pavement ends and the Gerstacker Bridge crosses the Río Grande to La Linda, the Heath Canyon Guest Ranch sits on your right (river runners note that downstream to your left on the Texas side is the put-in/take-out point at Heath Crossing). Homesteaded over a century ago by Tom Heath, the present quarters come with your choice of bunkhouse rooms at $35 per night for doubles or campsites from $3 per night per person and offer four thousand feet of frontage along the Río Grande as well as miles of border with Black Gap Wildlife Management Area. The ranch is reached by boat from the Río Grande at the Heath Crossing put-in/take-out which has vehicle access, by car from Big Bend National Park or Marathon via Highway 385 and FM 2627, and by plane on the 2,900-foot paved airstrip.

Once you make it to the ranch, the opportunities are endless. Get a Texas fishing license and hit the river. Whip out your binoculars for prime birding; this country sits right in the center of a north-south flyway. Bring your own raft or rent one from Río Grande Outfitters (371-2424) in Terlingua. Hike in and around the ranch or head over into Mexico—it's literally a stone's throw away. Bring your horse and some feed; you can use owner Andy Kurie's corral. Pets are welcome, too, as long as they're supervised. Cross the single-lane bridge—no toll or papers required—and travel a bit farther into Mexico along the dirt roads. The white *iglesia,* dedicated to Our Lady of Guadalupe and visible from the ranch's Open Sky Cafe, is a few minutes away.

Owner Kurie first came across the ranch during his tenure as a geologist at the nearby fluorspar mines, *Aguachile* and *Cuatro Palmas.* Fluorspar, once valued for its use in aerosol and freon, is in little demand these days. That's why La Linda supports only two families, the church is unused, and the town has no baseball team. As the mining slowed down, Kurie's interest didn't. When DuPont moved out, he moved in. His house stands directly across from the bunkhouse and always seems to welcome new friends.

Camping rates include water. The rate of $35 per night in the bunkhouse is single or double occupancy and the entire facility (three rooms sleeping six) is available for $100. With a full kitchen (bring your own groceries), living room, and dining room, the bunkhouse is not as primitive as it may sound, especially once the air conditioner starts to cool off the Mexican tile floors and encourages you to wrap up in a handmade bedspread. If you stay more than a single night, Andy will escort you to the mines for a first-hand tour as part of the package. When you return from Mexico, dine at the ranch's Open Sky Cafe (see **RESTAURANTS** below). You'll be able to trace much of your day's progress from the open-air seating. Catering for larger parties can be accommodated with advance notice.

SANTA ELENA, CHIHUAHUA

Located across the Río Grande from Castolon.

Located downstream from its namesake canyon, Santa Elena is a typical Mexican town of less than 300 people and comes complete with a plaza, church, and school. Originally settled as an *ejido* by a group of 30 families from Juarez (1935), droughts, crop failures, and insects ended all hopes of cotton farming, and by the late 1950s Santa Elena became the ranching community it is today. Avoid the heat of the day and cross later in the afternoon. It's not only cooler but gives you the opportunity to savor some of the fine cooking from the kitchen of María Elena Ceniceros. Ask anyone in town for directions.

ANNUAL EVENTS

October

INTERNATIONAL GOOD NEIGHBOR DAY FIESTA

Río Grande Village • 477-2251 • Free

Organized by the Interpretation Division of the Big Bend National Park, this day-long event celebrates the distinctive culture of the borderlands. Cultural demonstrations and entertainment that reflect traditional themes and customs of border folk are highlighted from noon till sundown. Colorfully costumed entertainers from both sides of the river perform traditional American and Mexican folk dances, musical programs, and authentic Mexican ballads. The Kid's Fiesta featuring *piñatas*, clowns, horseshoes, and a ring-toss is always popular. Concessionaires offer burgers, barbecue, Mexican delicacies, and cowboy cooking along with drinks and handcrafted items.

RESTAURANTS

($ = Under $7.50, $$ = Under $15, $$$ = $15+ plus tax & tip)

BIG BEND MOTOR INN RESTAURANT & STORE

Study Butte • 371-2483 • Daily • Breakfast, lunch, and dinner $-$$ • Cr

The main reason to stop here for a burger, some Mexican food, or a chicken-fried steak is because it's 80 miles to Alpine and 30 miles to Big Bend National Park. Breakfast includes eggs, hotcakes, breakfast *burritos*, and cereal. The Roadrunner Deli has a better kitchen but closes mid-afternoon.

CHISOS BASIN LODGE RESTAURANT

Daily • Breakfast, lunch, and dinner • 477-2291 • $-$$ AE MC V • W

The dining room is only open for meals and serves better-than-average burgers as well as steaks and a good chef's salad. The coffee shop stays open all day long making sandwiches, malts, milk shakes and the like.

OPEN SKY CAFE

Heath Canyon Ranch • 376-2235
Just north of Persimmon Gap, take FM 2627 all the way to the Mexican border **• Wednesday–Sunday • Dinner • $-$$ • Checks**

Mexican and border regional specialties like *asado*—lean pork served with red *chile*—and *chile verde con carne* always taste better with homemade tortillas. Any size table is welcome, but groups larger than 10 should give several days notice. Be sure to call. Special arrangements can be made for Monday or Tuesday meals as well as lunch or other catering.

ROADRUNNER DELI
By the Study Butte Store • 371-2364
Daily • Breakfast and lunch • $
Plenty of fresh coffee, hearty sandwiches, and delicious cheesecake. You can't go wrong at breakfast: good omelettes, breakfast sandwiches, muffins, and scones. Call or stop by to order a picnic basket for two or twenty. They also offer the only capuccino and espresso down south.

ACCOMMODATIONS

($ = Under $40, $$ = $40–$75, $$$ = $75–$100)

BIG BEND MOTOR INN and MISSION LODGE
Study Butte • 371-2218 or 800-848-2363 • $$
These spartan, single-story inns are located on opposite sides of the intersection of Highway 118 and FM 170 three miles north of the western entrance to Big Bend National Park. There are 76 smoking and non-smoking units including six suites. All rooms have phones and satellite TV featuring the major networks, and some come with microwaves and refrigerators. Also on the property are a restaurant, convenience store, service station, and a 75-unit RV park with full hookups. All guests have access to the outdoor unheated pool. Small pets OK.

CHISOS MOUNTAIN LODGE
Chisos Basin • Big Bend National Park • 477-2291 • $$
The only lodging in the park is located in the heart of the Chisos Mountains. There are 72 units including six stone cottages with bath and three double beds and the newer Casa Grande Lodge which has non-smoking rooms and handicap access. Amenities include the Chisos Mountain Lodge Dining Room, a gift and curio shop, and free parking. Pets are welcome, but the maid staff doesn't service rooms with pets inside. The property runs 100% occupancy during the high seasons—October to New Year's and during Spring Break.

LONGHORN RANCH MOTEL
15 miles north of the west entrance to BBNP • 371-2541 • $$
A one-story motel, the Longhorn Ranch sits alone in the desert surrounded by mountains on Highway 118 about 12 miles north

of Study Butte going towards Alpine. There are 24 smoking and non-smoking rooms, all with two double beds and satellite TV featuring the major networks. An outdoor unheated swimming pool, a pay phone, and El Matterhorn restaurant are all located on the property. El Matterhorn is open daily except Monday and has no liquor license, but it does permit patrons to bring in their own alcoholic beverages. AAA and summer rates are available.

TERLINGUA RANCH
From Study Butte, take Highway 118 17 miles north to the
ranch entrance and head east 16 miles to the property
371-2416 • $

One of the most solitary settings in America, the Terlingua Ranch is heaven for many. Head north from Study Butte or south from Alpine to the well-marked turnoff or ignore the directions and use the 4,800-foot gravel strip. Eight wooden buildings with three or four units make up the 31-room complex. None are designated smoking or non-smoking, and none have TV or telephone. The hotel restaurant serves seven days a week from 8 a.m. to 9 p.m. and has a beer and wine license. Also on the property are about 20 RV hookups (12 of which are full ones), campsites, an outdoor unheated pool, a gift shop, and a coin-operated laundry. Pets OK.

Recreational Vehicles

With the exception of Green Gulch (which leads up to the Chisos Basin) and Ross Maxwell Scenic Drive, most paved roads in Big Bend National Park are suitable for RVs. Steer clear of all dirt roads. The only campground with hookups in the park is at the Río Grande Village (477-2293). Operated on a first-come, first-served basis, there are 25 sites with electric, water, and sewer connections. Full hookup capability is required. Register at the Río Grande Village Store from 9 a.m. to 6 p.m. year-round except when they stay open longer during Spring Break. Other locations with RV hookups include the Stillwell RV Park (376-2244) by the park's east entrance (see **SIDE TRIPS**), the Big Bend Motor Inn (371-2218) in Study Butte (see above), the Terlingua Ranch (371-2416) north of Study Butte (see above), the Big Bend Travel Park (371-2250), and the Lajitas RV Park (424-3471) at Lajitas on the Río Grande (see **LAJITAS**).

BIG BEND RANCH STATE NATURAL AREA

PRESIDIO AND
BREWSTER COUNTIES   ★   (915)

At close to 300,000 acres, the State Natural Area is the largest component of the Parks & Wildlife Department of the State of Texas. Acquired in 1988 after years of negotiation, it is meant to be the showpiece of the state's park system. Because of its unique archaeologic, biologic, geologic, and historic resources, Parks & Wildlife has committed substantial funds, personnel, and time in preparation for its presentation to Texans and the world.

To protect its primitive nature, catalog its resources, and develop a master plan, access to the State Natural Area has been limited till recently. Also, policies to protect the many private parcels adjacent to or surrounded by the Natural Area had to be developed. During the past few years, offerings to the public were limited to two visitor centers, 30 miles of hiking trails, guided bus trips into the ranch, and three put-in points along the Río Grande. Most of the hiking and the guided bus trips required Texas Conservation Passports ($25) for participants 17 or older.

Long-awaited changes are now being implemented at the Big Bend Ranch. TP&W is tripling the amount of hiking trails from 30 to 100 miles. Activities other than hiking, rafting, camping, and bus tours will be permitted including mountain biking, horseback riding, car camping, ecotours, and tours by private guides in buses, vans, and four-wheel-drive vehicles. Most day trips will require the standard park entrance fee, and most overnight visits will require a Texas Conservation Passport ($25). This includes several innovative programs that Parks & Wildlife now sponsors (see **SPORTS AND ACTIVITIES** below).

One element that hasn't changed is getting to the Big Bend State Natural Area. A single thoroughfare, Farm-to-Market Road 170, offers the only access. It parallels the Río Grande from Lajitas (east) to Presidio (west) and is easy to get to from Big Bend National Park, Alpine, and Marfa. Known as *el Camino del Río* (the

River Road), it serves both visitor centers and offers unmatched views of the Río Grande, several of its canyons, the Big Bend Ranch, and Mexico. *Drive carefully.* The combination of the beautiful views and the treacherous terrain makes for trouble. Among the many hazards are plenty of loose livestock, grades in excess of 15 percent, sharp curves with limited sight distance, poor shoulders, and numerous low-water crossings.

Future Plans

Several concepts are likely to be integrated into the development of the State Natural Area in the near future. All of them are designed to preserve the State Natural Area's resources and to maintain its primitive character. Under consideration are plans to focus development on projects and locations that will serve the greatest number of visitors, i.e., along FM 170. This will mean enhanced facilities at the Warnock Center, Fort Leaton, and other high-traffic zones while minimizing impact in more primitive areas. An example of this low-impact strategy will include no construction of facilities similar to Big Bend National Park's full hookup RV campgrounds. Private campgrounds exist in both Lajitas and Presidio and will be augmented per the market.

TOURIST SERVICES

**BARTON WARNOCK ENVIRONMENTAL
EDUCATION CENTER
HCR 70, Box 375 • Lajitas • 79852 • 424-3327
Daily 8–5 • Adults $2.50, children under 12 $1.50**

The Warnock Center sits several hundred yards east of Lajitas. Named for the distinguished Sul Ross professor emeritus, it is the eastern gateway to the State Natural Area. Well staffed, its gift shop offers numerous titles on the Big Bend and Trans-Pecos as well as maps and other items. Bus tours of the Big Bend Ranch leave here and travel 136 miles round trip compared with the 74-mile tour from Fort Leaton. The additional mileage along the River Road is quite spectacular and allows for commentary, question and answers (and naps).

(text continued on page 40)

BIG BEND RANCH STATE NATURAL AREA
Management Plan for Expanded Public Use

PRESIDIO

FORT LEATON
STATE HISTORICAL
PARK

170

ENTRY GATE

Cienega Mountains   TERNEROS CREEK

PALO AMARILLO
POUR-OFF

Alamito Creek

LAS CUEVAS

TEXAS

Bofecillos Mountains   The Solitario

REDFORD

Fresno Canyon

Rio Grande

170   THREE DIKE HILL
WAYSIDE

ARENOSA
group camping

TAPADO CANYON

HOODOOS
primitive camping

COLORADO
CANYON
primitive camping

CHIHUAHUA

ROADS
El camino del Rio / FM 170
Casa Piedra County Road
BBRSNA Interior Road

TRAILS
Mountain Bike
Equestrian
Hiking only

PERMITTED ROADS AND TRAILS
Permitted 4 Wheel Drive
4 Wheel Drive Guided Tour
Equestrian Guided Tour

Road/Trail Mileage

⊞   Towns
◆   Backcountry Access
●   River Access
▢   Equestrian Access
▲   Wayside Exhibit, Guided Tour
     or Overlook
★   Visitor Contact Points

Bus tours originate at both Lajitas
and Fort Leaton with stops at
Las Cuevas, Sauceda and
Solitario / Fresno Canyon overlook

SOLITARIO / FRESNO CANYON OVERLOOK

SAUCEDA

TRES PAPALOTES FIELD RESEARCH STATION

GUALE MESA OVER-LOOK

MEXICANA POUR-OFF

MADRID FALLS

Rancherias Trail

WEST RANCHERIAS
CLOSED CANYON
EAST RANCHERIAS

SOLITARIO-CONTRABANDO CANYON WAYSIDE

170

PANTHER CANYON
primitive camping

MADERA CANYON
primitive camping

GRASSY BANKS
primitive camping

CONTRABANDO CANYON
movie house

170

WARNOCK EDUCATION CENTER

LAJITAS

1 2 3 4 5
MILES

200 FOOT
CONTOUR INTERVALS

Map courtesy of Texas Parks & Wildlife Department.

(text continued from page 37)

FORT LEATON STATE HISTORICAL PARK

Three miles east of Presidio along FM 170 • **229-3613**
Park Superintendent • P.O. Box 1180 • Presidio • 79845
Daily 8–4:30 • Adults $2, children $1 • W

Fort Leaton serves as the western gateway to the Big Bend Ranch State Natural Area and stands almost 60 miles west of the Warnock Center along FM 170. A complete description of its history is included under the **PRESIDIO & OJINAGA** listing. Tours of Fort Leaton include 25 of the fort's 40 rooms with exhibits and programs detailing the history of the Spanish, Mexican, Texan, and American colonizers.

OTHER POINTS OF INTEREST

SOLITARIO

This classic geologic dome was uplifted by an intrusive igneous body and runs about eight miles east to west and nine miles north to south. The sides or rim of the Solitario are composed of Cretaceous limestone and have been tilted to a near-vertical position. For decades, geologists thought that the Paleozoic formations at the center of the Solitario were exposed by erosion, but the most recent studies indicate that the Solitario actually erupted, taking off the dome's crest. This makes it one of the world's few laccocalderas. Contact the Warnock Center or Fort Leaton for information on tours and access.

SPORTS AND ACTIVITIES

Bus Tours

The most popular way to see most of the park is via one of the two bus tours operated by Texas Parks & Wildlife. Tours depart the first and third Saturdays of the month on air-conditioned, battle-tested buses each complete with restroom. Reservations and a deposit are required. Contact TP&W central reservations at 512-389-8900. A discount is available to Texas Conservation Passport holders. Each tour begins at 8:00 a.m.; show up early to check in and take care of any loose ends (like paying). Departures alternate from the Warnock Center (424-3327) and Fort Leaton (229-3613). Both are excellent tours. The one that departs Fort Leaton ventures farther into the interior of the State Natural Area and includes a view of the Solitario. The one that departs the Warnock Center goes into the heart of the Big Bend Ranch as far as the park headquarters but spends more time on the River Road, rated by *National Geographic* as perhaps the prettiest drive in America (June 1985). All trips are guided, have plenty of rest breaks including iced beverages, and include lunch at Sauceda, the ranch headquarters.

Fishing

Fishing along the Río Grande is allowed. Unlike the national park, however, a fishing license and a park permit are required. Trotline and jug fishing are discouraged.

Hiking and Camping

The expansion of the State Natural Area's trail system is underway. As new trails are developed they will be incorporated into future editions of the *Big Bend Ranch State Natural Area Trail Guide*, produced by the Texas Parks & Wildlife Department and available at the Warnock Center or Fort Leaton. Used in conjunction with a separately available trail map and a compass, the guide is easily the best resource for the trails and includes suggested itineraries. It also has a complete list of guidelines about water usage, critical management zones, private property, and other topics. *Portions of all trails include areas subject to flash flooding.* None of the routes are improved or marked with signs, only rock cairns. Routes can vary from old wagon roads to modern jeep trails and animal paths—wild as well as livestock.

The Closed Canyon Trail (1.4 miles round trip) is a good trek for families with older kids. It follows a narrow, shaded drainage carved through Santana tuff to a series of impassable pour-offs overlooking the Río Grande. With its steep walls, smooth sides and sandy bottom, it's an ideal escape from the heat of the day. The entire trail is in the bottom of this water-worn canyon and *highly susceptible to flash floods.* So, too, is the Rancherias Canyon Trail (9.6 miles round trip). A full day's hike, the route passes remnants of ancient lava flows 20 and 30 million years old and terminates at the fourth highest waterfall in Texas, Rancherías Falls. The Rancherías Loop Trail (19 miles from trailhead to trailhead) makes an ideal three-day hike with two nights out on the trail. It can be accessed via two trailheads, the East and West Rancherías Trailheads, and travels through three different canyon systems. It is best enjoyed beginning at the east trailhead and hiking through to the west one. About three miles along FM 170 separates both trailheads, so try to set up a shuttle or ride before you hit the trail. Numerous arroyos and canyon bottoms form major portions of the trail. Like the other two trails, *beware of flash flooding.* Both suggested camps are convenient to natural water sources, but bring your own and don't get caught dry. Budget about a gallon a day per person (one gallon weighs approximately eight pounds), and be prepared to purify any water you gather.

River Rafting

Refer to **River Trips** under **BIG BEND NATIONAL PARK** for a complete listing of guide services, trips, and suggestions. As in Big Bend National Park, you can run the river on your own or with a commercial service. Within the State Natural Area, access is offered at seven points. In order, heading west from the Warnock Center, they are Contrabando Canyon, Grassy Banks, Madera Canyon, Panther Canyon, Colorado Canyon, Arenosa, and the Hoodoos. Each of these is right off FM 170 and is marked on maps available at the Big Bend Ranch State Natural Area. Some have primitive campsites with self-composting outhouses, but none offer potable water, electricity, or much shade.

Seminars

Seminars at the Big Bend Ranch typically last two or three days, cost around two to three hundred dollars, and range from desert survival to rock art to useful plants of the Chihuahuan Desert. Administered at the Big Bend Ranch, they have been led by eminent botanist Barton Warnock (for whom the Warnock Center is named); Bob Mallouf, the Texas state archaeologist; David Alloway, interpretative naturalist for Texas Parks & Wildlife; and Kelly Bryan, Texas Parks & Wildlife ornithologist and superintendent of Davis Mountains State Park. Call 915-424-3327 or fax 915-424-3404 for more information. Keep in mind that Texas Conservation Passport holders enjoy discounted seminar rates.

SIDE TRIPS

COPPER CANYON, MEXICO

See separate listing under **PRESIDIO & OJINAGA.**

RESTAURANTS and ACCOMMODATIONS

See separate listings under **BIG BEND NATIONAL PARK, LAJITAS, PRESIDIO & OJINAGA,** and **TERLINGUA.**

CARLSBAD CAVERNS NATIONAL PARK

EDDY COUNTY, NEW MEXICO
MOUNTAIN TIME   ★   (505)

Nearly a century ago, a lone cowboy became intrigued by the nightly flight of hundreds of thousands of Mexican free-tail bats from the mouth of the caverns. Jim White's curiosity led to years of pioneering exploration and ultimately the designation of the caverns as a national monument (1923) and a national park (1930). Carlsbad Caverns National Park continues to be a fascinating subterranean wilderness with more than 80 caves in the park. Recent discoveries within the Caverns include the Bifrost Room and Storm Cloud Chamber (1982), the Rim Room (1984), and Chocolate High (1992). In 1986, a collapsed opening in Lechugilla Cave was cleared, and exploration began on what has become the deepest cave in America (1,593 feet) and the eighth longest cave in the world (68 miles).

TOURIST SERVICES

SUPERINTENDENT
CARLSBAD CAVERNS NATIONAL PARK
3225 National Parks Highway • Carlsbad, NM • 88220
505-785-2232 or 505-785-2107 (recorded info line)
8–5:30 (Mountain Time) • Closed Christmas Day
The most visible aspect of the National Park Service is the Visitor Center through which all cavern tours depart. Located seven miles west of White's City, New Mexico, and 27 miles southwest of Carlsbad, New Mexico, it includes kennels for pets, a gift shop with an extensive collection of books and other cavern items, and a restaurant.

GUIDEBOOKS AND PUBLICATIONS

CARLSBAD CAVERNS NATIONAL PARK:
SILENT CHAMBERS, TIMELESS BEAUTY
By John Barnett
Carlsbad Caverns/Guadalupe Mountains Association • $3.00
   This 32-page magazine-style piece includes simplified explana-
tions of cavern formation and superb photos of the caverns and
the surrounding Chihuahuan Desert.

STORIES FROM STONES:
THE GEOLOGY OF THE GUADALUPE MOUNTAINS
By David H. Jagnow and Rebecca Rohwer Jagnow
Carlsbad Caverns/Guadalupe Mountains Association
   Guadalupe Mountains and Carlsbad Caverns national parks
are the best known natural legacies of the Permian era. However,
many know the Permian name because of the enormous oil fields
that initially formed during this period. This booklet provides a
detailed explanation of the unique geological conditions that led
to the formation of the Permian reef and a better understanding
of modern geography as well as subsurface mechanics. Available
at both parks and through the Carlsbad Caverns/Guadalupe
Mountains Association at 505-785-2318.

SPORTS AND ACTIVITIES

Cavern Tours

Daily except Christmas • Admission: Adults $5, under 16 $3
   The National Park Service has done a great job of facilitating
access to the caverns. Visitors can either walk from the Visitor
Center to the cave's natural entrance and descend by foot (the
Natural Entrance Tour) or take an elevator to a point 750 feet
below the Visitor Center and begin in the heart of the caverns (the
Big Room Tour). A third option is the King's Palace Tour, which is
guided. All three tours are about a mile long and take roughly an
hour. All tours exit via elevator. The paths, including the walk
into the cave, are on paved trails that are well lighted. Plenty of
handrails and rock benches are available for safety and comfort.
Park rangers are available to answer questions, offer explanations, and render assistance. Wear a light jacket or sweater; the
caverns maintain a temperature of 56 degrees all year long.

It would be a catastrophic mistake not to spend 50¢ to rent a hand-held radio at the Visitor Center. Shaped like a wand, it picks up low-level transmissions at different points in the cave and broadcasts explanations of the cave's history and exploration, the geology of the caverns, and the nature of the different formations. These radios are available for adults in English or Spanish and for children.

Cavern Hours

	Summer	Non-Summer
Visitor Center Opens	8:00 a.m.	8:00 a.m.
Visitor Center Closes	7:00 p.m.	5:30 p.m.
Natural Entrance Route Opens	8:30 a.m.	8:30 a.m.
Natural Entrance Route Closes	3:30 p.m.	2:00 p.m.
Big Room Route Opens	8:30 a.m.	8:30 a.m.
Big Room Route Closes	5:00 p.m.	3:30 p.m.
King's Palace Guided Tours	Call Park	See below
Last King's Palace Guided Tour	Call Park	3:00 p.m.
Last Elevator to Surface	6:30 p.m.	5:00 p.m.
Bat Flight	Call Park	Go to Mexico

King's Palace Guided tours are scheduled four times daily during the summer months: 9:00 a.m., 11:00 a.m., 1:00 p.m., and 3:00 p.m.

Slaughter Canyon Cave or New Cave Tours

Admission: Adults $6, under 16 $3, under 6 not allowed

Slaughter Canyon Cave is new in the sense that it was discovered after the Caverns in 1937. Tours are available by reservation only (505-785-2232) and are offered daily from June through August and on weekends the rest of the year. All tours are guided, and several requirements are made of the participants, including one flashlight per person, good walking shoes or hiking boots, drinking water, and transportation to the cave parking lot at the mouth of Slaughter Canyon. A much more strenuous venture than the Caverns, only the physically fit should consider the 1.25-mile tour which lasts about 2½ hours. The most taxing part of the entire trip is the thirty-minute hike from the parking lot to the cave which is where your guide awaits you, the tour begins, and actual tour distances are calculated. All tour times are scheduled from the cave entrance and not the parking lot. To reach the parking lot at the mouth of Slaughter Canyon, drive five miles south-west of White's City on US 62-180 (towards Texas and Guadalupe Mountains National Park). The Slaughter Canyon turnoff to the west is clearly marked. Eleven miles down this road is the park-ing lot. Once you leave your vehicle, budget 3½ to 4 hours for the hike up, the tour, and the hike back. Cave temperature is 62 degrees, humidity is 90 percent, and photography is permitted (no tripods).

Hiking and Camping

About 750,000 people visit the park, and almost all go not a sin-gle step beyond the Visitor Center and the Caverns themselves. The 30 miles of primitive backcountry trails and 33,125 acres of designated wilderness that lie west of the Visitor Center are com-pletely overlooked. They are rugged, formidable, even unforgiv-ing, and never crowded. A backcountry permit is required (no charge), and a topographic map is essential. Both are available at the Visitor Center. Bring plenty of water—none is available on the trail. Because these trails are completely ignored, you'll find park personnel more than willing to suggest itineraries and to discuss possible hazards like summer storms, winter lows, flash floods, and the parched conditions.

Scenic Drive

At just under ten miles, the Walnut Canyon Desert Drive offers ample opportunity to enjoy a backcountry excursion including views of Rattlesnake Canyon and upper Walnut Canyon. The gravel, one-way loop is fine for passenger cars but not recom-mended for trailers or motor homes. Stop by the Visitor Center for a self-guiding booklet. The drive begins just west of the Visi-tor Center.

OTHER POINTS OF INTEREST

BAT FLIGHT
Outdoor Amphitheater at the cave's natural entrance behind the Visitor Center • Late May to October just before sunset

During the warmer half of the year, sundown signals feeding time for thousands of Mexican free-tail bats. This nocturnal pro-cession led to the discovery of the caverns by Jim White in 1901. The bats winter in Mexico and summer at the caverns. About 30 minutes before they emerge, a park ranger makes a brief presentation on the bats including their prey, their migratory habits, and their highly developed sonar system known as echolocation. *Bats of Carlsbad Caverns National Park* is a brief and colorful 32-page guide available at the gift shop.

SIDE TRIPS

LIVING DESERT STATE PARK
P.O. Box 100 • Carlsbad, NM • 88220 • 505-887-5516
22 miles north of White's City and 2 miles north of Carlsbad via US 285 • **Daily except major holidays • Admission $3**

Atop the Ocotillo Hills, Living Desert is a 1,120-acre botanical and zoological collection featuring native Chihuahuan Desert species. The Visitor Center offers detailed explanations of species and the ecosystem, and the Desert Arboretum houses more than 300 different succulents from around the world as well as the desert southwest. The 1.3-mile self-guided trail takes about 90 minutes.

RESTAURANTS & ACCOMMODATIONS

($ = Under $40, $$ = $40–$75, $$$ = $75–$100)
Room Tax 11%

After touring the Caverns, everyone assumes that White's City was named for or started by Cavern discoverer Jim White. It actually was founded in 1927 by a friend of Jim's, C.L. White, who forecasted the park's popularity. By 1936, White had developed a 13-unit lodge, ran a Texaco station, and was the lone resident. Fifty years later, the Texaco station is still in place as are three lodges with a combined 132 rooms as well as two restaurants, several gift shops, a museum, and year-round population of 27. The easiest way to get to White's City (and the Caverns) is to land at the seven-tenths of a mile improved strip outside White's City. White's City sits astride the entrance to the National Park; you literally have to drive through it to go the last seven miles to the Caverns. Reasons to stay here include the close proximity to the caverns, the variety of facilities and range of prices (from campsites to RV hookups to rooms), and your alternatives. Carlsbad, New Mexico, is half an hour north and Van Horn, Texas, is more than an hour and a half south. Gas, gift shops, and groceries are all within walking distance of the town's several properties.

BEST WESTERN CAVERN INN
White's City • 800-CAVERNS • $$–$$$

This two-story inn has 63 smoking and non-smoking rooms with satellite TV (HBO), phones with free local calls to Carlsbad, and thermocuzzis in some. There are two restaurants: Fast Jacks, and the Velvet Garter Restaurant and Saloon. There are also two pools—an Olympic-sized unheated one and a smaller heated one, two hot tubs, an arcade on the boardwalk, a tennis court and a basketball court, several gift shops, a laundry room, and plenty of free parking. The melodrama theater runs from May through September and by special appointment. A shuttle runs to the Caverns (fee). No pets. AAA, AARP, and military rates offered.

BEST WESTERN GUADALUPE INN
White's City • 800-CAVERNS • $$–$$$

Right across the street from the Cavern Inn, the Guadalupe Inn offers 42 non-smoking rooms. All amenities are similar. No pets.

WALNUT CANYON INN
White's City • 800-CAVERNS • $$

The oldest of three properties and more convenient for families. The 27 units at this single-story property are two-and three-bedroom suites. Guests are welcome to make use of the pools, hot tubs, and other amenities at the other properties. No pets.

Recreational Vehicles and Other Accommodations

PARK ENTRANCE RV AND CAMPERS PARK
White's City • AAA approved • 800-CAVERNS

Pull-through hookups (water, sewer, and electric). Bathrooms and showers surrounded by a grassy picnic area with tables and barbecue pits. Controlled access via coded gate (changed daily). Access to the pools, hot tub, and laundry at the other facilities.

The city of Carlsbad and its hundreds of hotel rooms and restaurants is 27 miles northwest of the Caverns via Highway 62-180. The Carlsbad Chamber (505-887-6516) offers a complete listing of hotels/motels as well as other attractions. Resources include the *New Mexico Vacation Guide* produced by *New Mexico* magazine in cooperation with the New Mexico Department of Tourism (800-545-2040) and *The Texas Monthly Guidebook To New Mexico* by Dave DeWitt, available from local booksellers or Gulf Publishing Co. (713-520-4444).

EL PASO & JUAREZ

EL PASO COUNTY SEAT   ★   515,342   ★   (915)

STATE OF CHIHUAHUA ★ 2,000,000+ ★ (011 52 16)

When people's thoughts turn to El Paso, a Marty Robbins ballad comes to mind. It's about a West Texas town whose *cantinas* are full of gunfighters and beautiful *señoritas*, and to millions *El Paso* is a catchy tune. But when you belly up to the bar at the L&J Cafe and listen as the proprietor tells you about Texas Rangers raiding his grandfather's cantina, the hitching post that used to be out front, and the gravesite across the street of a preacher's son who killed thirty men, keep in mind that Robbins sang a ballad and not a song.

DOWNTOWN EL PASO

N

STANTON
MESA
NEVADA
KANSAS
CAMPBELL
ARIZONA
OREGON
RIO GRANDE
EL PASO
MONTANA
YANDELL
WYOMING
MISSOURI
YANDELL
FRANKLIN
MAIN
MILLS
TEXAS
MYRTLE
MAGOFFIN
10
SAN FRANCISCO
SAN ANTONIO
CHAMBER OF COMMERCE
CIVIC CENTER PLAZA
OVERLAND
FIRST
PAISANO
DURANGO
LEON
CHIHUAHUA
SANTA FE
EL PASO
OREGON
MESA
STANTON
KANSAS
CAMPBELL
FLORENCE
THIRD
OCHOA
TO CORDOVA BRIDGE
FOURTH
TO JUAREZ
TO JUAREZ

CIUDAD JUAREZ

STANTON ST BRIDGE
SANTA FE ST
EL PASO
STANTON
LINCOLN
CORDOVA FREE BRIDGE
EL PASO, TEXAS
N
SANTA FE ST BRIDGE
BLVD DIAZ ORDAZ
AV MALECON
AV RIBERENA
BORDER HWY
RIO GRANDE
AV JUAREZ
LERDO
CONSTITUCION
5 DE MAYO
URUGUAY
COSTA RICA AV
AV DE LOS AMERICAS
AV LINCOLN
AV LOPEZ MATEOS
CALLE P. ELIAS CALLES
AV DEL CHARRO
AV RAFAEL P. SERNA
JUAREZ, CHIHUAHUA
JUAREZ MARKET
AV 16 DE SEPTEMBRE
GUADALUPE MISSION
HISTORY MUSEUM
PASEO TRIUMFO DE LA REPUBLICA
PLAZA MONUMENTAL BULLRING

El Paso has more than its share of beautiful señoritas (including a recent Miss USA), enjoys the most convenient snow skiing for Texans (three hours away), and serves as the home of the Scud-buster (Fort Bliss). El Paso and Juarez retain the crown as Mexican food capital of the world, and bullfights are just a cab ride away. But there's a lot more to the fourth largest city in Texas than most people (including some locals) give it credit for.

El Paso is commonly referred to as a Texas city. Though its origin dates back to 1598, *it wasn't until the Compromise of 1850 that El Paso was located within the bounds of the state of Texas.* For almost two centuries, El Paso was administered as a part of New Mexico (first by Spain and then by Mexico). Its location and orientation are still closer to the capitals of Arizona, Chihuahua, and New Mexico than to Austin. Notice how regional news and weather from Las Cruces or Tucson replace talk about Texas in the *El Paso Times.* The Pacific coast is closer than Galveston Bay, and the El Paso perspective refocuses accordingly. Unlike Houston, Dallas, or even San Antonio, El Paso blends its Spanish heritage, Mexican legacy, and thoroughly western orientation to produce an outlook and a visit found nowhere else in Texas.

Locals and savvy travelers rarely stay put in "the Pass." When you take for granted crisscrossing El Paso to get to old Mexico, to New Mexico, as well as around town, you'll begin to enjoy El Paso. Stay in the heart of the downtown, and a bullfight and dinner in Juarez are closer than a baseball game and hot dogs at Cohen Stadium. If the west side is your base, a day at Sunland Park, New Mexico, playing the ponies is far more convenient than a tour along the Mission Trail. This natural mix of cultures and function as a crossroads is the hallmark of historic El Paso as well as its future.

El Paso's origin centers on *el Camino Real* and the imperial goals of conquest and spreading the faith, not on dry goods or real estate speculation. The Royal Road wound its way from Mexico City via Chihuahua City to the most northerly outpost of the Spanish Empire—Santa Fe. Traversing nearly two thousand miles, *el Camino* was among the longest conquest and trade routes in North America, with branches forking off through the Big Bend and Davis Mountains to San Antonio and on to the Gulf of Mexico. Much of Interstate 10 and Interstate 25 north of El Paso follows its course. Nearly four centuries ago (1598), Spanish colonization of the American Southwest advanced significantly when Juan de Oñate led a colonizing expedition across the Chihuahuan Desert of what is now northern Mexico to the Río Grande, trailblazing the route for el Camino. Where the Río Grande sliced through the Franklin Mountains, he named this crossing *El Paso del Río del Norte.* Half a century later, another Spaniard, Fray Garcia de San Francisco y Zuniga, built the Mission of Our Lady of Guadalupe and founded a fledgling settlement (1659). This landmark is typical of El Paso; the construction of Our Lady of Guadalupe is recognized as the founding of the 24th largest city in the United States, even though the site of the mission is the main square of Juarez.

Across the river on what is now American soil, only small and scattered settlements like Coon's Ranch, Concordia, Franklin, and Magoffinsville existed as late as the American Civil War. During its early years, El Paso was often overlooked as a commercial or political hub. When El Paso County was organized (1850), more established communities like San Elizario and Ysleta vied for the county seat. It wasn't until the railroads reached west to El Paso that the focus of the valley shifted upriver. Soon El Paso boasted five rail lines. This combination of interstate and international arteries made El Paso as natural a choice as a distribution center in the nineteenth century as it does today. Many of the economic forces that propelled El Paso into the twentieth century are now permanent elements of the community. Mineral deposits in Mexico, New Mexico, and Arizona and smelters (which dot the El Paso skyline) led to the founding of the State School of Mines and Metallurgy (known today as the University of Texas at El Paso). Centuries of cotton farming along the Río Grande created a textile industry that produces millions of garments for American and global markets. Fort Bliss, once the headquarters of America's southern flank, has evolved into America's air defense headquarters.

Here is a quick look at things to come. Individually, both El Paso and Juarez are the largest border cities in the United States and Mexico. Together, they have no match from Brownsville to San Diego and stand to be catapulted economically into the twenty-first century. *Maquilas* are the engine of this growth. The *maquiladora* program relies on factories situated south of the border where components produced elsewhere are assembled using less expensive Mexican labor. The finished good is then exported to the world's largest consumer market, America, or shipped to another plant for final assembly. Juarez has no equal in Mexico when it comes to the number of maquiladoras or the number of people employed by maquilas. The list of maquilas in Juarez numbers about 300, the number of employees exceeds 100,000, and the roll call of American and international companies in Juarez includes companies like A.C. Nielsen, Briggs and Stratton, Honeywell, Murata, Proctor-Silex, Sylvania, and TDK. Eighty percent are American-owned. Both El Paso and Juarez will be important components of the success of free trade on a broader scale. Already the spillover from the maquila program affects numerous facets of El Paso today: increased employment and housing starts, the development of new businesses, and higher enrollment at local universities. But the most fortunate by-product from the standpoint of this book has been that as prospects for El Paso's future have brightened, awareness of the unique attributes of this region and renewed interest in cultural attractions like the historic Mission Trail grows stronger among locals and visitors like yourself.

Going Across

A roadtrip to Juarez is easier than driving around parts of Dallas these days. For you it might be the first time, but going over to shop or grab a bite has been a way of life out here for centuries. Stroll across or take a shuttle (see **TOURIST SERVICES**). Driving is not a bad idea, it's just not the best one if you are unfamiliar with Mexico's largest border city. Why put up with the hassle of directions, roundabouts, and the Mexican penchant for demolition-derby driving when someone else will do it for small change?

Walking Across. Park your car at one of the lots by the Santa Fe Street Bridge. An attendant collects the $3 to $5 per day fee. Hoof it over and pay the quarter toll. Stroll down Avenida Juarez with its hundreds of shops, restaurants, bistros, and bars heading south from the base of the Santa Fe Bridge. The intersection with Avenida de 16 de Septiembre is the heart of the city. The Juarez market is several blocks east; the Cathedral, the Guadalupe Mission, and the History Museum are directly to the right.

Driving Across. Several miles southeast of downtown, the Cordova Bridge of the Americas permits auto and pedestrian traffic both ways and is free. Downtown, take the Stanton Street bridge into Mexico and the Santa Fe Street Bridge back to the states. Your toll is a dollar going over and about two coming back. Wherever you pull up you'll find gentlemen directing, guiding, and otherwise doing their best to convince you how crucial their parking skills are. You don't have to buy this routine but they'll be with your car when you're gone. A dollar tip is customary.

On any trip south of the border, remember that American dollars are accepted as readily as Mexican pesos and that the recent devaluation has produced a new currency as well as modified the old one. The existing denominations are now utilized *minus* three zeros, for instance, 20,000 old pesos equals 20 new pesos. It is quite acceptable to haggle over prices in markets and with cabbies but not at restaurants or department stores. Quite often, the bill is presented with a dollar sign. Treat this as pesos until you are told otherwise. If you need to convert your money to pesos or vice versa, consider the following houses or stop at one of the ubiquitous *casas de cambio* that are sprinkled throughout downtown El Paso.

EL PASO INTERNATIONAL AIRPORT
El Paso Foreign Currency Exchange
Open daily all year • 779-1098

DOWNTOWN
Texas Commerce Bank • Main and Mesa Streets
Weekdays • 546-6500

GREATER EL PASO STATE NATIONAL BANKS
Eight locations • Varying hours
532-9922 for locations and hours

TOURIST SERVICES

EL PASO TOURIST INFORMATION CENTERS
Civic Center Plaza • Daily 8–5 • 544-0062
El Paso International Airport • Daily 9–5 • 772-4271 ext. 275
Well staffed and full of brochures, flyers, and magazines, these centers can do more than answer questions. The Civic Center Plaza location is also the headquarters for the El Paso-Juarez Trolley Co. and the site for departures on the trolley tour.

EL PASO-JUAREZ TROLLEY CO.
One Civic Center Plaza • 544-0062
Daily • $8 weekday, $10 weekend adult fare
Mission tours on Thursday during the summer only
There is no better way to see Juarez than via the trolley. The convenience and value of this service make it the best way to familiarize yourself with the area (see **DRIVING TOUR**). The charge is a lot less than any of the costs or hassles associated with driving your own vehicle into Mexico.

TEXAS TRAVEL INFORMATION CENTER
Anthony Exit on Interstate 10 (Mile Marker 0) • 886-3468
Open daily 8–5 except New Year's and Christmas
If you haven't stopped at one of the Texas Department of Transportation Centers before, do so now. After quizzing a trained travel counselor about your itinerary, pick up the *Texas State Travel*

Guide, a 272-page gold mine produced by the Texas Department of Transportation, regularly updated, and handed out free of charge.

TOUR BUS OPERATORS
EZ Way Lines • 591-4565
Golden Tours • 779-0555
Rancho Grande Tours • 544-1661
Río Grande Tours • 564-0493
Rocky Mountain Tours • 599-1451
Half- and full-day tours of El Paso/Juarez are conveniently scheduled by these coaches. Shopping, sightseeing, the Juarez Race Track, and bullfights are more easily enjoyed while someone else does the driving. Pick-up and drop-off to major hotels. Group and children's rates available.

Other Helpful Numbers

American Express Office: Sun Travel. 3100 N. Mesa Suite B. 532-8900. Monday through Friday from 7:30 a.m. to 5:00 p.m.
Airport: 772-4271.
Local Bus Service: Sun Metro. Union Depot at 700 San Francisco. 533-3333. El Paso's local transit system covers the entire city and begins service daily at 4:41 a.m. with the last bus returning by 11:06 p.m. Fares range up to 75¢.
Bus Terminal: Greyhound Bus Lines. 200 W. San Antonio. 532-2365.
Train Station: Union Station. 700 San Francisco St. 545-2247.
Automobile Rentals: Advantage, Avis, Budget, Dollar, Enterprise, Hertz, National, Thrifty.
Emergencies/Medical Assistance: 911.
American Consulate (Juarez): (0115216) 13 40 48.
Mexican Consulate: 910 E. San Antonio Ave. 533-3644.
U.S. Customs: 9400 Viscount. 540-5800.
Time and Temperature: 532-9911.

DRIVING TOUR

Head to the **El Paso-Juarez Trolley Company** office at the Civic Center or, if you're staying at one of the following hotels, call in advance for a complimentary shuttle: the Airport Hilton, El Camino Real Paso del Norte, Embassy Suites, Holiday Inn Sunland Park, Howard Johnson, Quality Inn, and the Radisson Inn Suites. Children four and under ride free; for kids under 13 it's always $8; adults pay $10 on weekends only. The trolley runs every day on an hourly circuit beginning at 10 a.m. with the final sweep picking up the stragglers beginning at 5 p.m. Allow at least three to four hours total for the nine stops on the tour (though you'll probably only visit one of the three restaurant stops). Keep in mind that the tour starts in the more modern section of Juarez and ends up in the oldest area. Consequently, American shopping habits are more common at the initial five stops and Mexican ones—for instance, negotiating prices—at the last four. This type of bargaining is acceptable neither at restaurants nor at the newer markets.

From the Civic Center, the trolley proceeds east to the Free Bridge and heads across to the **Pueblito Mexicano**. Within walking distance of the next four stops, this mall is a replica of a colonial Mexican village, complete with a Subway sandwich shop and a Benetton outlet. With numerous vacancies, the three-story complex is still a good place to get your prescriptions filled or to enjoy lunch at **Viva Mexico,** a bright, colorful restaurant with breakfast and lunch buffets and a dinner menu. The restaurant also offers banquet facilities for larger groups.

Plaza de las Americas is where the tour gets going. Located in the old Pronaf shopping center, it has been rebuilt as an indoor mall with a leather store, an oriental shop, and a cinema that shows American movies with Spanish subtitles. Within walking distance are **Decor,** which features furniture, furnishings, and glass blowing, **FoNart,** the national artisan center, with wonderful, hard-to-find, hand-crafted gifts, the **National Institute of Fine Arts,** which offers permanent and changing exhibits of fine art and primitive artifacts (Tuesday through Sunday), and **Casa del Sol,** a well-established, moderately expensive Juarez restaurant.

The **JJ Market** offers the only opportunity to haggle in the Pronaf area. This small shop specializes in curios, and the ladies behind the counter are tough negotiators. Ask for the owner. He cuts a much better deal.

If you take the trolley to **Salon Mexico,** you'll pass one of Mexico's largest bullrings (see **SPORTS AND ACTIVITIES**). Serving breakfast, lunch, and dinner during the day, **Salon Mexico** is one of the least expensive eateries on the trolley route with a menu in English and prices in dollars. With plenty of brass and polish, it comes alive after nine in the evening as a restaurant, bar, and disco with three dance floors and bands on busier nights.

Chihuahua Charlie's is the liveliest restaurant on the tour and one of the more expensive. Breakfast, lunch, and dinner as well as 16-ounce *margaritas* keep it hopping. Trolley riders receive a second margarita on the house. During the summer, a fiesta is held between 1:30 and 2:30 Saturday afternoons featuring *mariachis* and *folklorico* dancing.

From Chihuahua Charlie's to **Casa Oñate** is ten safe but boring city blocks. Everyone gets back on for the ride to this large leather factory and jewelry store where prices are negotiable. The password is "handtooled": purses, boots, briefcases, luggage, and golf bags.

City Market or **Centro Mercado** is one vendor after the next selling every item imaginable and haggling with customers new and old over price, quality, and breeding (see **SHOPPING**). There are over a hundred stalls vending fresh food, packaged Mexican staples, handcrafted items, clothing, jewelry, knick-knacks, leather, and produce; there is also a restaurant.

The final stop is for duty free goods: perfumes, name-brand cosmetics, etc. On heavy traffic days, instead of being retrieved here, you'll walk down to the Santa Fe bridge and be picked up and transported back to the Civic Center.

BIRD'S-EYE VIEW

SCENIC DRIVE
Take the Downtown Exit from I-10. Take Mesa north to Rim Rd. and take a right. Follow Rim Rd., which becomes Scenic Dr., two miles to the Murchison Park pull-off.

After the view itself, the best part about the vista from Murchison Park is that the City of El Paso has placed a dozen explanatory tablets that describe the different sights—Fort Bliss, downtown, Juarez, the University of Texas El Paso, etc. Pass on the pay-per-view telescopes if it's one of the many hazy days. Sunset is best (and safest).

MUSEUMS

AMERICANA MUSEUM OF SOUTHWEST CULTURAL HISTORY
**Convention & Performing Arts Center • 5 Civic Center
542-0394 • Tuesday–Friday 10–5 • Free • W+ • Gift shop**

Featuring a permanent exhibit entitled *The Art and Legacy of a Vanished People,* the Americana Museum presents a comprehensive display of pre-Columbian pottery of the Southwest. The many examples of Sedentary Culture craftsmanship are augmented by numerous annual exhibits of local and regional artists. Creations by local artists and Indian artisans from the Apache, Cherokee, Navajo, and Ute tribes are available in the gift shop.

BORDER PATROL MUSEUM

4315 Transmountain Drive • 759-6060
Tuesday–Saturday 9–4:45 • Free • Gift shop

This museum recently moved into a new building right next to the Wilderness Park Museum (see below) and houses 30,000 artifacts. With no funding from the federal government, an extensive collection of acquired and donated memorabilia pertaining to the Border Patrol and its founding in 1924 has been assembled. Rotating exhibits highlight the various Border Patrol sectors and aspects of fulfilling the Border Patrol's mission, such as firearms and smuggling techniques.

CENTENNIAL MUSEUM OF THE UNIVERSITY OF TEXAS EL PASO

UTEP Campus at the corner of Wiggins Way and University
747-5565 • Tuesday–Saturday 10–5 • Free • W

Displays include pottery, stone tools, and shell jewelry of prehistoric Mexico, mineral and rock specimens, dinosaur bones, fossils, and other relics from the Ice Age.

CHAMIZAL NATIONAL MEMORIAL

800 San Marcial • 534-7273 • November–May daily 8–5
June–October daily 10–7 • Free • W+

The Chamizal Memorial is a monument to the peaceful settlement of the minor changes in the course and character of the Colorado and Río Grande rivers. The name *chamizal* refers to the *chamiza* (salt bush) which prevails along the river plains where the changes in course took place. Those changes were remedied by the Chamizal Settlement, initiated in 1962 by Presidents Kennedy and Mateos, and were implemented by a concrete-lined channel that prevents the river from changing course. In addition to a historical museum, the 55-acre park grounds boast a 500-seat performing arts theater, a 1,000-volume reference library, and Los Paisanos Gallery, which exhibits different artists from Mexico and the United States. Quite often Chamizal is the site of Ballet El Paso, fiestas, festivals, and commemorations including the annual First Thanksgiving Reenactment and the Border Folk Festival (see **ANNUAL EVENTS**).

EL PASO MUSEUM OF ART

1211 Montana • 541-4040 • Tuesday–Saturday 10–5
Sunday 1–5 • Free (donations accepted) • W+

Set in one of the largest private houses designed by Henry Trost, the museum's collection is best known for the collection (and gift) of Samuel Kress, which is housed in the west wing's three galleries. With nearly 60 pieces, it includes works from the Early Renaissance (1300-1500), High Renaissance (1467-1600), and the Baroque-Rococo (1600-1800). Changing exhibits are on display in the east wing. Contact the EPMA for information on the exhibit schedule, art classes, lectures, concerts, and access to their reference library.

EL PASO MUSEUM OF HISTORY

Interstate 10 East at Avenue of the Americas North • 858-1928
Tuesday–Sunday 9–4:50 • Guided group tours by appointment
Free (donations accepted) • Gift shop • W

Much history has settled in El Paso's dust. For more than four centuries, explorers, conquerors, gunfighters, and settlers found a natural all-weather passageway where the Río Grande could be crossed and the southernmost Rocky Mountains relented. The mission of the El Paso Museum of History is to chronicle this heritage and interpret its many historical artifacts. The scope of this museum is apparent in the cultures it examines: Spanish, Mexican, and Anglo. In addition to providing workshops, lectures, classes, and special exhibits, the Museum's collections include blacksmithing and leatherworking tools, fans and shawls, cavalry items, bottles, Victorian era furniture, and historic clothing.

EL PASO SCIENCE MUSEUM—INSIGHTS

505 N. Santa Fe at the corner of Santa Fe and Missouri
542-2990 • Tuesday–Saturday 9–5
Adults $5, seniors and military $3, students $2

Each year, more than 100,000 guests visit this popular El Paso museum. Insights is designed to be interactive, i.e., visitors must activate the displays by performing some kind of activity like touching, jumping, or pushing. With over one hundred exhibits, it's as much fun for adults as for kids. Topics include the senses and other phenomena like electricity, gravity, shadows, and—a favorite—bubbles. Traveling exhibits are often featured.

FORT BLISS MUSEUM COMPLEX

An unusual mix of old and new, Fort Bliss was Black Jack Pershing's headquarters while trying to capture Pancho Villa, as well as Werner von Braun's laboratory when beginning Operation Paperclip. With over 1,700 square miles in and around El Paso, America's air defense center is a vital component of the El Paso economy. The present location—La Noria Mesa—is number six. When first garrisoned in 1849 by Brevet Major Jefferson Van Horne, only six companies were detailed. All operations were relocated to Fort Fillmore, New Mexico, and it wasn't until 1854 that Fort Bliss was reestablished. Now more than 300 students from 22 nations study at the U.S. Army Air Defense Training Center. The German Air Force Defense School is also based at Fort Bliss. Take the Airway exit off Interstate 10, proceed north, and veer left past El Paso International Airport. You'll run right into the main gate. No pass or fee is required to enter the base to visit any of the museums, however, proof of insurance and a driver's license are required. Entry at night is restricted to base personnel.

Fort Bliss Museum
Buildings 5051-5054 • Pleasonton and Pershing Roads
568-4518 • Daily 9–4:30 • Closed holidays • Free
This adobe replica of the first Fort Bliss uses a Sutler's Store for visitor orientation and as a gift shop. A six-minute slide show presents a brief overview of early El Paso. Seven period rooms feature reproductions of uniforms, equipment, and furnishings accurate to 1857. The collection in the north building contains artifacts from the history of Fort Bliss beginning with the Civil War, the occupation and torching of the fort by Confederate troops, and other El Paso area locations of the post including Concordia Ranch, Garrison Town, and Hart's Mill. Ask about the one-of-a-kind American flag that flies over the museum before you head inside for a look at Black Jack Pershing's riding crop.

Third Armored Cavalry Regimental Museum
Bldg. 2407 • Forrest and Chaffee Roads • 568-1922
Monday–Friday 9–4:30 • W
Like the Fort Bliss Museum, a visit starts with a brief introduction to the museum at the Orientation Gallery. Third Cav has an unparalleled heritage in the U.S. Army. The second oldest regiment in active service, it was first "baptized in fire and blood" (Winfield Scott) as the Regiment of Mounted Riflemen during the Mexican-American War (1847). Formed at the Jefferson Barracks, Missouri, the Regiment later became the Third United States Cavalry. Now known as the Third Armored Cavalry, its history

includes 39 campaigns in eight wars as well a list of over 50 generals who have emerged from its ranks. The Main Gallery houses most of the collection as well as timelines that pinpoint the history of the regiment within the broader scope of American history. The collection of Third Cav Regimental Standards (battle flags) is the most comprehensive of any unit in the U.S. Army. Also on display is a history of Third Cavalry military weapons, equipment, and uniforms from its earliest days to modern high tech gizmos that amaze and annihilate.

United States Army Air Defense Artillery Museum
Bldg. 5000 • Pleasonton Road • 568-5412
Daily 9–4:30 • Closed holidays • W
   This one is easy to find; look for the huge missiles out front. The history of air defense is featured beginning with the development of U.S. Army antiaircraft guns to combat the Red Baron and his fellow aces during World War I (1917) and continuing up to the most famous weapon of post-Vietnam warfare, the Patriot Missile aka the Scudbuster. Efforts to contain and control World War II's best known land-to-land missile, the V-1 or Buzz Bomb, are examined. In addition to defense-oriented land-to-air projectiles, other technologies depicted by dioramas, photographs, models, and graphics include radar, searchlights, sound locators, and fire control equipment.

MAGOFFIN HOME STATE HISTORICAL PARK

1120 Magoffin Avenue • 533-5147 • Wednesday–Sunday 9–4
Adults $2, children $1 • W+ but not all areas
   In 1875, Joseph Magoffin built the present 19-room territorial-style house of sun-dried adobe on a site settled by his father decades earlier. It stands on more than an acre of landscaped gardens. The Magoffin family occupied the house for more than a century, even after the City of El Paso and the State of Texas jointly acquired the house and property in 1976. Furnishings, paintings, and other family treasures are displayed as well as other items relating to historic El Paso.

WILDERNESS PARK MUSEUM

2000 Transmountain Road • 755-4332
Tuesday–Sunday 9–4:45 • Free • W
   Numerous dioramas, accurate and vivid, describe man in the Southwest during prehistoric, pre-Columbian, as well as more modern times. The permanent collection is full of eye-catching displays: arrowheads, ceremonial feathers, and turquoise jewelry. Each is presented with its own vista on historic cultures. If your

tribe is too restless to remain indoors, take them outside to the Nature Trail which winds its way around the museum and past replicas of a kiva, a pithouse, and a pueblo.

HISTORIC PLACES

CONCORDIA CEMETERY

Located between US 54, Interstate 10, Yandell Drive, and Stevens Street • 542-1591

Right next to the spaghetti bowl—where Interstate 10 and Highway 54 mesh—stands row after row of headstones, tombstones, and El Paso history. Since the nineteenth century, Concordia has served as the final resting place for all of El Paso—Gentile and Jew, famous and infamous. Perhaps the most notable occupant is John Wesley Hardin, murdered at the Acme Saloon (1895) by John Selman. The son of a Methodist minister, Hardin took to homicide at the tender age of 15, killed three soldiers sent to arrest him, and never kicked the habit. More than 30 men met their maker after meeting Mr. Hardin. To catch up with John Wesley, find the western entrance to the Chinese section of the cemetery and head just west and north (towards New Mexico and the Franklin Mountains).

EL PASO MISSION TRAIL

I-10 East, Avenue of the Americas Exit south to Zaragosa

These three missions are located in the oldest part of El Paso, an area locals call the Lower Valley. Though most of the original settlement of this area by the Tigua Indians and the now extinct Piros was on the south side of the Río Grande in El Paso del Norte (Juarez), the course of the Río Grande has changed over the centuries and so has the international status of the missions (see **CHAMIZAL NATIONAL MEMORIAL**).

YSLETA DEL SUR PUEBLO (TIGUA INDIAN RESERVATION)

108 S. Old Pueblo Rd. • 859-3916 • Summer: Daily 8–4:30 Winter: Wednesday–Sunday 8–5 • Admission • W

Tiguas (pronounced TEE-wahs) are the descendants of settlers who arrived in Texas three hundred years ago and are recognized as the oldest identifiable ethnic group in the state. Their heritage is the Pueblo grouping of native North Americans which includes the Hopi, the Taos, and the Zuni tribes. Soon after fleeing Santa Fe during the Pueblo Revolt (1680), the Tiguas built the Ysleta mission. Today, their 37-acre reservation offers demonstrations of native crafts, browsing through shops, and perhaps lunch at the Tigua Restaurant (order the *fajitas*).

MISSION YSLETA

Zaragosa and Alameda • 859-9848

Originally built on the south bank of the river in 1691, the first mission was destroyed by a flood. The second church was named in honor of the patron saint of the Tiguas, San Antonio de la Ysleta, and sits next to the present-day Tigua Indian Reservation. A century later, the river had changed course and the Mexican-American War had been fought. Mission Ysleta was in ruins as well as in the United States. The third sanctuary, visible today, was constructed on even higher ground. This one has endured its share of calamities including fire that destroyed the silver dome roof and bell tower (1907).

SOCORRO MISSION

Socorro Road (FM 258) at Nevarez • 859-7718

This is the oldest continuously active parish in the United States (1681). When the Tiguas settled Ysleta, other tribes such as the now-extinct Piros settled to the east and built the Socorro Mission. Though the earliest structures (1691) were destroyed by floods, the hand-crafted *vigas* (ceiling beams) survived and have been incorporated into the design of the present mission (1843). Socorro is an outstanding example of Spanish Mission architecture, yet the vigas and the *latilla enrejados* (smaller branches), which form a distinctive herringbone pattern, evidence notable Indian influences. Nearby archaeological excavations have led to the discovery of the foundation of the original structure.

CHAPEL SAN ELIZARIO

San Elizario Plaza off of FM 258 • 851-2333

Presidio San Elizario, named for French Saint Elcear, was established by the Spanish government in the 1780s to protect *el Camino Real* from Apaches. Soon after its construction, the *presidio* (fort) was moved 37 miles north to this location (1789) where it protected the growing community of San Elizario from Indian attacks for over half a century. When this portion of old Mexico became American territory (1848), the importance of San Elizario was evident in its selection as county seat. The present church was constructed in 1877 and serves as the focal point of the plaza. A graceful combination of European and Southwestern styles, it was used by Steven Spielberg as the setting for the final scene of *Fandango* starring Kevin Costner.

EL PASO UNION DEPOT

700 San Francisco • 533-3333 (Sun Metro) • 545-2247 (AMTRAK)
This red-bricked, high-steepled masterpiece shines from its 1981 renovation. Union Depot was built at the turn of the century (1906) when El Paso was coming of age as the junction of the Southern Pacific, the Atchison, Topeka & Santa Fe, and the Mexican Central railroads. It serves as the downtown terminal for Sun Metro, El Paso's local transit system, and as the AMTRAK station. Each holiday season the depot hosts performances of El Paso's concert choir and chamber orchestra, El Paso Pro-Musica.

GUADALUPE MISSION

Avenida 16 de Septiembre at the Plaza • Juarez
Located in the heart of Juarez, this mission is the soul of the region. It was from this church and the plaza before it that Juarez and El Paso began. Completed in 1668 after almost ten years of construction by Mansos Indians, this is the initial component of the Mission Trail and predates Ysleta, Socorro, and San Elizario.

OTHER POINTS OF INTEREST

EL PASO ZOO

4001 E. Paisano Dr. (across from the County Coliseum)
544-1928 • Daily except New Year's, Thanksgiving, and
Christmas • Monday–Friday 9:30–4 • Weekends and holidays
9:30–5 • Adults $2, seniors $1, children $1
Over 400 species are featured at this 18-acre facility. The showstoppers are the sea lion shows at 11 a.m. and 4 p.m. and the elephant feeding between 9:30 and 10:00 a.m. and at 2 p.m.

FRANKLIN MOUNTAINS STATE PARK

Downtown El Paso to the New Mexico border • 877-1528
The Franklins divide El Paso into east and west. Over 24,000 acres of this rugged range is located within the state park (and the El Paso city limits). There are plenty of hiking trails, picnic shelters, and numerous access points, but Franklin Mountains is one of the most undervisited parks in the state given its urban setting.

LOS MURALES ("THE MURALS")

El Paso's many cultures are nowhere better and more vividly expressed than in its numerous murals. The colorful creators range from well-known mainstream artists like Tom Lea, who got a federal contract to produce *Pass of the North* at the Federal Courthouse (1938), to the unknown muralist whose *Lagrimas* ("tears") graces the wall of a building in the historic Chihuahuita district. Stop by the El Paso Juarez Trolley Company office at the Civic Center and pick up a copy of the El Paso Junior League's four-color, 20-page brochure *Los Murales*. With maps, addresses, and descriptions of the murals, it's the essential guide.

MOUNT CRISTO REY (SIERRA DEL CRISTO REY)
Interstate 10 West, Sunland Park Exit to Doniphan

Where the states of Chihuahua, New Mexico, and Texas meet stands a towering 27-foot statue of Christ beckoning his flock, particularly on the Feast of Christ the King (the last Sunday in October). Unfortunately, unless you travel in a large enough group, you can fall victim to the numerous thieves who infest the slopes of Sierra de Muleros. Quarried of Cordova cream limestone near Austin, it was sculpted by Urbici Soler in the late 1930s. The trail up the mountain is 5,650 feet long (about a two-hour hike) and includes the fourteen stations of the cross. The sculpture stands atop a nine-foot base, is perched 4,675 feet above sea level, and includes a 33½-foot-high cross.

SPORTS AND ACTIVITIES

Amusement Parks

CHAMPIONS SPORTSPLEX
1780 N. Zaragosa off Interstate 10 E. • 857-7676

This private outdoor facility has lighted softball fields, lighted volleyball courts, T-ball and youth baseball diamonds, softball and hardball batting cages, a playground, and a two-story clubhouse with concessions and televisions tuned to ESPN.

PUTT-PUTT GOLF & GAMES
8836 Montana at Hawkins • 779-2226 • Sunday–Thursday 9 a.m.–12 a.m. • Friday–Saturday 9 a.m.–1 a.m.

Three 18-hole lighted miniature golf courses for golfers of all levels. Also available are a video game arcade, bankshot basketball, and a snack bar.

WESTERN PLAYLAND
Ascarate Park • 6900 Delta Drive • 779-3914
Open summers Wednesday through Sunday • Admission varies: one price for all or entrance fee and per ride

For bigger kids, Western Playland features rides, wet and dry, with intimidating names like El Bandido, Snake Mountain, and the Himalaya. Youngsters have their choice of rides, and the video arcade attracts quarter pushers of all ages.

WET-N-WILD WATER WORLD
Interstate 10 Exit 0 at Anthony • 886-2222
Open from mid-May to mid-September • Admission
Kind of like a combination Jurassic Park/Noah's ark theme: volcanic gardens inundated with tons of water. With free-fall slides, flumes, and tubes, it's just south of the Texas/New Mexico state line by I-10.

Baseball

EL PASO DIABLOS
Cohen Stadium • 9700 Gateway North • 755-2000
Ticket prices: $3.75, $4.75, $5.25 • Game time: 7 p.m.
For over 20 years, El Paso's home team has been the Diablos of the Texas League, a farm team in the Milwaukee Brewers organization. The Diablos host visiting squads from within the Western Division—Midland, San Antonio, and Wichita—as well as interdivision rivals from Jackson, Shreveport, Arkansas, and Tulsa. Promotions like free lottery tickets, giveaways, and post-game concerts run all season long. As the sun sets behind the Franklin Mountains and things begin to cool off, a night at the ballpark can be pleasant as well as inexpensive. Located on the east side of town in a first-rate facility.

Basketball

UTEP MINERS
UTEP Special Events Center • 747-5265 • W+ but not all areas
It wasn't long ago (1966) that Texas Western, now known as the University of Texas at El Paso, shocked America by winning the Final Four and bringing the NCAA crown home. A member of the Western Athletic Conference, each December the Miners host the Sun Bowl Tournament. Previous invitees include Indiana, Michigan, Ohio State, Iowa, Iowa State, USC, Pepperdine, and Tennessee. Tickets for Miners games start as low as $5.

Betting

JUAREZ TURF CLUB
One block south of the International Bridge • 775-0555
Open from 9 a.m. daily
Pick your poison—baseball, basketball, football—they cover them all including college and pros. Greyhounds are featured Wednesday through Sunday nights with matinees in season. Full service restaurant and bar.

Bullfighting

PLAZA MONUMENTAL
Pan American Highway • Juarez • April through September
In the interior of Mexico at the great arenas or *plazas de toros*, bullfights are held from October through March. Along the border, however, the opposite holds. In Juarez, *corridas* are held during the heat of the year beginning in the spring and lasting all summer long at one of Mexico's largest arenas. Pay the extra dollar or two to be seated on the *sombra* (shady) side and leave the *sol* seats for those who can take the heat. Don't get suckered into buying a sunny or a shady seat for the late corrida. If you feel your negotiating skills (in Spanish, no less) are not sufficient, contact **Victor Garcia** at 915-525-5341. His services include transportation to and from the arena as well as securing tickets.

Charreada
(Mexican Rodeo)

CHARRO ASSOCIATION RODEOS
Lienzo Charro Lopez Mateos Arena • Juarez
½ mile beyond Plaza Monumental off Avenida 16 de Septiembre
Like bullfights, *charreadas* are another great Hispanic tradition. This one draws from the tradition of the *vaquero*, whose skills led to the development of the American cowboy. Charreadas are composed of seven *suertes* (rounds), all of which are designed to demonstrate the talents of the vaquero.

Dog Racing

JUAREZ RACETRACK
Pan American Highway • 542-1942
Wednesday through Saturday
Year-round dog racing in an enclosed, climate-controlled area. Wagers are accepted in dollars and in pesos. Food and beverages available at the Jockey Club.

Fishing

There's plenty of fishing around El Paso. Unless you're traveling towards the Big Bend and can budget some time for catfish near Tornillo, your best bet is north to New Mexico. Remember that Texas and New Mexico require fishing licenses. More information about licensing is available from the Texas Parks & Wildlife Department at 915-598-4741 and the New Mexico Department of Game and Fish at 505-524-6090.

El Paso Area:

HIDE-A-WAY LAKES
40 miles south from El Paso off Hwy 20 near Tornillo • **764-2555**
Private. Catfish. $5 a hook and $5 a vehicle.

PLAIN VIEW LAKES
40 miles south from El Paso off Hwy 20 near Tornillo • **764-2750**
Private. More catfish but $6 a hook and $6 a vehicle.

New Mexico:

ELEPHANT BUTTE RESERVOIR
70 miles north of Las Cruces off I-10 (90 miles from El Paso)
Public. Now we're fishing. Elephant Butte is the largest reservoir on the Río Grande and popular for all water sports. Elephant Butte Reservoir and the adjacent State Park enjoy a national reputation for striped bass with some over 50 pounds. Other catches include white bass, smallmouth and largemouth bass, catfish, and crappie.

CABALLO LAKE
60 miles north of Las Cruces off I-10
Public. Less than 10 miles south of the southern tip of Elephant Butte Reservoir, Caballo Lake is not as popular or as crowded as its upstream neighbor. Head either to the lake or below the dam at its south end for largemouth bass, white bass, crappie, and walleye.

Football

UTEP MINERS
Sun Bowl Stadium at UTEP • 747-5234
Admission • W+ but not all areas
Western Athletic Conference football is showcased each fall featuring teams like Air Force, Brigham Young, and those mighty Wyoming Cowboys. In addition, the John Hancock Bowl highlights El Paso's Sun Carnival. Tickets for Miner games start as low as $10 for adults and $7 for kids.

Golf

With its abundant sunshine and plentiful water, El Paso does not want for golf courses. Private ones such as Coronado Country Club (584-3841) or the El Paso Country Club (584-0511) require guests to be escorted by a member. Fort Bliss offers military personnel and retirees the Underwood Golf Course (562-1273) at moderate rates of $8 during the week and $10 on weekends. The following list includes public courses and the semi-private Horizon Golf and Tennis Club.

ASCARATE MUNICIPAL GOLF COURSE
Ascarate Park • 772-7381 • Weekdays: $8 or $5 for seniors
Weekends: $10 or $5 for seniors after 12:30 p.m.

CIELO VISTA MUNICIPAL GOLF COURSE
1510 Hawkins • 591-4927 • Weekdays: $10 • Weekends: $12

HORIZON GOLF AND TENNIS CLUB
Horizon City • 852-3150 • Weekdays and weekends: $25

PAINTED DUNES DESERT GOLF COURSE
12000 McCombs Road • 821-2122
Weekdays: $10 or $7 after 4:30 p.m. • Weekends: $12 or $8 after 4:30 p.m. • Juniors and seniors: $7 during the week

Horse Racing

SUNLAND PARK RACETRACK
Interstate 10 West, Sunland Park Exit west • 589-1131
Live Meet October through May • Simulcast May through September • General admission $1 • Turf Club $5 • W+
A trip to Sunland Park is an El Paso tradition, particularly given the natural affinity of Texans for horse flesh. Located just

inside the New Mexico state line, the view of the Franklin Mountains over the infield lake is memorable and so are the races. Catch stakes races such as the Riley Allison Thoroughbred Futurity and the Sun Country and West Texas Futurities in the spring. Or if you time it right, show up for Derby Day with a live transmission (and wagering) from Churchill Downs. In addition, a host of car shows, wine tastings, and handicapping seminars make a trip to Sunland Park a memorable one.

Tennis

El Paso's dry, sunny days keep courts packed year-round save in the summer months during the heat of the day. The real treat is serving them up at night when the cool evening makes playing a pleasure. Both the east side YMCA at 2044 Trawood (591-3321) and the west side YMCA at 7145 N. Mesa (584-9622) have courts and welcome guests as does the more centrally located YWCA at 1600 N. Brown (522-7475). The City of El Paso offers an enormous number of courts at more than a dozen parks all across town. Call Parks and Recreation at 541-4331 for locations, conditions, and hours. In addition, lighted courts are open to the public at the following El Paso high schools from 5:30 to 7:30 p.m. during the school year and from 10 a.m. to 7:30 p.m. during the summer: Austin, Coronado, Del Valle, El Paso High, Irvin, and Montwood. El Paso's traditional tennis bastion, the El Paso Tennis Club (2510 N. Vrain, 532-4373), hosts clinics and tournaments year-round including the Eric Alwan Celebrity Invitational/Chicken-Fried Steak Cook-Off.

COLLEGES AND UNIVERSITIES

UNIVERSITY OF TEXAS EL PASO
747-5000 • W+ but not all areas
To any visitor, the most visible feature of UTEP is its unusual Bhutanese architecture, one of a kind nationwide and a tribute to El Paso architect Henry Trost. What strikes the eye but eludes the mind are the battered walls which slope outward by seven inches from top to bottom. Bhutanese design elements in many of the 76 buildings on campus include deep-set lower windows, ornamental friezes of brick and tile below the roof line, and the low-hipped roofs. Other notable structures on campus include the 52,000-seat Sun Bowl Stadium and the 12,222-seat Special Events Center (see **SPORTS AND ACTIVITIES** below).

To any follower of higher education, the most notable aspect of the University of Texas El Paso is its commitment to Hispanic students and graduates. Six out of every 10 students are Hispanic, an estimated 50 percent are first generation university students, and more Hispanic UTEP graduates go on to pursue doctoral degrees than from any other institution nationwide. A growing strength at UTEP is its unique bilingual and binational programs, offered to over 17,000 students enrolled at this second oldest component of the University of Texas system. Founded by the Texas Legislature (1913) as the State School of Mines and Metallurgy, the present 366-acre site and architectural theme were selected three years later after fire destroyed the original eastside location. The mineral-laden areas around El Paso—New Mexico, southern Arizona, northern Mexico, and far west Texas—were ideally suited for mining research. The School of Mines became the College of Mines (1919), Texas Western College (1949), and ultimately the University of Texas El Paso (1967).

PERFORMING ARTS

BALLET EL PASO
University at Hawthorne • 533-2200 • Tickets from $5 to $22
The second oldest of El Paso's performing arts organizations, Ballet El Paso gave its first performance in 1960. Different venues host Ballet El Paso's three annual productions including one just for children.

EL PASO CONVENTION & PERFORMING ARTS CENTER
1 Civic Center Plaza • Santa Fe at San Antonio • 534-6000
Located in the heart of downtown El Paso and within walking distance of major hotels, Mexico, and City Hall (considered a part of the complex). Facilities include the 2,500-seat Abraham Chavez Theatre, a Grand Hall flanked by large meeting rooms, and the 60,000-square-foot Exhibit/Convention Hall, site of several trade shows annually.

EL PASO COUNTY COLISEUM
4100 E. Paisano Drive (Paisano at Boone) • 534-4229
The coliseum hosts many El Paso events including concerts, ice capades, tractor pulls, the Southwestern Livestock Show and Rodeo (February) and the NARC Championship Rodeo (November).

EL PASO PRO-MUSICA
532-7653
Founded to present quality choral and instrumental chamber compositions, Pro-Musica presents musical selections ranging

from Renaissance to contemporary during its October to March concert season including Christmas concerts at historic Union Depot (see **HISTORIC PLACES**) and the International Chamber Music Festival each January (see **ANNUAL EVENTS**).

EL PASO SYMPHONY ORCHESTRA

Abraham Chavez Theatre • 532-3776
Tickets from $5 to $20 (performance) or $44 to $132 (season)

Each season, the El Paso Symphony Orchestra presents a varied series from September through April featuring eight paired concerts in addition to KinderKonzerts, a pops concert series, and six Young People's concerts.

McKELLIGON CANYON COUNTY PARK & AMPHITHEATER

McKelligon Canyon Road • 532-0981 (Park) • 565-6900 (Theater)

Set high in the east side of the Franklin Mountains, this 90-acre park is found by taking Interstate 10 to Highway 54 (also called the Patriot Freeway). Head north towards Alamogordo and exit Fred Wilson Avenue. Take a left under the freeway and you'll be going towards the Franklins. When you run into McKelligon Canyon Road, follow it to the 1,500-seat Amphitheater.

ROSA GUERRERO INTERNATIONAL BALLET FOLKLORICO

566-5084

A unique manifestation of Southwest heritage, Rosa Guerrero's company has won national acclaim for its folkloric dances and has performed before Presidents and international dignitaries at the Kennedy Center for the Performing Arts in Washington, D.C.

SPECIAL EVENTS CENTER

UTEP Campus • 747-5234 (Tickets) • 747-5330 (Basketball)
Admission varies • W+

Used for basketball games, concerts, and other programs, the UTEP Special Events Center seats 12,222.

SUN BOWL STADIUM

UTEP Campus • 747-5234 (Tickets) • 747-5330 (Football)
Admission varies • W+

The site of the John Hancock Bowl, Sun Bowl Stadium is home turf for UTEP, a member of the Western Athletic Conference.

SHOPPING

One Of a Kind

EL PASO CHILE COMPANY

909 Texas Avenue • El Paso • 79901 • 915-544-3434
Monday–Friday 9–5 • Saturday 10–2

For over a decade, this El Paso specialty foods company has dominated the market for *chile* products nationwide. The Kerr family offers what is undeniably the most authentic memento from El Paso/Juarez: chile peppers, chile powders, chile *salsas*, chile wreaths, and, of course, *ristras* (hanging bunches of chiles). Pick up a copy of Park and Norma's bestselling *The El Paso Chile Company's Texas Border Cookbook* or the sequel, *Burning Desires*. Gift boxes start at less than $20 and are packed with your choice of marinades, powders, salsas, spices, tortilla chips, and BBQ sauce. Or serve up chiles in a variety of spicy fettucinis, linguinis, and pestos. The El Paso Chile Company School of Cooking hosts nationally known chefs and culinary experts like Mark Miller, Laura Brodey, Lucinda Hutson, and Tommy Tang. Call for upcoming programs. Not surprisingly, El Paso Chile Company does a booming mail order business. Stop by or call for a catalog.

EL PASO SADDLEBLANKET

601 N. Oregon (Exit 19 off I-10) • 544-1000
Monday–Friday 9–5 • Saturday 10–4 • Closed Sunday

Cash, checks, pesos—*no le hace*—it's just like Old Mexico. And well it should be. El Paso Saddleblanket is the largest wholesale and retail distributor anywhere of Mexican *artesanias* including ceramic, textile, and *talabarteria*. Follow the billboards across West Texas and southern New Mexico to plenty of parking and huge showrooms of baskets, clothes, glassware and tinware, jewelry, pots, rugs, serapes, skulls, and horns. Dozens of different hand-crafted Mexican saddles, saddlebags, saddleblankets, and saddle purses are piled from floor to ceiling, and no one is long without assistance from attentive staffers. Handcrafted Navajo and Zuni items are displayed next to handwoven oriental rugs, Guatemalan goods, and Pendleton woolens. Tens of thousands of pieces are stacked on shelves, displayed in cases, and piled on the floors of the 36,000-square-foot, two-story building. An interesting final note: Only 20% of El Paso Saddleblanket's business is retail trade. Wholesale accounts range from mom-and-pop operations to major retailers in America and overseas.

ELODIA
5410 N. Mesa • 581-8771 • 1331 N. Lee Treviño Dr. • 595-1997
Spend next to nothing or a small fortune; the level of service and the high quality of merchandise don't vary. One-of-a-kind clothing imports, evening gowns, even custom wedding dresses are popular, but many come to Elodia to be pampered at the facial or nail salon. Parties of six or more call for Elodia's limo service.

JUAREZ CITY MARKET
Avenida 16 de Septiembre • Daily from sunrise to sunset
This is a true *mercado* in the heart of Mexico's fourth largest city. The number of handmade and hand-crafted items is endless: aisle after aisle of household furnishings, decorative items, kitchen utensils, raw produce, Mexican cheeses, packaged foodstuffs, and other essentials and non-essentials unique to Mexico like *metates*. Stop before, during, or after your visit for a drink at *Neveria Camacho* on the market's east side as Tony "The Whistler" pokes fun at tourists and locals. After you run the gauntlet and make it inside, most of the proprietors are patient, friendly, and easy to deal with. See the lady at the cheese counter for *mole poblano* and rich, flavorful Mennonite and asadera cheeses. Choose from scores of *chiles: Ancho, arbol, mirasol, mulato, pasilla, piquin* and *poblano* are a few. Other great food items include dried shrimp for soups, *nopalitos* and *tunas* (cactus palms and fruits), *piñon* nuts, pumpkin seeds, raw sugar, raw tamarind, and bottled vanilla. If a vendor doesn't have what you need, he or she will either find it for you or convince you to buy something in stock. Much of Mexico's commerce has been traditionally transacted this way. To the north of the market is another Juarez institution, **Casa Mendoza.** In business since the early 1940s, this is your opportunity to snap up household and kitchen items at a fraction of what you'd pay in the States, including blue-rimmed glasses in every size and shape imaginable, all sorts of galvanized products, and cheap *talavera*. Also nearby is the **Rio Grande Pharmacy** where legions of American shoppers buy moderately priced, high quality pharmaceuticals. All products are produced by the same parent companies—Eli Lilly, Pfizer, et al—but are sold at substantial savings. The Río Grande Pharmacy is a reputable business dating back to the 1950s. The staff speaks English. Catch a cab, walk across, or take the trolley to enjoy the sights and sounds of the market.

ROCKETBUSTERS
115 Anthony • 541-1300 • Monday–Friday 7 a.m. to 5 p.m.

The next time you bump into Tom Cruise, ask him how he likes his Rocketbusters. Mr. Cruise was among Tinsel Town's first Rocketbuster fans; a short list of those partial to Marty Snortum's works of art (also known as cowboy boots) includes Billy Crystal, Steven Spielberg, Oprah Winfrey, and Eric Clapton. Rather than head to Paris, Munich, Tokyo, or New York for your pair, mosey on over to the Rocketbuster factory a few blocks east of the Union Depot (see **HISTORIC PLACES**) on Anthony. More than likely, you'll have to ring the doorbell to be admitted.

Rocketbusters may well be the the the last bootmaker in the United States to handcraft boots from start to finish including the heels and the toe boxes. Consequently, production runs about 4,000 pairs a year. Compare that with America's largest bootmaker, Justin, which makes that many in a day. It's a welcome surprise to learn that a pair can be had for as little as $350 (most handcrafted boots run several times that amount). If you get a hankering for the limited edition James Dean, Roy Rogers, Gene Autry, or Dale Evans styles, plan on dropping several thousand bucks. Either way, Marty stands behind his staff's work—in a pair of Rocketbusters.

Factory Outlets

Unlike the rest of the United States, the idea of a factory store out in El Paso is not a picturesque shopping center filled with designer seconds. It's either the factory itself or a retail facility nearby. Lower labor costs, the Río Grande River, and local cotton farms are reasons why this city dominates many manufacturing industries, in particular, western wear. Bootmaker Tony Lama got his start in downtown El Paso after a stint at Fort Bliss. The business he started is one of several major bootmakers operating locally. El Paso is the world's denim capital with two million pairs of jeans trucked out each week sporting labels like Levi, Wrangler, Lee, Calvin Klein, Guess?, and Jordache. Though you won't find a Levi factory outlet, listed below are some of the better known, high volume retailers as well as the factory outlets that make shopping El Paso a bargain.

AZAR NUT FACTORY STORE

1800 Northwestern Drive • 877-4079 • *I-25 west to Transmountain Exit, head east, take a right on Northwestern* Monday–Friday 10–6 • Saturday 10–2 • All major cards

Almond, Brazil nut, cashew, filbert, pecan, pistachio, black walnut, white walnut—they're all at Azar's headquarters. A sampling of other items includes candied nuts, yogurt peanuts, clusters, gift baskets, cocoa, coffees, and teas.

FARAH FACTORY STORE

**8889 Gateway West • 593-4481
Monday–Friday 10–7 • Saturday 10–6 • Sunday 11–5 • Cr**

Right at the factory, the Farah line is best known for men's and boy's labels like John Henry, Savane, and Farah. The savings on casual wear and dress wear, including slacks and sport coats, run from 30 to 60 percent off suggested retail.

LUCCHESE BOOTS

**6601 Montana Avenue • 778-8585
Monday–Saturday 9–6 • AE MC V**

Handmade lasts, hand-stitched uppers, and an all-leather boot have earned Lucchese its reputation. Save up to 40% on boots pulled from shipment for minor defects.

SAHARA SPORTSWEAR

**Colony Cove I Center • 7040-V N. Mesa • 833-8169
Monday–Saturday 10–6 • MC V**

Shirts, shorts, sweaters, warm-ups, bags, and hats by Sahara are on sale as well as Sahara's line of products for colleges and professional baseball.

TONY LAMA BOOTS

7156 Gateway East at the factory • 772-4327

12151 Gateway East (I-10 at Zaragosa Exit) • 858-0124

4900 Interstate 10 West at the Mesa Exit • 581-8192

M–F 9–7 • Saturday 9–6 • Sunday 12–6 • Major credit cards

El Paso's own Tony Lama went from soldier to cobbler to master bootmaker during the course of a career that spanned the better part of this century. Same selection at all three stores.

Galleries

GALERIA LAS VIGAS

9173 Socorro Road (half block east of Ysleta Mission)
860-0789 • Tuesday–Saturday 10–5 • Sunday 1–5 • D MC V

Located in the heart of the historic Lower Valley, the name *las vigas* refers to the ceiling beams that support the roof of this renovated adobe structure which is believed to be the original customs house in Ysleta. Owners Hank and Vicki Goodman represent a variety of nationally known craftsmen. In addition to Hank's own hand-thrown pots, look for pottery by Alan Day, Janice Gregory, and Jeannie Rundell, jewelry by Thomas Mann, and woodworkers like contemporary furniture craftsman Charlie Thompson, puzzle box designer Duane Dallas, and wooden vessel maker Craig Lossing.

GALERIA SAN YSIDRO

10300 Socorro Rd. (Lower Valley) • 858-5222
Thurs.–Sun. 10–5
2021 E. Yandell (Downtown) • 544-4455
Tues.–Sat. 10–5

If you've admired the furnishings at the Gage Hotel (Marathon), the Inn of the Anasazi (Santa Fe), or the Cibolo Creek Ranch (Shafter), then you already know the Galeria San Ysidro. Decorative furnishings range from cowboy to country to all styles of Mexican—provincial, Indian, even a little Colonial. Exquisite wrought iron from neoclassic to Pueblo Deco is available and can be designed and made to order. Both locations are retail facilities; however, the Lower Valley studio is the site of all repairs, refurbishing, and construction while the downtown warehouse offers a better selection of finished products.

Malls

BASSETT CENTER MALL

I-10 at Geronimo • 772-7479
Monday–Saturday 10–9 • Sunday 12–6

Anchored by Mervyn's, the Popular, Ross, Service Merchandise, and Target, Bassett Center boasts 80 specialty stores and restaurants as well as a six-screen movie theatre.

CIELO VISTA MALL
I-10 at Hawkins • 779-7070
Monday–Saturday 10–9 • Sunday 12–6

Anchored by Dillard's, J.C. Penney, Montgomery Ward, and Sears. General Cinema operates a 10-screen movie theater at Cielo Vista.

LA PLACITA
El Paso International Airport • Daily

Better than most airport arcades, La Placita can cover you in case you need a last-minute souvenir as well as other essential and non-essential items. The knife shop is tops.

PLACITA SANTA FE
5024-5034 Doniphan Drive • *Take the Mesa Exit from Interstate 10, head south, and take a right just before the railroad tracks on Doniphan. Right behind Furr's.*

More than a dozen different boutiques, galleries, shops, and *tiendas* crowd the site of the old Paradise Motel. The story of the Paradise includes a clandestine meeting between Black Jack Pershing and Pancho Villa. Doniphan used to be the primary route north and west out of El Paso, and the Paradise, built at the turn of the century, holds the distinction of being the first motel in town. Long known for its vices, the reputation of the Paradise began to wane as hookers, gun runners, and bootleggers took over. Now revitalized and restored for shoppers, Placita Santa Fe has handmade clothing and accessories, handcrafted spurs and jewelry, fine art, teddy bears, and antiques, all at the top of a long list of items available.

SUNLAND PARK MALL
Interstate 10 at the Sunland Park Exit • 833-5595
Monday–Saturday 10–9 • Sunday 12–6

Anchored by Dillard's, J.C. Penney, Mervyn's, and the Popular, Sunland Park Mall is one of El Paso's newest and was developed by the same company that brought the world the Mall of the Americas. One of the more interesting shops is the **Cooking Place** (833-0222) on the second level. All sorts of kitchen items related to local cuisine like mini *ristras*, Southwestern tiles, and regional cookbooks are on sale. The mall has a six-screen cinema.

SIDE TRIPS

CARLSBAD CAVERNS NATIONAL PARK, NEW MEXICO
Take Montana Street east out of El Paso. It soon becomes Highway 62-180. Follow the signs 42 miles past Guadalupe Mountains National Park and into New Mexico to the White's City intersection. Carlsbad Caverns is to your left about seven miles. Total drive time is less than four hours from El Paso's east side.
See separate listing under **CARLSBAD CAVERNS NATIONAL PARK.**

GUADALUPE MOUNTAINS NATIONAL PARK, TEXAS
Take Montana Street east out of El Paso. It becomes Highway 62-180. Take 62-180 straight to the Visitor Center at Guadalupe Mountains National Park. Drive time is approximately three hours.
See separate listing under **GUADALUPE MOUNTAINS NATIONAL PARK.**

HUECO TANKS STATE HISTORICAL PARK
Highway 62-180, 24 miles east from El Paso • Ranch Rd. 2775 north • 6900 Hueco Tanks Rd. #1 • El Paso • 79936 • 857-1135
Daily 8–5 • Gate is locked at 7 p.m. • Admission: Over 12 yrs. $2, 6–12 yrs. $1 • Camping sites $8–$11
The Hueco Tanks stand just outside El Paso and centuries removed from the scores of rusting cars, scattered construction sites, and real estate sales offices that line the eastern reaches of Montana Street (which becomes Highway 62-180). Three low rock masses nestled beneath the limestone and granite Hueco Mountains dominate the park. These intrusions are syenite porphyry, a type of granite intruded into a softer layer of rock about 34 million years ago; they gradually became exposed as the overlying rock eroded. During millions of years of erosion, depressions were formed, called *huecos* by the Spanish, that trap late summer rains (there are no springs). It is this phenomenon in the middle of the northern reaches of the Chihuahuan Desert that has brought man to the Hueco Tanks for thousands of years to replenish his canteens, to water his mounts, and to hunt game. This legacy is preserved in thousands of pictographs (rock paintings) and, on a much smaller scale, petroglyphs (designs carved or chipped into the rock) of human, animal, and mythological figures. Three cultural periods are represented—the Desert Archaic, the Jornada Branch of the Mogollon Culture, and the more recent

Apache, Comanche, and Kiowa. Inscriptions are also visible by 49ers and travelers making use of the Butterfield Overland Trail station whose ruins are also located in the park.

Twenty multi-use campsites, a sewage dump station, showers, and restrooms are available. Hueco Tanks is known for its outstanding birding as well as some of the best rock climbing in Texas. Refer to the *Birds of Hueco Tanks State Historical Park* checklist and *Hueco Tanks: A Climber's and Boulderer's Guide* (Chokestone Press: 1991).

INDIAN CLIFFS RANCH

I-10 East to Fabens Exit (Mile Marker 49) then north four miles
P.O. Box 1056 • Fabens • 79838 • 544-3200 or 764-2283

Practically self-contained, the Indian Cliffs Ranch boasts everything from hayrides to movie sets to mesquite-smoked barbecue at the Cattleman's Steakhouse. Groups of two to two thousand make tracks for Indian Cliffs which has extensive catering and party facilities as well as on-site activities like a children's zoo, longhorn and buffalo, and the Fort Apache playground. Most El Pasoans have enjoyed a steak dinner at Cattleman's, whose reputation has earned mention in several national publications in addition to sweeping local honors for best steak. Plenty of bus and RV parking.

LINCOLN, NEW MEXICO

Highway 54 northeast from El Paso through Alamagordo to
Tularosa • Right (east) on Highway 70 past Ruidoso to Hondo
Left (west) on Highway 380 to Lincoln • Drive time is
approximately three hours by car • **505-653-4025 (Lincoln**
County Heritage Trust)

Almost untouched by development, the town of Lincoln's only street is lined with century-old stores and adobe homes whose quiet ways belie Lincoln's violent past. The Lincoln County War pitted the rival cattle operations of James Dolan and L.G. Murphy versus those of John Chisum, Alexander McSween, and John Tunstall. The catalyst was the murder of Tunstall. A devoted admirer, Billy the Kid (William Bonney), set out to avenge his death, and the war began. The culmination was a five-day shootout. Much of Lincoln is operated by the State of New Mexico and the Lincoln County Heritage Trust, including the Lincoln County Courthouse, the San Juan Mission, the Tunstall Store Museum, Dr. Wood's House, and the Wortley Hotel.

OLD MESILLA at LAS CRUCES, NEW MEXICO

Take I-10 west past Las Cruces and Exit Avenida de Mesilla
south • Drive time is approximately one hour by car
800-343-7827 (Las Cruces info) • 800-545-2040 (NM info)

The signing of the Gadsden Purchase took place in Mesilla, which was bigger than Las Cruces and El Paso and the largest city between San Antonio and San Diego. Mesilla flourished during the mid-1800s as a supply center for Fort Fillmore and as a changing station for the Overland Mail. Mesilla's wild side was apparent with events like Billy the Kid's first murder trial, his conviction, and his escape. Fortunately for present-day visitors, Mesilla's charm and integrity were preserved when the Santa Fe Railroad chose Las Cruces for its route. Mesilla's day as Doña Ana County's first city had ended. The easy drive from El Paso proceeds north and then west along Interstate 10 and south at the Avenida de Mesilla exit. Drive over and stop at **La Posta (505-524-3524),** one of only two Overland Mail Route changing stations in existence. It's located right off the Plaza and is open Tuesday through Sunday for lunch and dinner (order the green chile enchiladas). Art galleries, gift shops, and other restaurants line the plaza whose soul is **San Albino Church,** originally constructed in 1855 and rebuilt in 1906. The well-known **Gadsden Museum (505-526-6293)** chronicles Mesilla's colorful past.

RUIDOSO, NEW MEXICO

Highway 54 northeast from El Paso through Alamagordo to
Tularosa • Right (east) on Highway 70 to Ruidoso and Ruidoso
Downs • Drive time is approximately 2½ hours • 800-253-2255

Long before Texans made Houston the air-conditioning capital of the world, they lowered the temperature by heading for high country getaways like Ruidoso, Taos, and Durango. The alpine meadows, pine trees, and light afternoon showers in the Sacramento Mountains make Ruidoso shine as the home of the world's richest horse race, the multi-million dollar All-American Futurity held Labor Day weekend (505-378-4431). The All-American culminates a meet packed with well-known stakes races, all highly competitive and many with enormous purses. Next door to Ruidoso Downs, the **Museum of the Horse** (505-378-4142) houses a collection of 10,000 artifacts, bridles, harnesses, sculptures, and spurs to tell the history of horse and men. By the time winter rolls around (and the horse races have gone south to Sunland Park), Ruidoso turns into one of America's southmost ski towns. Many stay here while schussing on nearby Ski Apache, the highest point on the 460,000-acre Mescalero Apache Indian Reservation. A wonderful way to get to know this area is at the **Inn of the Mountain Gods (800-545-9011 or 800-545-6040).** With its own golf course, tennis courts, and other amenities, this high-altitude getaway is a perfect reason to visit Ruidoso regardless of season. For those who haven't visited in a while, the treacherous municipal airport has been converted into a Jim Colbert golf course, the Links at Sierra Blanca.

WAR EAGLES AIR MUSEUM
Santa Teresa Airport • Santa Teresa, NM • 589-2000
Admission $4, seniors $3, under 13 free • Closed Mondays
Take exit 11 off Interstate 10 (Mesa Street) and go west several miles into New Mexico. Avoid the right fork onto FM 260 which stays in Texas. Follow the signs to the Santa Teresa Airport, and to your left stands the War Eagles hangar. Dozens of planes, most of them flyable, are on display including some gems. The showstopper is a P-38 Lockheed Lightning, one of only eight remaining worldwide of this fast, high-flying WWII interceptor. Other notable craft include the two fighter-bomber warhorses of the Korean Conflict—the Soviet Mig-15 and the American F-86—and a Stealth Fighter (no photos allowed). The gift shop specializes in model aircraft and has a selection of books, caps, patches, pins, and t-shirts. An informal air show featuring an assortment of planes is scheduled the first Saturday morning of the month from May through September.

WHITE SANDS NATIONAL MONUMENT, NEW MEXICO
Highway 54, 88 miles north and Highway 70, 14 miles west
Daily except Christmas • Summer 8–7 • Winter 8–4:30
$4 per vehicle • W+ • Gift shop • Concessions • 505-479-6124
For those familiar with Great Sand Dunes National Monument in Colorado's San Luis Valley, get ready for an entirely different experience. Located in the heart of the world's largest gypsum dune field, White Sands is huge—almost four times as large as its Colorado counterpart. Consequently, the dunes are not so crowded and only a tenth as tall, e.g., 50 to 60 feet high versus almost 700 in Colorado. White Sands is located in the northernmost portion of the Chihuahuan Desert as compared to Great Sand Dunes, which sits in a corner of the fertile San Luis Valley. Finally and most vividly, White Sands dazzles, its dunes a finely ground gypsum rather than the wind-blown topsoil that accumulated to form Great Sand Dunes. Stop at the Visitor Center for an explanation of this area's geologic past and the unique biosystem that has evolved around it. If a short hike is in order, walk the one-mile

self-guided Big Dune nature trail. If behind the wheel with the a/c full blast sounds more appealing in this desert setting, take her for a spin on the sixteen-mile Heart of Sands loop drive. Parking areas along this paved route allow for short walks, and pullouts for wayside exhibits explain the nature of the dunes and their origin as well as some of the animal and plant life that have adapted to this harsh environment. If you're timing this visit closely, be sure to call in advance to find out whether missile testing at the adjacent White Sands Missile Range conflicts with your schedule. Occasional delays of up to two hours can close the Dunes drive. Note, however, that the Dunes drive has longer hours than the Visitor Center: 7 a.m. to 10 p.m. in the summer; 7 a.m. to sunset in the winter.

ANNUAL EVENTS

January

INTERNATIONAL CHAMBER MUSIC FESTIVAL
First Baptist Church • 805 Montana • Admission varies
532-7653
While the rest of America looks to summer festivals for first-class chamber music, El Paso has established a series of concerts each January that brings some of the music world's brightest stars to the Sun City.

February

SOUTHWESTERN INTERNATIONAL LIVESTOCK SHOW & RODEO
El Paso County Coliseum • Admission • 532-1401
This ten-day extravaganza features one of America's top 15 PRCA rodeos (based on total payout). Cowboys and cowgirls from 34 states, Mexico, Canada, and Australia vie for over $150,000 with additional prize money for the final day's Bull Busters. The rodeo makes the Southwestern Livestock Show possible for thousands of exhibitors. Other activities include a horse show, a county fair and market, an exotic snake show, a children's barnyard, a western gala, and a chili cook-off.

March

SIGLO DE ORO FESTIVAL
Chamizal National Memorial • Admission • 534-6277

Different troupes from throughout the Spanish-speaking world come to El Paso to compete in this international classical drama competition. Spanish operas and literature are featured.

April

JUAN DE OÑATE FIRST THANKSGIVING FESTIVAL
Chamizal National Memorial • 532-7273 or 800-351-6024 • Free

Each year on the last Sunday in April, El Pasoans gather to commemorate the First Thanksgiving, a celebration of the expedition of Don Juan de Oñate. In 1595, Oñate was granted the right to conquer New Mexico by the King of Spain. Three years later, he led over 100 men, their families, servants, and herds north from Chihuahua into the great desert. This colonizing effort, the first in America, occurred before many Mayflower passengers were born. Oñate's pioneering route went due north from Chihuahua to El Paso rather than following the Río Conchos to its confluence with the Río Grande and then northwest. The four-mile-long train took four blistering months to reach the Río Grande and the future site of El Paso (April 20, 1598). After ten days of rest, the expedition celebrated with America's first play, America's first Thanksgiving, and a proclamation (*La Toma*) claiming the land for the King of Spain.

June/July/August

VIVA EL PASO!
McKelligon Canyon Amphitheater • 565-6900
Tickets: $6–$10 for adults • $3–$7 for children

After you take your seat high on the east side of the Franklin Mountains, the cast of 50 professional singers, actors, and dancers brings to life El Paso's multi-cultural heritage. Dinner, snacks and drinks are served. Bring a sweater for the cool summer nights.

September

BORDER FOLK FESTIVAL
Chamizal National Memorial • 532-7273
Labor Day weekend • Free
A celebration of El Paso's multicultural heritage staged on the lush lands of Chamizal National Memorial, Border Folk Festival features music, dance, poetry, storytelling, and workshops. Many tasty foods and other concessions are available.

October

AMIGO AIRSHO
Biggs Army Airfield at Fort Bliss • 532-5387
Admission: Adults $6–$18, children $3 • W but not all areas
Be sure to bring your camera or video equipment because the list of demonstrators is as good as any nationwide. Expect the Navy's Blue Angels and the Army's Golden Knights to be joined by professional aviators performing heart-stopping stunts. Walk the show grounds and view military and civilian aircraft, vintage autos, and classic Harleys. Many non-aviation activities are scheduled around the busy two-day show, including a kick-off concert and bowling, golf, racquetball, softball, and volleyball tournaments. Contact the Amigo Airsho for dates, prices, and information on reasonably priced hotel and air packages.

EL PASO JUAREZ INTERNATIONAL CLASSIC
Downtown El Paso/Juarez • 544-9400
This 15-kilometer (9.3 mile) run winds its way back and forth across the border twice en route to proclaiming a champion.

KERMEZAAR
El Paso Convention Center • 533-0837
The largest arts and crafts show in the Southwest features hand-crafted goods including textiles, paintings, and ceramics.

November

WORLD FINALS RODEO
El Paso County Coliseum • 545-1188
Nine days of rodeo and a tenth day that's all bullriding bring 600 cowboys and cowgirls in from across the country and around the world. All are members of the 12,000-strong North American Rodeo Commission and are competing for a $25,000 added purse.

October, November, December

SUN CARNIVAL SPORTS FESTIVAL & PARADE
Citywide • 533-4416 • Admission varies • W
In late October, John Hancock sponsors the All-American Golf Classic featuring outstanding collegiate golfers from the U.S. and Japan. In late November, over 300,000 spectators line Montana Street from Campbell to Copia for the Thanksgiving Day parade. December features the Sun Bowl basketball tournament as well as the nationally televised post-season football classic.

RESTAURANTS

($ = Under $7.50, $$ = Under $15, $$$ = $15+ plus tax & tip)

The self-proclaimed Mexican food capital of the world seems destined to hold onto its crown as the popularity of this cuisine expands along with El Paso and Juarez themselves. Other traditional assumptions about dining in El Paso and Juarez no longer apply. Several well-known establishments not listed below are ongoing concerns, but have let standards fall to the extent that they can be considered health risks.

American

JAXON'S
1135 Airway • 778-9696 • 4799 N. Mesa • 544-1188 • Daily
Lunch and dinner • $–$$ • Cr • W+ but not all areas
An El Paso power lunch starts with tortilla soup or an order of *quesadillas*. Don't pass up the blue corn tostadas, the fajitas, or the unbeatable burger. If you have room left share a mud pie or, better yet, order a single slice for the table. It's that big. At dinner, hand-cut steaks are their forte. Bar.

SAN FRANCISCO GRILL
Downtown at San Francisco, El Paso, and Mills • 545-1386
Daily • Lunch and dinner • $–$$ • Cr • W+ but not all areas
With less than 20 tables and a dozen seats at the bar, this is as clubby as El Paso gets. Stick to the hearty sandwiches. If you're considering the San Francisco Club Sandwich, go for the soup and sandwich combo (the club is monstrous). Best dessert? Go for the crème brûlée (the key lime pie runs a close second). The full bar stocks Anchor Steam.

Barbecue

EL PASO CITY LIMITS

8838 Viscount • 598-7722 • Monday–Saturday
Lunch and dinner • Closed Sunday • $–$$ • AE D MC V W
   City Limits is known for its dollar rib night and specializes in mesquite-smoked barbecue, steaks, and catfish. City Limits (located near the airport) has a sports bar. Their sister restaurant on the west side is the **Rib Hut** at 2612 N. Mesa at UTEP (532-RIBS). Order the baby back ribs and ask for extra sauce for ribs and fingers. Bar.

STATE LINE

1222 Sunland Park Drive • 581-3371 • Daily except Saturday lunch • Lunch and dinner • $–$$ • Cr • W+
   A popular stop for families with its large patio courtyard, booths and tables indoors, and lively decor straight from *Back to the Future*. It only gets more crowded right after a day at the track. Favorites include El Paso's biggest (and arguably best) beef ribs, the well-marinated brisket, an all-you-can-eat country-style platter, and the burgers. Don't order the popular cobbler with ice cream till you see how much of an appetite you have left.

TEXAS BAR-B-Q CO.

1316 Texas Ave. • 546-9051 • Monday–Friday • Breakfast and lunch • $ • Major credit cards for catering orders only • W
   For most barbecue fans, the picture of John Wayne says it all. These folks have their priorities, and mesquite-smoked brisket is tops on their list. The breakfast menu boasts nearly a dozen different *burritos* as well as two servings that'll carry you till Santa Fe: the Mexican Plate and the Country Plate. Consider trying your favorite portion served as a burrito rather than ordering a sandwich. Texas Bar-B-Q Co. caters, custom smokes, and serves to-go brisket, chicken, hash, hot links, or pork any way you want—by the pound, as a plate, or in a sandwich.

Bistro

CAFE CENTRAL

1 Texas Court across from the Paso del Norte Hotel • 545-2233
Monday–Saturday • Lunch and dinner • $$–$$$ • Cr • W
   This is the best restaurant in the book. Changes in season and inspiration prevent any set menu from being printed, but pray that *frutas del mar* is being served when you are seated: green lip

mussels, calamari, scallops, and shrimp reduced with garlic, white wine, butter, and fresh herbs. The only thing closer to perfection is Art Lewis on the saxophone Friday and Saturday nights. Anything served with the *chinois* sauce is superb—soy sauce, cilantro, ginger, and garlic. The entire menu lists favorites like the superb Caesar salad and the *Tacos Tres Colores* (lobster, chicken, and beef). Bar.

Chinese

UNCLE BAO'S

5668 N. Mesa • 585-1818 • 9515 Gateway West • 592-1101
Daily • Lunch and dinner • $–$$$ • Cr • W+

Several years ago, the folks at *Texas Monthly* ranked Uncle Bao's as good if not better than anyplace in San Francisco's Chinatown. Since then, Uncle Bao's has opened up a second location on the west side and has only increased in popularity. If you pass on the Citrus Beef, know that Uncle Bao offers tremendous portions and consistent, Americanized Chinese cuisine. Weekend buffet from 11:30 a.m. to 4:00 p.m. Bar.

Continental

MARTINO

417 Avenida Juarez • 011 52 16 12 33 70 • Daily
Lunch and dinner • $–$$ • Checks

Martino's is the sole surviving bistro on Juarez's once-great strip. With several hundred choices, it's simplest to ask for Oscar as your waiter and enjoy his selections as well as his mean Stoli martini, shaken right at the table. Pass on the salad and the soup course (dramatic but weak) and save room for your entrée—the quail or the *carne asada a la tampiqueña*. A basket of shoestring fries is mandatory. Yes, they are cooked in beef fat. Bar.

Italian

BELLA NAPOLI

6331 N. Mesa • 584-3321
Tuesday–Saturday dinner • Sunday lunch and dinner
Closed Monday • $–$$ • AE MC V • W but not all areas

El Paso comes to Bella Napoli for veal entrées like *ossobucco*, *picata*, and the specials. Try the eggplant parmigan—*magnifico*. Live opera on Thursday nights. Beer and wine.

CAPPETTO'S

5229 Sanders near Cohen Stadium • 755-1304
2716 Montana Ave. off Piedras • 566-9357 • $–$$ • Cr • W
Great meals get off to good beginnings at Cappetto's because
of its excellent Italian salad. Loaded with olives, pepperoni, sala-
mi, and scallions, it's the perfect complement to the piping hot
bread. An outstanding heavy red sauce enhances the many pasta
dishes. Bar.

Border Regional
Mexican Food

There are all kinds of restaurants in El Paso, but only one great
cuisine. This is it. The neighborhood, the building, the decor, they
don't matter. The *salsa* tells you more about the operation than
any guidebook can. Is it prepared onsite, is it fresh, does it have
character? Salsa also tells the style of cuisine. Have a seat at Griggs and sample the traditional red salsa; it's typical of the New
Mexican recipes that the Griggs family has passed down for over
a century. Their servings favor milder palates and feature less
fiery peppers. Just like their salsa.

Restaurants listed in Juarez often go to extremes to ensure a
pleasant dining experience by using filtered water. As with all
cases in Mexico, stick to Mexican food and save the flambé for the
country club. Seafood is a judgment call. There are usually
enough enticing alternatives that the choice doesn't come up. El
Paso-based chains like Avila's and Leo's are included, recommended, and offer good food and good value.

AVILA'S

East side: 10600 Montana • 598-3333 • West side: 6232 N. Mesa
584-3621 • Daily • Lunch and dinner • $ Cr • W
The *salsa*—a green one—is hot, rich, and thick. Always follow
the chips and salsa with an order of *chile con queso*. It goes well
with all of Avila's time-tested entrées: rolled meat tacos and any
enchilada plate. Be sure to save room for an order of El Paso's best
sopapillas.

CASA JURADO

4772 Doniphan • 833-1151 • Bar • Closed Monday
226 Cincinnati • 532-6429 • Beer & wine • Closed Sunday
Lunch and dinner • $–$$ • Cr
The spicy bite of the tortilla soup is tempered by cool avocado
slices. The distinctive orange *salsa* is full of *chiles*, tomato, and

oregano. Entrée recommendations include *chili verde con carne* and the *flautas*, beef or chicken.

DELICIOUS MEXICAN EATERY

3314 Fort Blvd. • **566-1396** • **1335 Montwood** • **857-1396**
Daily • **Breakfast, lunch, and dinner** • **$** • **Checks** • **W**
Continual efforts throughout West Texas and New Mexico have yet to uncover a better *gordita* than at Delicious. Literally "little fat one," these deep-fried corn patties are hollowed out, stuffed with every imaginable filling, and quickly gobbled up. The *chile rellenos* make you wonder what you've been eating all these years. In order to serve up the freshest possible relleno, the Borrego family buys chiles in season from New Mexico, California, and Mexico. If you've never had *relleno burrito*, this is your chance.

FORTI'S MEXICAN ELDER

East side: 321 Chelsea • **772-0066** • **West side: 7410 Remcon Circle** • **585-0086** • **Daily** • **Lunch and dinner** • **$–$$** • **Cr**
The best of the big boys. No one in El Paso has run a restaurant as well as Consuelo Forti has for the past twenty years, and one of the reasons is that no one has run her kitchen except chef Robert Loya. Try the chicken *salpicón*. Served cold, this shredded chicken salad is prepared with a lime and cilantro vinaigrette. For a bite of everything, skip breakfast and order the Combination Plate #3—an *enchilada*, a *taco*, a *tamale*, a *chile relleno, chile verde* or *rojo, guacamole*, beans and rice. Beautiful presentation, better food. Don't pass up the *flan* (dessert custard) or the Mexican lemonade (regular or strawberry *margaritas*).

GRIGGS NEW MEXICAN FOOD

9007 Montana • **598-3451** • **5800 Doniphan** • **584-0451**
Daily • **Lunch and dinner** • **$–$$** • **D MC V** • **W**
Just because George Bush used to visit doesn't mean you should write it off. Not surprisingly, Mr. Resumé preferred New Mexican style cooking—milder and less forceful. The flavorful red *salsa* has little bite and makes a wonderful introduction to Mexican food for first timers apprehensive about steam coming out their ears. For a safe entreé, order a plate of green enchiladas.

GUSSIE'S TAMALES AND MEXICAN BAKERY

2200 N. Piedras • **566-8209**
Daily 8 a.m. till 8 p.m. • **$** • **Checks**
Don't be deceived: this is not your typical *panaderia* (bakery). In addition to *biscochos*, corn cookies, *pan de huevo, polvorones*, and *timbales*, eastside El Pasoans know Gussie for her heavenly

tamales. They're full of her wonderful spirit, and Gussie tolerates no shortcuts like *maseca* or animal fat. If you need the cure, enjoy the excellent *menudo.* Take-away only.

H&H CAR WASH
No. 1: 701 E. Yandell at Ochoa • 533-1144
No. 2: 8630 Dyer St. • 755-2131 (No food service)
Daily except Sunday • Breakfast and lunch • $
A true cross-section of El Paso can be found at H&H. Witness the parade of Mercedes, Lexus, and beat-up Isuzu Troopers. The concept, a combination 1950s car wash, gas station, and diner, embodies the American dream. A leading reason the food is so good is because of the brisk traffic in the garage. Sit at the bar and worship the *carne picada,* the best breakfast in the book—chopped sirloin tips, onions, tomato, and chiles, stir-fried and served with a side of *salsa* prepared fresh at H&H. The milder green salsa is a jalapeño blend, and the higher octane red is made with *chile de arbol.* In the *carne picadillo,* the sirloin is replaced with ground beef. By the time you finish eating, your car is washed, starched, and ironed for $8.50 plus gas.

JULIO'S CAFE CORONA
Avenida 16 de Septiembre • (0115216) 13 33 97 or 13 08 33
Daily • Lunch and dinner • $–$$ • MC V
Pass on the El Paso location and head straight to Juarez for a bowl of *Tlalpeño* soup, a hearty chicken broth made with much too much chicken, cilantro, lime, and a hint of *chipotle* (dried, smoked red jalapeño). Someone must order *salpicón*—cold, shredded beef salad in a chipotle, lime, cilantro vinaigrette and tossed with red onions, tomato, cheese and avocado. Or try the *machaca* with egg—shredded, dried beef prepared with scrambled egg and a red chile sauce. Dessert is easy: *cajeta crepes*—three rolled crepes, smothered in cajeta (a Mexican caramel sauce) and topped with toasted pecans.

L&J CAFE
3622 Missouri by the Concordia Cemetery • 566-8418
Exit Copia off I-10, go north to Missouri, and take a right
Restaurant: Mon.–Fri. 11–8 • Saturday 11–6 • Closed Sunday
Bar: Mon. Tue. Thu. 10 a.m.–12 p.m. • Wed. Fri. Sat. 10 a.m.–2 a.m.
Sun 12–12 • $ • Cr
With great food, good prices, and a long bar, the L&J boasts a crew of regulars who make the cast of *Cheers* look like new kids on the block. Founded in the 1920s by Tony Flores (grandfather of Leo, the present owner), it first opened for business with a hitch-

ing post out front, endured Prohibition, and survived countless raids by the Texas Rangers. The wonderful red sauce on the stacked enchiladas blends red *chile, chile de arbol,* and *pasilla* to perfection. They taste even better at the bar. Diehards order them *montado*—with an egg (sunny-side-up on top). Try the *caldillo* or the *chile verde* the second time around. Beer and wine.

LA HACIENDA CAFE

1720 W. Paisano • 532-5094
Tuesday–Sunday • Lunch and dinner • $–$$ • Cr • W
The locals have been grumbling that the dirt-cheap prices are now only reasonable, but as long as Carlos keeps serving up cold Tecates, they'll be back. Try the *tampiqueña* or go off the menu for the chicken-fried steak. Season it with the tasty *salsa,* blended with cilantro, onion, and red and green peppers. Other favorites include the green *chile enchiladas,* the stacked red *enchiladas,* the *chile rellenos,* and the excellent *flan* (dessert custard). Recent changes at La Hacienda include an expanded patio area and live music. If the food wasn't so consistently good, the restaurant would be a museum. *El Camino Real* crossed the Río Bravo near La Hacienda, which was built in 1849 or 1850. Known as Hart's Mill or *el Molino,* it served one of El Paso's earliest settlements and was adjacent to Fort Bliss later in the nineteenth century. Unfortunately, finding La Hacienda can be a substantial undertaking. Call for directions (or stay at the nearby Sunset Heights Bed & Breakfast). Beer and wine.

LEO'S

7872 N. Loop • 593-9025
5315 Hondo Pass Ave. • 757-0505
5103 Montana Ave. • 566-4972
2285 Trawood Dr • 591-2511
8001 N. Mesa • 833-1189
Daily • Lunch and dinner • Each location closes on a different day • $ • AE MC V
If the food at El Paso's best-known Mexican restaurants reminds you of Avila's, it's because they're family. The *salsa* is similar, too, but with more cilantro. Excellent *burritos* and *chile con carne.*

RUBIO'S RESTAURANT

5734 Alameda near Paisano • 772-5354 • Tuesday–Friday 11–6
Weekends 7–4 • Closed Monday • $ • MC V • W
Don't be surprised if the whole Rubio family is at work cooking, waiting tables, or working the cash register. Start off with El Paso/Juarez's best *chile con queso.* Made with white cheese, flame-

roasted chiles, chicken broth, tomato, and onion, all the Velveeta in the world won't prepare you for this one. Though the *flautas* are legendary, their specialty is beef *fajitas*, and their secret is a different cut of meat. Add a side of *frijoles rancheros*, and all you'll need is a slice of coconut cream pie to end the perfect meal. Beer and wine.

Steaks

BILLY CREWS

1200 Country Club Rd. • 589-2071
Dinner daily • Reservations suggested • $$–$$$ • Cr • W+

Don't be intimidated by the first-class wine list (rated as one of the Top 100 worldwide by the *Wine Spectator*). Ask for assistance and order by the glass. For tenderness, order the filet. For flavor, choose the ribeye. Big appetites go to the New York. All the dessert pies are baked at the restaurant.

CATTLEMAN'S STEAKHOUSE

At Indian Cliff Ranch (see SIDE TRIPS above) • 544-3200
Monday–Friday 4:30–10 • Saturday 4–10 • Sunday 12–9
$–$$$ • AE DC MC V • W+

Listed as serving the Best Steak in America by *People* magazine and a perennial choice for the best steak in El Paso, Cattleman's is El Paso's best-known steakhouse. The monstrous portions and two-pound T-Bone can satisfy the biggest appetites, and there is more to do before, during, and after dinner at the Indian Cliff Ranch than at most amusement parks. Fort Apache, a grist mill, a children's zoo, hayrides, an Indian maze, and movie sets are all within walking distance.

CLUBS AND BARS

BIG WALLY'S SPORTS BAR & GRILL

2514 N. Mesa • 532-0333 • Daily 11 a.m. to 2 a.m. • Cr • W+

Start with over a dozen televisions (including three big-screens), add El Paso's best wings as well as *fajitas*, burgers, and steaks, and throw in live music Thursday through Saturday nights. All you're missing are the daily drink specials, Happy Hour beginning at 3:00, and throngs of business people, college kids, and assorted El Paso locals who make Big Wally's happen. Bar.

CHIHUAHUA CHARLIE'S
P.T. de la Republica • (0115216) 3 17 80 or 3 99 40 • Daily
Lunch and dinner • AE MC V
   Their slogan is "We don't speak English but we promise not to laugh at your Spanish." Live music, massive 16-ounce *margaritas*, and the lively binational crowd make Chihuahua Charlie's a noisy favorite. Easily reached by crossing the Cordova Bridge of the Americas. Bar.

COMIC STRIP
6633 N. Mesa • 581-8877 (Hotline)
Tuesday–Saturday after 6:30 p.m.
   If you're tired of spending six or seven dollars on first-run movies, drop three bucks some weeknight and head to the Comic Strip. You'll get more than your money's worth, and that's not including Tuesday night's two-for-one specials. Friday and Saturday nights cost more but that's when top national touring comedians make it to town. One show nightly at 8:00 Tuesday through Thursday; Friday and Saturday shows start at 8:30 and 10:45. Open seating. Alcoholic and non-alcoholic beverages. Must be 17 or older if not accompanied by an adult. Bar.

DENIM & DIAMONDS
9505 Viscount 595-0036 • Tuesday–Sunday 5 p.m. till 2 a.m.
   The horseshoe-shaped dance floor gives the place away. Put on your Wranglers, step into your boots, and scoot on over to El Paso's busiest country & western club. Plenty of live music, drink specials, and a packed dance floor are regular nightly fare. Must be 21 or over.

EL PASO SURF CLUB
2500 N. Mesa • 544-7873 • Daily • Lunch and dinner • Cr
   Never a dull moment here. Pat Devlin continues to think up new promotions while keeping favorites going including the 16 de Septiembre fiesta, beach parties, 80-ounce party buckets, the ever-popular Shoot-the-Worm Club, and, for the first time in Texas, female professional boxing. The pro boxing nights run during the summer and most bouts are ten rounds. Tickets run from $5 to $50 with prime rib and drinks included with the best seats.

KENTUCKY CLUB
629 Avenida Juarez • Juarez • (0115216) 20647
The legend. Enjoy this last vestige of a bygone era in Juarez's history at the Kentucky Club's enormous hand-carved bar, staffed by barmen in black tie whose tenure at the Kentucky Club routinely exceeds the age of their patrons. Worth a trip in themselves are the Ramos gin fizz and the *margarita*, shaken over ice and served neat.

ACCOMMODATIONS

($ = Under $40, $$ = $40–$75, $$$ = $75–$100, $$$$ = Over $100)
Room Tax 14%

With over six thousand hotel rooms available in the El Paso/ Juarez area, every budget and style can be matched. This list is broken down by area and should not be viewed as all-inclusive.

East Side

AMERISUITES HOTEL
8250 Gateway East • 591-9600 or 800-255-1755 • $$
This two-story hotel located on the south side of Interstate 10 has 126 units, each with kitchen, bedroom, and bath, all with cable TV, pay-per-view movies, and room phones (charge for local calls). Amenities include pool and spa, free airport shuttle, and complimentary breakfast.

LA QUINTA LOMALAND
11033 Gateway West • 591-2244 or 800-531-5900 • $$
This two-story motor inn has 138 units including non-smoking rooms with cable TV (Showtime), pay-per-view movies, and free local calls. Denny's and Guenther's Edelweiss are right next door. Amenities include outdoor heated pool, complimentary continental breakfast and free coffee in the lobby, and free parking. Small pets OK. Discount rates for AAA and Sam's Wholesale Club available.

Airport/Mid-City

EL PASO AIRPORT HILTON
2027 Airway Blvd. • 778-4241 or 800-742-7248 • $$$–$$$$
With spade at the ready, Conrad Hilton led the groundbreaking ceremonies at the four-story Hilton right as you leave El Paso

International (200 yards away). With 121 units and 151 suites, there is also an Executive Level ($$$$). All rooms feature cable TV (Showtime), pay-per-view movies, and room phones (charge for local calls). Amenities include Magnim's restaurant, lounge, and piano bar, heated outdoor pool, jacuzzi, health club with sauna, courtesy airport shuttle around the clock, and free parking. Small pets OK.

EL PASO MARRIOTT
1600 Airway Blvd. • **779-3300 or 800-228-9290** • **$$$$**

This six-story Marriott has 296 units including two-bedroom suites and non-smoking rooms with cable TV (HBO) and pay-per-view movies, and room phones (charge for local calls). Amenities include two restaurants—Chatfield's and La Cascada—and McGinty's lounge, indoor/outdoor pool, health club with sauna, gift shop, courtesy shuttle to airport, free parking, and an American Airlines ticket office. Pets on the first floor only.

EMBASSY SUITES
6100 Gateway East • **779-6222 or 800-EMBASSY** • **$$$$**

This eight-story hotel located right by I-10 has 185 suites with satellite TV, pay-per-view movies, a microwave or stove and oven, coffee maker, and refrigerator. Amenities include Chloee's restaurant and lounge, indoor pool, health club with jacuzzi, sauna, and steam room, gift shop, courtesy shuttle to airport, complimentary cooked-to-order breakfast, manager's reception each afternoon featuring open bar and complimentary hors d'oeuvres, and free parking. Pets allowed for $50 non-refundable fee (ouch!).

LA QUINTA GERONIMO
6140 Gateway East • **778-9321 or 800-531-5900** • **$$**

This two-story motor inn has 121 units including suites and non-smoking rooms with cable TV (Showtime) and room phones (no charge for local calls). Amenities include two adjacent 24-hour restaurants, Denny's and the Kettle, heated outdoor pool, courtesy shuttle to airport, complimentary coffee and complimentary continental breakfast. Small pets OK. Discount rates for AAA, Allstate, and Sam's Wholesale Club members.

RADISSON SUITE INN
1770 Airway Blvd. • **772-3333 or 800-333-3333** • **$$$**

Each of the 150 rooms at this three-story hotel is a suite. Located right by the El Paso International Airport, smoking and non-smoking suites are available. All rooms include cable TV, a VCR, access to a complimentary video library, and no charge for local calls. Amenities include a complimentary cooked-to-order breakfast or continental breakfast, complimentary cocktails during the week, the Cafe at the Radisson restaurant and lounge, heated outdoor pool, health club with sauna, exercise room, game room, gift shop, same-day valet laundry, laundry room, courtesy shuttle to and from the airport, and free parking. No pets allowed. AAA, government, and limited AARP discounts available.

Downtown/Medical Center

CLIFF INN
1600 Cliff Drive • 533-6700 or 800-333-2543 • $$$

Antiques fill the lobby of this gracious establishment located within walking distance of Sierra Medical Center and other hospital facilities. The elegant single-story hotel emphasizes convenience while enabling guests to look after medical needs. Guests are offered complimentary transportation to and from doctor's appointments, as well as airport shuttles. The Cliff Inn has 78 guest rooms, kitchenettes, and suites including non-smoking rooms with cable TV (HBO) and room phones (charge for local calls). Amenities include the Three Continents Restaurant and Lounge, pool with jacuzzi, lap pool and tennis nearby, complimentary breakfast, complimentary hors d'oeuvres, and free parking. No pets.

CAMINO REAL PASO DEL NORTE
101 S. El Paso St. • 534-3000 • $$$$

What the Waldorf is to New York and the Adolphus is to Dallas, the Paso del Norte is to El Paso. Located right across from the Convention Center, this is not only El Paso's largest hotel, with 375 rooms and 32 suites, but it's a landmark in its own right. Designed by Henry Trost, the Paso del Norte opened with a lavish gala on Thanksgiving Day in 1912 and is still the first name in El Paso accommodations. Built of brick, steel, and terra cotta, the interior was done in fire-proof gypsum from nearby White Sands, and the lobby, mezzanine, and dining rooms were finished with cherrystone, golden scagliola, and black serpentine marble and solid mahogany. Non-smoking and handicap rooms are available, and all rooms have cable TV, pay-per-view movies, and room phones (charge for local calls). On property are the Dome Grill, Cafe Río for more casual dining, and Uptown's club. Complementing any dining experience is a round of drinks at the historic Tiffany Dome Bar (perhaps the best bar in Texas). The dome is encased in its own temperature-controlled room and insured for over $1 million. Amenities include an outdoor heated pool and health club, gift shop, courtesy shuttle to El Paso International Airport, secured parking (fee), and a Delta ticket counter on the premises.

HOLIDAY INN PARK PLACE

325 N. Kansas Street • 533-8241 or 800-HOLIDAY • $$–$$$

This 12-story hotel is located in the heart of downtown El Paso about 12 blocks from Mexico and has 119 units including suites and non-smoking rooms with cable TV (HBO) and room phones with no charge for local calls. Be sure to ask for a room with a balcony. Amenities include the Park on Five restaurant and the Main Street Bar and Grille, an outdoor pool on the fifth floor, a health club affiliation, complimentary shuttle to and from the airport, complimentary coffee and newspaper, and free parking. Pets under 20 pounds welcome as long as they are not left unattended. AAA rates available.

INTERNATIONAL HOTEL

113 W. Missouri (Exit 19) • 544-3300 • $–$$

Good rates might attract you to this convenient downtown property, but Elvis Presley fans take note: the King booked most of the 7th floor for his final El Paso appearance (1976). Seventeen stories tall, the International has 209 smoking and non-smoking units including suites. All rooms have cable TV and phones with free local calls. Amenities include the Starr Room restaurant ($) and bar, room service, View at the Top club on the 17th floor featuring *mariachi* entertainment and a happy hour buffet, an outdoor unheated pool on the 7th floor, courtesy shuttle to air, train, or bus connections and doctor's appointments, banquet and meeting facilities, and free indoor covered parking. Pets OK (deposit).

West Side

HOLIDAY INN SUNLAND PARK

900 Sunland Park Drive • 833-2900 or 800-446-4656 • $$

This two-story property located right off Interstate 10 at the Sunland Park exit has 166 units including non-smoking rooms, cable TV (HBO), pay-per-view movies, and room phones with free local calls. Amenities include the Sierra Grill restaurant and coffee shop, the Tack Room lounge, an outdoor pool, free airport shuttle, golf and tennis affiliations, and free parking. Small pets OK. AAA and AARP rates available.

Bed & Breakfasts

SUNSET HEIGHTS BED & BREAKFAST INN
717 W. Yandell • 544-1743 or 800-767-8513 • AE MC V • $$–$$$$
You'd think from what Richard Barnett and Dr. Roni Martinez offer that you were ensconced in a resort hotel: poolside hors d'oeuvres, hot tub and sauna, cable TV, air conditioning, phones, and fireplaces. Try a renovated 1905 brick Victorian National Historic home full of Victorian furnishings, solid brass fixtures, and surrounded by wrought iron fencing. As far as convenience goes, this one can't be beat. El Paso's hardest-to-find Mexican restaurant, **La Hacienda,** is just down the street, and after a night in Juarez you can walk across the Santa Fe Bridge, get in your car, and arrive in two minutes without taking a single turn (a helpful plus after a night on the strip). There are five rooms (including a honeymoon suite) and a cottage, each with private baths including immense claw-foot tubs. A full five- to eight-course breakfast is served in the dining room or the rose garden. Gourmet French dinners are available by reservation with a six-person minimum. Take the Porfirio Diaz exit from Interstate 10, and a right on Yandell to Randolph. Check in by appointment. Check out by noon. No smoking. No pets.

YOUTH HOSTEL

GARDNER HOTEL—EL PASO INTERNATIONAL YOUTH HOSTEL
Member AYH • 311 E. **Franklin** • 532-3661 • **$**
One night's rent + tax required for any reservation
Cash, check, money order, or MC V accepted for deposit
No charge for cancellation up to 72 hours in advance
You'll be right in the middle of downtown El Paso when you stay at the Gardner. It's convenient to Union Depot with eastbound and westbound service three times weekly and to the Greyhound bus terminal with daily arrivals and departures. If you're flying into El Paso, either take a cab downtown (about $15) or hop on the #33 bus to San Jacinto Park. The Gardner is a block north to Franklin Avenue and less than two blocks east. Though the oldest continually operating hotel in town (1922), it's not a dump. The recent lobby renovation reeks of oiled wood, polished marble, tanned leather, and gilded antiques. The Gardner has 50 rooms, ten of which are dedicated to the hostel ($12 per person per night) along with a kitchen, dining area, common area, and

laundry. The scoop on the hostel is that it's better than average. Points are added for the common area, the laundry, overall convenience, and round-the-clock access to the property as well as to the bunk rooms. Points are deducted for the smaller than average bathrooms, the cramped kitchen, and the nagging list of AYH rules and regulations. Right next door is one of the city's better-known burger stands, the **Big Bun.** Nothing on the menu tops two bucks. From El Paso to the Big Bend, forget about hitching a ride. You'll only get sunburnt and disappointed. Either take Amtrak from nearby Union Depot (three times a week) or catch a Greyhound bus from the downtown terminal located across from the Civic Center (daily). Cars can be rented in Alpine upon arrival. Commissary.

FORT DAVIS

JEFF DAVIS COUNTY SEAT   ★   900   ★   (915)

For over four centuries, visitors to the Davis Mountains have marveled at this mountain island in the desert. Black bear and cool mountain breezes are found in stands of pine and oak that surround the tallest town in Texas. Winter snows are welcome. It's still ranching country here, but tourism is taking over as the old Fort, Davis Mountains State Park, and the University of Texas McDonald Observatory and nearby Big Bend National Park attract more visitors each year.

Spanish explorer Antonio de Bermejo journeyed through Limpia Canyon less than a hundred years after Columbus discovered America (1583). His countrymen, however, preferred to settle closer to *el Camino Real* which led from Mexico City to El Paso and then north to Santa Fe. Something about Apaches and Comanches. Too far removed to be of much interest to Mexico or the Republic of Texas, it was only when Fort Davis was garrisoned that Anglo-Americans began to settle the Apache Mountains (as they were then called). Those who recall Jeff Davis remember him as President of the Confederacy. During the Pierce

Administration, he was Secretary of War and ordered the fort to be established (1854). It was also as a result of his efforts (the Civil War) that the fort was abandoned. His name now graces the fort, the town, and the county. During the War Between the States, neither blue nor grey triumphed here; it was the Apache who burnt the yellow and limber pine fortress to the ground. Regarrisoned two years after Appomattox, Fort Davis became the headquarters for the Army's Department of the Pecos. The arrival of the railroad and the subjugation of the Native Americans led to the fort's closure. The town of Fort Davis survived as county seat for an immense ranching region and now as one of the most enjoyable tourist destinations in Texas.

TOURIST SERVICES

FORT DAVIS CHAMBER OF COMMERCE
Hotel Limpia • P.O. Box 378 • Fort Davis • 79734
426-3015 or 800-524-3015 • Daily 7 a.m. to 10 p.m.
Located in the lobby of the Hotel Limpia, the Fort Davis Chamber has plenty to offer visitors planning to come or already in town. The toll free number is a good start, but even better are the hours the Chamber keeps—the same as the hotel's front desk. Call for info packets, event schedules, and restaurant and accommodation updates. Also available are several publications on Fort Davis, flyers on local and area attractions, and complimentary coffee.

GUIDEBOOKS AND PUBLICATIONS

JEFF DAVIS COUNTY MOUNTAIN DISPATCH
P.O. Box 1097 • Fort Davis • 79734 • 426-3077
Annual subscription: $21
If you want to make the most of your visit or enjoyed it enough to keep in touch, get a subscription to the *Dispatch*. A weekly, it runs about 12 pages and covers local events, area activities, and the seasonal changes that occur at the fort, the observatory, and other attractions.

FORT DAVIS APACHE ROCKET
By the Fort Davis Historical Society • Free
This complimentary 16-page publication is packed with Fort Davis history. Original sources are quoted, a historic tour is mapped, and plenty of background on the post and the town is included. Grab a copy as soon as you get to town. Available at most shops and restaurants.

BIRD'S-EYE VIEW

SKYLINE DRIVE

Davis Mountains State Park
Four miles northwest of Fort Davis via State Highway 118

Pay four dollars at the park's entrance (or show a valid Texas Conservation Passport), meander down Park Road 3 until you see the Skyline Drive arrow pointing left, and put it in low gear. By the time you drive to the hill's crest, you'll come to a fork in the road. Bear right. When you kill your engine, the quiet will be deafening and the vistas amazing. The view from atop the Skyline Drive is unbeatable. Some rave about the Window at the Basin in Big Bend National Park, others extol the River Road along the Río Grande, but if you want to experience what comes to mind when people say the word "TEXAS," look no further. Depending on the season and the rains, the thousands of square miles that surround you can range from straw-colored to shades of green or even snow white. Though gentle, snowfall is no rarity along these southernmost Rockies. Clearly visible to the north stands the University of Texas McDonald Observatory. The prominent knob on the mountain off to the left of the observatory is Old Baldy. It sits atop Mount Livermore, the tallest peak in the Davis Mountains at 8,378 feet. Proceeding clockwise or to your right from the observatory are the Glass Mountains over by Marathon, pyramid-shaped Mount Ord on the far side of Alpine, closer and steeper Mitre Peak, Haystack and the Puertacitas, Chinati Peak down by Mexico, and Blue Mountain along the road to Valentine.

MUSEUMS

NEILL DOLL MUSEUM

On Court St. seven blocks west of the courthouse • 426-3969
Open June 1 through Labor Day • Tuesday–Saturday 10–5
Sunday 1:30–5 • Closed Monday • Off-season by appointment
only • Admission

Built as a summer house for Galveston resident Henry Trueheart, over 350 dolls from the nineteenth and twentieth century are displayed, with the oldest dating back to the 1830s. The collection also includes antique doll buggies, quilts, toys, and bottles. For an unusual treat, consider staying overnight. Bed and breakfast accommodations are available (no children).

OVERLAND TRAIL MUSEUM
Go two blocks west from sign on Main Street by the Stone Village • **Tuesday–Saturday 10–5 (summer)** • **By appointment (winter)** • **Adults $1, children 50¢** • **426-3904 (Historical Society)**
Owned and operated by the Fort Davis Historical Society, this museum is located on the longest existing stretch of the Overland Trail still in use as an improved dirt road. Most portions of the Trail are either paved or have been passed over by progress. Set in the former residence of local barber, tinkerer, and Justice of the Peace Nick Mersfelder, the numerous exhibits detail Jeff Davis County's early days. The original post office from nearby Valentine is set up as are local artifacts including spurs, saddles, furnishings, and firearms. Photos, many from the 1800s, depict life at the fort, on pioneer ranches, and in town.

HISTORIC PLACES

FORT DAVIS NATIONAL HISTORIC SITE
P.O. Box 1456 • **Fort Davis** • **79734** • **426-3224**
Daily except Christmas • **8–6 (summer), 8–5 (winter)**
Admission: $2 per person • **W+ but not all areas**
Fort Davis was established in 1854 by the Eighth U.S. Infantry to protect travelers and mail coaches on the San Antonio-El Paso Road. It was named for the then current Secretary of War, Jefferson Davis. Fort Davis was abandoned for most of the Civil War and left to the Apaches who destroyed many of the original buildings. In 1867, it was reestablished by units of the Ninth U.S. Cavalry, one of the newly formed regiments consisting of soldiers of African-American descent. Known as buffalo soldiers, these troops served at Fort Davis from 1867 to 1885. The death of the Mescalero chief Victorio (1880) signaled the end of the Indian Wars in Texas and, too, the mission of the post.

In 1891, Fort Davis, having "outlived its usefulness," was abandoned by the military and reverted back to private ownership. The officers' quarters became some of the best rent houses in town, and by the turn of the century the Post Hospital was a favorite spot for picnics and dances. In the late 1920s, the property was leased by cowboy movie star Jack Hoxie as a movie set. In the 1950s, the Fort Davis Historical Society leased the property. The society was instrumental in having Fort Davis authorized as a National Historic Site (1961).

Today a visitor center, museum, and auditorium are located in restored barracks. A slide program is presented in the auditorium every half hour, and the sounds of a Dress Retreat Parade can be heard on the grounds at scheduled times. During the summer, park rangers and volunteers dressed as soldiers, officer's wives, and servants keep open and interpret some of the restored and refurnished buildings. In winter, these buildings are open for self-guided tours.

There are several miles of hiking trails on the grounds, and a shaded picnic area is a perfect place to have lunch. Electric carts are available to handicapped or restricted visitors. Special events include an Easter Sunrise service, Fourth of July Celebration, and the Friends of Fort Davis NHS Festival on the Saturday of Labor Day weekend. Special evening tours are held in the spring and fall. These tours take visitors back in time and give a glimpse of what life was like at Fort Davis in the 1870s and 1880s.

JEFF DAVIS COUNTY LIBRARY
Just south of the County Courthouse
Tuesday, Thursday, Friday 12–6 • Saturday 9–1 • 426-3802
"Get Booked" is the fitting slogan of the county's public library (located in the former Jeff Davis County jail).

PIONEER CEMETERY
Take Highway 118 south from Fort Davis ½ mile to cemetery sign • **Open daily** • **No admission fee**
A big blue highway department sign points across from the 118 Cafe to a rickety old gate. Open it and walk down the paved path several hundred feet to the grassy field that contains the graves of Fort Davis pioneers, soldiers of the Confederacy, and many whose tombstones have disintegrated and whose names have been forgotten. Quite common are wooden crosses, mute memorials in this abandoned meadow. For a town of less than a thousand, it's hard to imagine but modern Fort Davis makes use of two other cemeteries these days.

OTHER POINTS OF INTEREST

CHIHUAHUAN DESERT RESEARCH INSTITUTE VISITOR CENTER
Three miles south of Fort Davis on Highway 118 • **837-8370**
April through August • Monday–Friday 1–5 • Saturday 9–6
Free • W
In the foothills of the Davis Mountains just south of Fort Davis, CDRI explores the enormous biotic province that extends from

near Mexico City in central Mexico north through the Trans-Pecos and into the Rio Grande Valley of central and southern New Mexico and adjacent southeastern Arizona. The Chihuahuan Desert is one of the four major deserts in the United States (the other three being the Great Basin, the Mojave, and the Sonora). Visitors learn about this vast and varied desert area at the Chihuahuan Desert Arboretum, a 40-acre area which has been divided into approximately 57 plant families, most of which were grown from seed. The 4,000-square-foot Cactus Propagation Greenhouse houses nearly 200 species of cactus and succulents that comprise the Institute's collection, among the world's largest. The Visitor Center also features the self-guided Modesta Canyon Trail System to a series of hidden springs at the mouth of a beautiful wooded canyon and another route to Clayton Peak, the highest point on the property. The loop through the Canyon takes about 1.5 hours to walk, and the top of Clayton Peak by itself is about a half-hour jaunt.

DAVIS MOUNTAINS STATE PARK

Superintendent • Box 786 • Fort Davis • 79734 • 426-3337
Four miles northwest of Fort Davis via Highways 17 and 118
$4 per vehicle weekday • W+ but not all areas

One of the most visited state parks, Davis Mountains State Park straddles the confluence of Keesey and Limpia Creeks and offers visitors a wide choice of activities, amenities and, above all, scenic splendor (see **BIRD'S-EYE VIEW**). Rising from 4,900 to 5,675 feet above sea level, the park provides numerous facilities to enjoy the cool summers and mild winters of the Davis Mountains, including campsites, trailer sites with electric or full hookups, and 39 hotel rooms at the Indian Lodge (see **ACCOMMODATIONS**). The park's interpretive center is open from 4 to 6 p.m. during the summer and from 3 to 5 p.m. the rest of the year. Hikers can take advantage of trails within the park as well as trek to nearby Fort Davis National Historic Site (3.5 miles one way). Texas Conservation Passport holders can enjoy trails in the recently acquired 1,400-acre Limpia Canyon Primitive Area. Passport holders can also participate in the park's unique bird banding program, which is offered from August to November and from March to May from 8 to 11 a.m. This is a rare opportunity in one of the state's top flyways. Reservations are suggested (426-3337).

MCDONALD OBSERVATORY
Highway 118, 17 miles north of Fort Davis • **426-3640**
**UT McDonald Observatory • P.O. Box 1337 • Fort Davis
79734 • Visitor Center open daily 9–5 except Thanksgiving,
Christmas, and New Year's Day • Longer hours during
summer for star parties**
William Johnson McDonald, a prosperous Paris (Texas) banker, willed to the University of Texas over $1,000,000 in 1925 for the creation of an observatory. Upon his death, this windfall caught everyone flat-footed including UT's Board of Regents and McDonald's heirs. As you can tell from the immense 82- and 107-inch reflector telescopes, housed in burnt orange and white domes, McDonald's wishes were carried out (though not without an out-of-court settlement to quiet his heirs). The facility search committee selected 6,800-foot Mount Locke high in the Davis Mountains, far from the lights of larger cities and the clouds of coastal Texas.

Recognized around the world for its research excellence, the University of Texas has once again focused attention upon the McDonald Observatory with the announcement that UT will join with Penn State University as principal partners in the construction of a massive new scope atop adjacent Mount Fowlkes, the William P. Hobby-Robert Eberly Telescope. Unlike more traditional optical telescopes, the Hobby-Eberly Telescope will be a *spectroscopic survey telescope* or SST. Spectroscopic astronomy measures the amount and composition of wavelengths (or colors) of light from astronomical objects. This light is captured at the focus of the 91 computer-controlled hexagonal segments that compose the primary mirror. Think of these segments as forming a Texas-sized honeycomb (more than 10 meters wide). In a separate room beneath the SST, a fiber optic cable transmits the incoming light to a mass of spectroscopic instrumentation. This is where the research begins.

SSTs can analyze data from more distant and fainter astronomical objects. They cost less, too: The $13.5 million SST is approximately 15% the amount spent on the recently constructed Keck telescope in Hawaii. With different phases for design, contracts, and construction, **the new telescope is scheduled for completion in late 1997.** Once operational, this "Arecibo type" telescope (named for a similarly configured Puerto Rican radio telescope) will look into many astronomical phenomena that present telescopes and observing schemes are incapable of studying. Opportunities include the measurement of astronomical distances and velocities, aspects of stellar evolution, dark matter, and variable stars such as R. Coronae Borealis, RV Tauri, and Algols.

The staff at the Observatory expects the number of visitors to double during the construction phase from the present level of more than 150,000 annually. The W.L. Moody, Jr. Visitors' Information Center, located at the base of Mount Locke, offers astronomy exhibits, films, a gift shop, and a bookstore. The Center is open year-round from 9 a.m. to 5 p.m. During the day, weather permitting, solar viewing is performed at the center at 11 a.m. and 3:30 p.m. From March 1 through October 31, the center stays open on Tuesday, Friday, and Saturday evenings from 5 p.m. until the end of the star party at the Public Observatory located just behind the Visitors' Information Center. With cooperation from the heavens, you can view the planets, the moon, galaxies, and other celestial objects through large telescopes. Bring your binoculars if you own some, and be sure to dress warmly—the mountain air gets cool after sunset. Because of the seasonal variance in time of sunset, the beginning times change monthly.

Tuesday, Thursday, Friday Star Party Schedule

January	6:30 p.m.	July	9:30 p.m.
February	7:00 p.m.	August	9:00 p.m.
March	7:30 p.m.	September	8:30 p.m.
April	8:30 p.m.	October	8:00 p.m.
May	9:00 p.m.	November	6:30 p.m.
June	9:30 p.m.	December	6:30 p.m.

Once a month, McDonald Observatory opens the 107-inch telescope for an evening program at no cost. Participation requires reservations six months in advance. The admission fee, schedule of dates, and complimentary tickets can be obtained by contacting the W.L. Moody, Jr. Visitors' Information Center.

SPORTS AND ACTIVITIES

Cycling

The Davis Mountains offer year-round cycling for all levels and at all distances. Most of the favored routes are on well-maintained state highways that are relatively free of traffic. A few basics: Watch for livestock—there is plenty of open-range (unfenced) grazing in Jeff Davis County. Make sure you have ample water, spare tubes, and tools for basic repairs. A cycling trip can be derailed for want of parts and/or service. Some repairs as well as mountain bikes and cruisers, van support, and tour planning is available at Fort Davis Bike Rentals (915-426-3916 during the day and 915-426-3461 at night). This cyclery is located in town at the Fountainbleau RV Park, where convenient camping and RV hookups, a washateria, and showers are available. The nearest full service repair shop is in Midland (Peyton Bikes 915-699-1718), several hours by car and two days by UPS ground delivery.

For the less ambitious, the shortest and easiest routes are in town or close by. An excellent (and brief) route heads south from town on Highway 17 towards Marfa but bears west on 166 to the Point of Rocks (five miles one way). Standard intermediate-length trips are to Marfa via Highway 17 (just over 20 miles) and the more demanding ride to Alpine via Highway 118 (around 25 miles). Though the one-way distance to Balmorhea on Highway 17 is 50 miles, there is a 2,000-foot elevation drop which makes much of this ride a breeze. The steepest portion is the section preceding Wild Rose Pass, which is not as tough as some hills in Austin.

Of course, the ultimate test is the 75-mile Scenic Loop. The highest road in the state, it offers long flats, scores of peaks and valleys, and gorgeous scenery. Texas doesn't offer any better cycling. If you ride clockwise from Fort Davis (Highway 17 south to Highway 166 to Highway 118 back to town), the toughest part comes last. Most choose to head counter-clockwise and face the music right off, past the Prude Ranch uphill to the Observatory and into, through, and out of Madera Canyon. The long ride downhill past Sawtooth Mountain leads into a few rolling hills and plenty of unfenced pastures before the lengthy, relatively level stretches around Blue Mountain and back into town. Many prefer to bite off pieces of this ride and enjoy a 20- or 30-mile hill workout or a series of sprints on the straightaways.

Guest Ranch

PRUDE RANCH
Six miles north of Fort Davis on Highway 118 • 800-458-6232

Since the 1920s, Texans have been heading to the mile-high Prude Ranch to escape broiling summers in the lowlands. The only difference is that the guests these days are from all across America and around the world, and now there's something going on almost year-round. The motto of the ranch is "we'll keep a horse saddled for you," and for starters, the Prude Ranch stables offer **horseback riding, trail rides,** and, for larger groups, **chuckwagon suppers.** On your own, there is **hiking** in and around several thousand acres of ranch property. If you're interested in **cycling,** the ranch is located right on the most scenic (and demanding) paved ride in Texas—the 75-mile Scenic Loop. Other facilities include a **basketball court, a rodeo arena,** a heated indoor **swimming pool,** and a **tennis court.**

Keep in mind that all of these activities are in addition to watching or participating in any of the scheduled events at the Prude Ranch, such as **rodeos,** including a recent Texas high school rodeo championship, **cycling** events, and the annual **Star Party,** which draws close to a thousand astronomers.

Horseback Riding

Mounts are available at several stables including the Prude Ranch. Most charge around ten dollars per hour with longer rides available. In town, Ron Beames runs Davis Mountains Horseback Tours (426-3016) out of Johnnie Fitzgerald's barn and offers one-hour, two-hour, half-day, and day-long rides.

Touring

See **SIDE TRIPS** below.

SHOPPING

FISHER HILL GALLERY

Main Street (Highway 17) • **426-3246**
Monday–Saturday 10–6

The house coffee at the Hotel Limpia is mixed here, and over a dozen different blends are available ground or whole bean at Fisher Hill. Several are brewed daily and served by the cup. Try the cool coffee de cream, served on ice with cream and sugar.

Dolls gussied up in bright ensembles with Spanish moss hair and other gourd crafts are the specialty of co-owner Sondra McAnally. Local artists like Kelly Bryan, Christi Dillard, and Ann Williams are featured in the gallery. Most of the antiques and hand-crafted items come from area ranches and homes.

HIGH COUNTRY NURSERY

Right across from Fort Davis National Historic Site • **426-3155**
Monday–Saturday 9–6 • **Sunday 1–6**

Browse past aisles of varietals native to the Trans-Pecos, like evergreen sumac, tecoma stans, purple sage, Chisos red oak, and madrone. Antiques, collectibles, and an ongoing flea market are inside, as is a selection of colorful Mexican imports.

HOTEL LIMPIA GIFTS
Hotel Limpia • 426-3241
Daily 10–9:30 except Monday till 5 p.m.
The area adjacent to the Hotel Limpia Dining Room is devoted to gifts, collectibles, and books. Home accessories include western candlesticks, picture frames, reproduction tin signs, wind chimes, bells and baskets. Everything imaginable having do with birds is on display—feeders, houses, blankets, and books. The shelves are stacked westerns, cookbooks, and southwestern titles.

LINEAUS ATHLETIC COMPANY
P.O. Box 2021 • Fort Davis • 79734 • 800-626-6456
Call or write for a catalog or stop by Lovegene's in Marathon
For over a decade, Lineaus Lorette has been designing, handcrafting, and marketing medicine balls and other leather training products to organizations like the New York Giants, the Denver Broncos, and the USC Trojans. Stressing speed as well as strength, medicine balls have been valued by generations of coaches for providing the ideal workout—aerobic as well as anaerobic. Lorette's standard medicine ball weighs 12 pounds, has a 14 inch diameter, and sells for $200. His latest twist, the rugby medicine ball, weighs three pounds (versus the traditional one-pounder) and retails for $95.

S.S. SAVAGE
Adjacent to Town Square on Main Street • 426-3311
On the first floor of the Hotel Limpia West, this gallery features handcrafted Mexican and Mescalero Apache collectibles, a wide selection of books, and works by local artists.

SIDE TRIPS

SCENIC LOOP
State Highways 17, 118, and 166
This is as good as Texas gets on paved public roads. Nearly 75 miles of rolling hills, winding canyons, and jagged peaks combine with open grassland for a memorable 1½-hour drive. And that's not counting stops. Head counterclockwise, i.e., from Fort Davis to Davis Mountains State Park on to the Prude Ranch. This route offers the best vistas: Mount Locke and the UT Observatory from the south and Sawtooth from the east. Good picnic sites along the way include Davis Mountains State Park just outside of Fort Davis, along Highway 118 below the Observatory, at Madera Canyon beyond the Observatory, and the Point of Rocks (at the end of the Loop). Much of the Loop is unfenced, and cattle graze, sleep, and herd on or near the road. Always avoid low-water

crossings during summer storms. And fork off to Kent, Valentine, or Marfa only if you are willing to enjoy added hours of scenery.

ANNUAL EVENTS

April–May

CHIHUAHUAN DESERT RESEARCH INSTITUTE ANNUAL PLANT SALES
CDRI Visitor Center • *3 miles south of Fort Davis* • 837-8370
Last weekend in April • Memorial Day
Drought-tolerant and heat-resistant ornamental plants native to the Chihuahuan Desert are the highlight of these fundraisers. Develop your garden with varieties unavailable at most nurseries. The growth in popularity of this sale has led to the separate cactus and succulent sale on Memorial Day.

May

HAMMERFEST
Prude Ranch • 800-458-6232 or 915-699-1718 (Peyton's Bikes)
Memorial Day Weekend • Registration fee
One of the major races statewide, Hammerfest is run by the United States Cycling Federation. Several hundred participants, from novice racers to nationally ranked riders, compete for points, trophies, and cash. In order to place, riders must race three times at distances varying from seven miles (from the Prude Ranch to the McDonald Observatory) to 75 miles (the Scenic Loop). A tough weekend of riding, Hammerfest has been used as a qualifying race for the U.S. Olympic Team. Less serious riders may sign up and pay a prorated fee to participate in a single day's race.

July

FOURTH OF JULY
In town and at the fort • 800-524-3015 (Chamber of Commerce)
Fourth of July weekend
Free: Courthouse Festival • Admission: Dance
The busiest weekend in Jeff Davis County. At the fort, a formal flag raising and retreat ceremony highlight a day full of uniforms, demonstrations, and pageantry. In town, the parade starts at St. Joseph's Catholic Church and heads down Main Street to the town square. Freight wagons, color guards, an infantry cadre from the fort, floats, and hundreds of mounted riders from area ranches participate. Everyone heads to the courthouse lawn for a good part of the late morning and early afternoon to eat, poke

around the booths, and catch up. Soon folks head out to the Prude Ranch for the team roping while others head home for supper and to get ready for a West Texas street dance. Show up early; by sundown it's elbow to elbow on the dance floor.

August

BLOYS CAMP MEETING
Skillman Grove • *17 miles west of Fort Davis on Hwy 166*
Early August • Free (donations accepted)
　　Many West Texans and people partial to West Texas who gather at Skillman Grove are second, third, and fourth generation attendees at this non-denominational camp meeting. Founded by Rev. Dr. William Benjamin Bloys, the first meeting (1890) lasted three days. Forty-seven attended. Campers slept on bedrolls and cooked in Dutch ovens, and the Reverend used an Arbuckle coffee crate for a pulpit. By 1909, 115 hacks and buggies, 450 horses and mules, and nine automobiles brought 575 campers to Skillman Grove. These days, several thousand attendees participate in the week-long meeting. Many spend a night (or the week) in one of the 350 permanent cabins, while others bring RVs or stay in Fort Davis. Bible study comes after a full cowboy breakfast (donations only) with services offered in the morning, afternoon, and evening.

September

FRIENDS OF FORT DAVIS FESTIVAL
Fort Davis National Historic Site • 426-3224
Saturday of Labor Day weekend • Free
　　For more than a decade, this annual day-long event has featured a wide variety of activities and is one of only two days each year when there is no admission fee to the fort. Some activities highlight the fort's history, like the cavalry-infantry patrol demonstrations, the military drills, and the field camps. Some are just plain fun like the door prizes, the children's games, the wagon rides, and a melodrama in the Cottonwood picnic grove presented by the Big Bend Players. Other activities you won't find anywhere else include an 1884 baseball game pitting the Fort Davis nine versus Fort Concho's team from San Angelo. Played in authentic uniforms and using rules of that era, these two posts enjoy a heated rivalry with games played at both forts during the year. A high point for many is the extensive Colt firearms exhibit at the auditorium. Also on hand are craftsmen demonstrating skills from the fort's heyday—broom squires, dollmakers, saddlemakers, blacksmiths, and photographers. Laundresses even set up Suds Row. Though the festival is a

major fundraiser for the Fort, there is no admission charge. Funds are raised at the noon barbecue which features music by the Corn-grinders and at the silent auction with items ranging from antiques to collectibles and books.

CYCLEFEST

Prude Ranch • 800-458-6232 or 915-699-1718 (Peyton's Bikes) Weekend varies • Fee

Not to be confused with Memorial Day's Hammerfest, Cyclefest is a two-day, family-oriented bicycling event at distances ranging from ten to 100 miles. All cycling is on portions of the beautiful 75-mile Scenic Loop. The long ride (you choose the distance) is scheduled for Saturday, and a shorter jaunt is planned Sunday morning to allow participants to head home early. The Prude Ranch, headquarters for Cyclefest, has activities for family members as well as bunks, meals, and entertainment for all comers.

September–October

HARVEST MOON AND TUNES FESTIVAL

In and around Fort Davis • 800-524-3015 (Chamber of Commerce) • Weekend of the Harvest Moon (call for exact weekend) • Admission fee to concerts

Celebrating the fall harvest with plenty of good bluegrass, country music, and fun-filled activities, this festival is a great way to see and enjoy Fort Davis during the off-season. Friday and Saturday nights feature top name entertainers with past performers including Asleep at the Wheel, Guy Clark, and the Dixie Chicks. Saturday's daytime events include presentations by local horticultural experts, tours of local vineyards, orchards, and farms, garden displays, a vegetable contest, arts and crafts, a community Walk/Fun Run, and a roping.

RESTAURANTS

($ = Under $7.50, $$ = Under $15, $$$ = $15+ plus tax & tip)

BLACK BEAR RESTAURANT AT THE INDIAN LODGE

Davis Mountains State Park • 426-3254
Four miles northwest of Fort Davis via State Highway 118
Monday–Saturday 7:30 a.m. to 9 p.m.
Sunday breakfast 7:30–9:30, brunch 12–2:30, dinner 4–9 • $

It's a West Texas tradition to corral the family, take a five-minute or maybe a fifty-mile ride through some of the state's prettiest country, and enjoy the inexpensive Sunday buffet complete with salad bar, choice of entrées, and homemade desserts. Pay the entrance fee (four dollars) to enjoy the Skyline Scenic Drive (see **BIRD'S-EYE VIEW** above). If you're considering the 75-mile Scenic Loop around breakfast time, stop in for the early morning specialties like the breakfast tacos with choice of potato, *chorizo* (Mexican sausage), bacon, country sausage, or ham with egg.

HIGHWAY 118 CAFE

Just south of town on Highway 118 • 426-3934
Tuesday–Sunday 6:30 a.m. to 8:30 p.m. • Closed from 2:30 to 5:30 p.m.
   Simple food, good service, excellent green *enchiladas*. If you need a change of pace, order them with an egg. The phrase is *montado* and means "on top." Superb *chile rellenos* can be coerced from the kitchen.

HOTEL LIMPIA DINING ROOM

Main Street at the Town Square • 426-3241
Dinner Tuesday–Saturday • Breakfast and lunch on Saturday & Sunday • $–$$ • AE D MC V • W
   The menu at the Limpia can satisfy all tastes and appetites. There's a vegetable plate, charbroiled steak, southwestern spaghetti, spinach lasagna, and several fish and chicken selections. All entrées are served family style with a selection of vegetables, soup or salad, biscuits, and mashed potatoes. With the exception of the special of the day and the steak, feel free to ask for seconds on your menu selection and any of the side dishes. Children are made welcome with plates like chicken-fried chicken or spaghetti, and all kids' meals include a beverage. If you care for a mixed drink with dinner, head upstairs to the Bandana Room and buy a temporary membership. Fee is waived for hotel guests.

RAUL'S BARBECUE

Intersection of Highway 118 and 17
Most days • Lunch and dinner (tends to close early) • $
   Any visit to the Davis Mountains is incomplete without paying homage to the finest barbecue in West Texas. Located in a nondescript house on the east side of town just before Highway 17 forks to Balmorhea, Raul's is operated at the discretion of the namesake owner. If it's not open the first time you stop by, do yourself a favor—try again. Show up before quitting time—7:00 p.m. Brisket lovers can order by the pound or enjoy a *tejano* (on a bun). Ribs by the plate or to go.

THE DRUGSTORE RESTAURANT
At the Old Texas Inn • 426-3118
Breakfast and lunch six days a week • Closed Wednesday
$ • AE MC V
   The highlight of the Drugstore is the old fashioned soda fountain featuring hand-mixed floats, malts, sodas, sundaes, ice cream, and phosphates. The chicken *fajita burrito* and the chicken-fried steak are the menu's bestsellers. Choices also include half a dozen burgers, sandwich baskets, BLTs, and salads.

CLUBS AND BARS

THE BANDANA ROOM
Upstairs at the Hotel Limpia • 426-3241
Nightly Tuesday–Saturday
   This full bar enjoys the distinction of being the only establishment in Jeff Davis County to serve alcohol. Enjoy the rustic setting upstairs over the Hotel Limpia Dining Room for drinks or dinner. State law requires nonmembers not staying at the hotel to buy a $3 temporary membership.

ACCOMMODATIONS

($ = Under $40, $$ = $40–$75, $$$ = $75–$100, $$$$ = Over $100)
Room Tax 10%

BUTTERFIELD INN
Main Street • 426-3252 • $$
   Each of the four brightly painted cottages comes with bath and ample living area at this centrally located inn. All have cable TV (HBO), a jacuzzi tub, and a wood fireplace to take the chill off in the cooler months. A pay phone is available at the main building, which houses the gift shop, the bedding plant shed, registration, and Jacques, a frisky chocolate poodle. No pets.

FORT DAVIS MOTOR INN
Highway 17 North • 426-2112 or 800-803-2847 • $$
   Up and going since the spring of '94, the motor inn sits between Highway 17 to Balmorhea and Limpia Creek. Two adobe-style buildings accented with gothic arches house 36 units. Smoking and non-smoking rooms are available as is a handicap unit. Phones with free local calls, cable TV, and pine furnishings come

with all rooms. Stop by the lobby for complimentary coffee in the morning. Leashed pets not left unattended are welcome. AAA and AARP discounts available. Three RV spaces with full hookups are on site, but no showers or restrooms are available.

HOTEL LIMPIA

On the Square • 426-3237 or 800-662-5517 • $$–$$$

The two-story main building was built in 1912 of pink limestone quarried near Sleeping Lion Mountain and has 14 rooms including suites. Across Main Street stands the two-story Limpia West annex, an eight-room rustic rock structure constructed in 1925. The most recent addition is the Hotel Limpia Suites (behind the main building). All rooms feature cable TV (HBO). As long as someone is at the front desk, a pot of fresh coffee, the Limpia Blend, is brewed in the lobby. Two spacious parlors and porches with rocking chairs await guests, as does the Hotel Limpia dining room, the Bandana Club upstairs (full bar), and a well-stocked gift shop with plenty of good books. Pets are welcome (charge). Like the Gage in Marathon, call early for springtime reservations. The Hotel Limpia has a busier summer season. Some weekends are booked years ahead, e.g., Fourth of July, the Star Parties, Harvest Moon and Tunes.

INDIAN LODGE

Davis Mountains State Park • 426-3254 • $$–$$$
Four miles northwest of Fort Davis via State Highway 118

Operated as a bed and breakfast by the Texas Parks & Wildlife Department, the original portions of the white adobe pueblo-style lodge were built by members of the Civilian Conservation Corps (1933). Note the pine *viga* and cane *latilla* ceilings, the 18-inch-thick walls, and some of the hand-carved furniture. The old and new wings have 39 rooms combined, each with cable TV, tile baths, and central heat and air. The air conditioning is the biggest surprise. Most nights, even in the summer, require a light blanket. Lodge guests can also enjoy the heated outdoor pool and recreation room.

An American-plan breakfast is served to overnight guests from 6:30 to 9:30 a.m.in the Black Bear Restaurant. Choose from bacon, sausage, eggs to order, pancakes, hashbrowns, cereal, juice, milk, and coffee. *Evenings at the Lodge,* featuring ethnic food and entertainment, are scheduled throughout the year and include Mardi Gras, St. Patrick's Day, Oktoberfest, and Halloween. Note that the lodge closes for the middle two weeks of January. Reservations are accepted up to one year in advance. Cribs, roll-aways, and room service not available. Pets not allowed in rooms.

PRUDE RANCH
Highway 118, six miles north of Fort Davis • 800-458-6232
$$–$$$
This famous guest ranch (see **SPORTS AND ACTIVITIES** above) offers 35 rooms with doubles or kings and private baths, 13 cabins with double and bunk beds, and seven bunk rooms that accommodate from 10 to 20 people (depending on age and familiarity). The Prude family goes out of its way to ensure you see it all and do as much as you possibly can. Part of that includes pulling the plug on all televisions and phones (though pay phones are available on the property). Wholesome portions of good ranch cooking are served in the dining hall. Other amenities include a heated indoor pool and a gift shop. Leashed pets only. AAA discount available.

Bed & Breakfasts

BOYNTON HOUSE GUEST LODGE AND BED & BREAKFAST
Atop Dolores Mountain • 426-3123 or 800-358-5929
$$–$$$ • W+
Perched atop Dolores Mountain, this white-bricked, red-tiled Mexican colonial (1985) is built around a solarium brimming with rose bushes, geraniums, and peach and banana trees. It offers views of Fort Davis, the Davis Mountain high country, and the open range heading towards Marfa and Alpine. Boynton House has four bedrooms, each with private bath, cable TV, and a phone by request. The common area includes a large family room and plenty of exercise equipment. The library is full of books, magazines, good games, an easel, and a piano. The breakfast bell rings by consensus, usually around 8:15 with coffee and tea brewing an hour earlier. The proprietor is a registered nurse, and special dietary needs are welcome. No pets. AARP discount available.

WAYSIDE INN BED AND BREAKFAST
426-3535 or 800-582-7510 • **$$–$$$$**
This country house (1941) has five bedrooms ($-$$) downstairs, each with private bath, and two larger bedrooms upstairs which share a bathroom and can be rented as a suite ($$$$). Quilts—antique and contemporary, furnishings—old and new, and Anna Beth and Jay Ward's full country breakfast can be found inside. Count on pancakes, biscuits from scratch, baked eggs, canadian or turkey bacon, and cereals. Anna Beth likes to use her china, silver, and cloth napkins but will accommodate those who prefer paper products. The private side entrance is for guests returning from star parties, the Marfa Lights, or a day on the river.

FORT STOCKTON

| PECOS COUNTY SEAT ★ 8,524 ★ (915) |

An important leg of the Comanche War Trail from the South Plains to northern Mexico each September included Comanche Springs (present-day Fort Stockton) and watering holes east of Marathon and around Persimmon Gap at Big Bend National Park, i.e, roughly the route of US 385 from Fort Stockton to Big Bend National Park. Plentiful water drew native Americans from many tribes, Spanish explorers like Domínguez de Mendoza (1684), and, ultimately, Uncle Sam (1858), who sought to protect the Government Road from San Antonio to El Paso with troops from Fort Lancaster (see OZONA below). Like most West Texas garrisons, the fort itself didn't last till the twentieth century, but the town survived and prospered. Fort Stockton is now the center of one of America's largest natural gas fields as well as a convenient gateway to the Big Bend. Though the Comanches are long gone, the importance of water to Fort Stockton remains clear. One of the town's biggest events is the annual Water Carnival, and millions of tourists know Fort Stockton as the biggest watering hole on Interstate 10 between Van Horn and Ozona—a 200-mile stretch.

TOURIST SERVICES

VISITOR INFORMATION CABOOSE
Interstate 10 and Highway 285 (Exit 257) • 336-8052
September–May: 11–6 Monday–Saturday • 12–6 Sunday
June–August: 10–8 Monday–Saturday • 12–8 Sunday
Right off I-10 by the golden arches, this is an easy way for travelers to pick up brochures and to check on upcoming events while beginning a stay in Fort Stockton or before going on. Parking is available for historic tours of Fort Stockton and winery tours at Ste. Genevieve via Roadrunner Bus Tours.

ROADRUNNER BUS TOURS
Pickup at Caboose, Chamber of Commerce, and other points in town • 336-8052 or 336-2264
Historical Tours M–F 1:30 and 4:00 • Weekends 2 p.m. only
Admission: Adults $6.50, children $3.50

Winery Tours Saturday morning only at 9:40
Admission: Adults $8, children $6.50

MUSEUMS

ANNIE RIGGS MEMORIAL MUSEUM
301 S. Main St. • **336-2167**
September–May: 10–12 and 1–5 Monday–Saturday; 1:30–5
Sunday • **June–August: 10–8 Monday–Saturday and 1:30–8**
Sunday • **Admission: Adults $1, children 50¢** • **W**

Built in 1900 by a group of local investors, the hotel is an excellent example of Territorial Architecture. The 14-room facility was built of adobe with wrap-around verandas and gingerbread trim. All rooms are well appointed: One features furnishings from the turn of the century, a second exhibits archaeologic finds from the area, a third covers the life of pioneer women, and others include Western memorabilia, geology, and rotating exhibits.

Annie Riggs came to Fort Stockton as an eight-year-old shortly after the Civil War. Several husbands and ten children later, she used the proceeds from the murder of her second husband (by her son-in-law) to buy out the original backers for $5,000. She owned and operated the hotel until her death in 1931.

WHEELS AND FRILLS MUSEUM
221 N. Main • **336-8421**
Admission: Adults $2, children $1

This museum combines two collections: vintage vehicles and exquisite dolls. Included in the auto collection are Model T's and Model A's, a Studebaker Champion, and stake-bed trucks. One-of-a-kind First Lady Dolls in inaugural gowns, china dolls, and fashion dolls are included in Frills section.

HISTORIC PLACES

HISTORIC FORT STOCKTON
Monday–Saturday 10–1 and 2–5 • **336-2400**
300 East Third Street • **Admission: Adults $1, children 50¢**

Owned by the City of Fort Stockton and managed by the Fort Stockton Historical Society, old Fort Stockton consists of original structures dating back to 1868 and reconstructed military buildings restored to 1870s appearance. The fort was initially garrisoned in 1858 but abandoned at the beginning of the Civil War. Confederate forces only briefly occupied the garrison, and Union forces reoccupied the post from 1867 to 1886. The Historic Fort Stockton Museum itself is located in Barracks #1. Start and view the informative video before you tour the rest of the premises. Afterwards, head to the four original buildings (out of 35) still standing: the Guard House and three of the eight Officers' Quarters. The Guard House is worth a closer look; it contains jailer's quarters, three solitary confinement cells, and a larger holding cell.

OTHER POINTS OF INTEREST

PAISANO PETE
Intersection of Main Street and Dickinson Blvd.

Paisano Pete, the world's largest roadrunner, stands 11 feet tall and 22 feet long and is available for viewing and photos round-the-clock all year long (including holidays).

STE. GENEVIEVE WINERY
I-10, Exit 285 McKenzie Road • *25 miles east of Fort Stockton*

The largest winery in Texas is also America's fifth largest. Ste. Genevieve marries University of Texas lands with the *savoir faire* of French winemakers. Over a thousand acres are under cultivation and produce more than a million bottles of wine.

SPORTS AND ACTIVITIES

Golf

PECOS COUNTY 18 HOLE MUNICIPAL GOLF COURSE
Highway 285 one mile northwest of Fort Stockton • **336-2050**
Open Tuesday through Sunday

The home course of PGA tour member Blaine McAllister offers a 50% senior citizen discount off normal rates. Weekday green fees are $10, and weekend fees are $15.

ANNUAL EVENTS

July

WATER CARNIVAL

Comanche Springs Pool at Rooney Park • 336-2264 (Chamber)
Third weekend of the month • Admission • W

Each year, a different theme is incorporated into more than a dozen different performances ranging from musicals and dancing to synchronized swimming. All can be viewed at the Comanche Springs Pool on Thursday, Friday, and Saturday nights, with different admissions each night.

RESTAURANTS

($ = Under $7.50, $$ = Under $15, $$$ = $15+ plus tax & tip)

STAGE COACH INN

1401 W. Dickinson • 336-2804
Tuesday–Sunday • Breakfast, lunch, dinner • $–$$

Find a friend, grab a seat at the bar, and split an order of *ratones* while your Monster Fireburger is on the grill. Ratones are *jalapeños* stuffed with cheese, battered, and deep-fried. There are none better than these; be sure to have a beer or a tall glass of sweet tea handy, gringo. Fireburgers are one of several house specialties, and are served with a flavorful *picante*. For Mexican food, order the green *enchiladas* in your choice of chicken, beef, or cheese, or the Combination Plate—a *chalupa*, a *taco*, three *enchiladas*, salad, *tostadas*, and *chile macho*. Beer.

SARAH'S CAFE

106 S. Nelson • 336-7124
Monday–Saturday • Lunch and dinner • $–$$ • MC V • W

Author James Michener and four-time Indy champ A.J. Foyt are among those privileged to have enjoyed a good Mexican plate from Doña Sarah's kitchen. Sarah Nuñez, a Shafter native, opened for business in 1929. Her children and grandchildren run Sarah's now. Lots of folks stick with Sarah's Special: a *chile relleno*, a *chalupa*, a *taco*, an *enchilada*, some *guacamole*, rice and beans. Be sure to savor the legendary green sauce. It goes best with chicken dishes like the enchiladas. Beer and wine.

ACCOMMODATIONS

($ = Under $40, $$ = $40–$75, $$$ = $75–$100, $$$$ = Over $100)
Room Tax 13%

BEST WESTERN SUNDAY HOUSE INN
3200 W. Dickinson • 336-8521 or 800-528-4234 • $$
This two-story lodge located on the west side of town has 112 smoking and non-smoking units including suites and family rooms. Rooms include cable TV (HBO), pay-per-view movies, and phones with no charge for local calls. Complimentary coffee is served in the lobby. Annemarie's Alpine Lodge Restaurant is on the property and serves an inexpensive lunch buffet. Other amenities include an outdoor unheated pool, courtesy car for local transfers, and free parking. Small pets OK. AAA, AARP, and corporate rates available.

COMFORT INN
2601 Interstate 10 at Exit 257 • 336-9781 or 800-592-4015 • $$
This two-story inn sits right on I-10 at Exit 257 and has 97 smoking and non-smoking units including suites. Rooms include cable TV (HBO) and phones (free local calls). Some have small refrigerators. Amenities include complimentary coffee in the lobby, El Corral restaurant and bar, an outdoor unheated pool, and free parking. Pets are welcome. AAA and AARP rates available.

GUADALUPE MOUNTAINS NATIONAL PARK

CULBERSON AND HUDSPETH COUNTIES
MOUNTAIN TIME   ★   (915)

Unlike many national parks, Guadalupe Mountains has almost no appreciable development either in its vicinity or within the park itself. Come prepared. Enormous salt flats and rugged mountain ranges surround this already desolate area. The nearest gas station is 35 miles north across the New Mexico state line near Carlsbad Caverns National Park. Conveniences like service stations and restaurants are even more distant in Texas: 75 miles south in Van Horn and 110 miles west in El Paso. Commercial air service and rental cars are available in Carlsbad, New Mexico (55 miles), El Paso (110 miles) and Midland-Odessa (170 miles). The nearest air strip is 34 miles north at White's City (800-228-3767). Improved but not paved, it's seven-tenths of a mile long.

Most of the park's limited development borders Highway 62-180 along the park's eastern edge. The Pine Springs Visitor Center, the nearby Pine Springs Campground, and the Ranger Station at McKittrick Canyon are all accessible via paved or improved dirt roads from this highway. Highway 62-180 is the route that the TNM&O Bus Line (806-765-6641) travels (ask for the Pine Springs stop). Some of the more remote areas, Dog Canyon, for instance, are more than 100 miles by car even though as the crow flies they are less than 15. Because of this lack of development, most of the highest country in Texas remains as pristine as it was when Spanish explorers first encountered the Mescalero Apache in the sixteenth century. This policy has been mandated by the designation of over half the park, 46,850 acres, as wilderness area. This has been the way of these mountains since before the Spanish and even up to its most recent residents, pioneering ranchers, who set up camps or headquarters in the lowlands and ventured into the high country only to herd strays or to hunt deer, elk, and bear. The sparse vegetation never supported much cattle; consequently, ranching operations were few, hands covered enormous

(text continued on page 126)

GUADALUPE MOUNTAINS
NATIONAL PARK

Dog Canyon
Campground

Dog
Canyon

Lost Peak

McKITTRICK   CANYON

McKittrick
Canyon
Visitor
Center

Smith Spring

CANYON

Hunter
Peak

TO CARLSBAD, NEW MEXICO

62   180

Visitor Center
and Headquarters

El Capitan

Pine Springs
Campground

Picnic Area

Historic site

Information Station

Campground

Backcountry campsite

Improved road

Unimproved road

Trail

N

54

TO VAN HORN

0   1   2   3

Miles

(continued from page 123)
ranges, and the infrastructure more common to greener pastures never developed.

Almost all of the present park is former ranch land that was donated expressly for a National Park or acquired with cooperation of ranch owners. The oldest structures standing are ranch headquarters such as the Williams Ranch which can be accessed only by four-wheel-drive roads or the Frijole Ranch (and nearby Manzanita Spring) right off Highway 62-180. For a more detailed historical explanation, see **HISTORIC PLACES** below.

TOURIST SERVICES

SUPERINTENDENT, GUADALUPE MOUNTAINS NATIONAL PARK
HC 60, Box 400 • Salt Flat, TX • 79847-9400 • 915-828-3251
8–4:30 p.m. except 7–6 p.m. Memorial Day through Labor Day
There is no park entrance fee although campground use fees are charged. Use this address and phone number when contacting the Park Service for information, however, don't go to Salt Flat, Texas, if visiting Guadalupe National Park is on the agenda (you'll only find a cafe and a post office). The visitor centers and ranger stations are located on the eastern and northern portions of the national park.

PINE SPRINGS VISITOR CENTER
Highway 62-180 • 828-3251 • Daily 8–4:30
Located adjacent to the Pine Springs Campground, this Visitor Center provides the full gamut of information, activities, and resources. Brochures and trail maps on the park, books covering regional history and natural sciences, exhibits, and a slide program are all available. Rangers not only provide the latest details on trails, campgrounds, and special conditions but also offer guided hikes and nightly programs at the Pine Springs Campground Amphitheater (seasonally).

MCKITTRICK CANYON VISITOR CENTER
Four miles west of Highway 62-180 from a turnoff 7½ miles northeast of Pine Springs • **Access closed nightly**
Gateway to McKittrick Canyon, learn more about this Texas treasure and one-of-a-kind relic forest before you begin your day hike. No overnight camping is permitted in McKittrick Canyon.

DOG CANYON RANGER STATION

Located at the Dog Canyon Campground, this remote facility can be reached by foot via the Pine Springs or McKittrick Canyon Trails or by car via State Highway 137, a paved road, which extends west 59 miles from Highway 285 approximately 12 miles north of Carlsbad. Even phone lines go the long route. Although the Ranger Station is in Texas, it has a New Mexico number (505-981-2418). The distance from the Pine Springs Visitor Center is 12 miles by foot and 105 miles by vehicle.

GUIDEBOOKS AND PUBLICATIONS

THE GUADALUPES

By Dan Murphy • Carlsbad Caverns/Guadalupe Mountains Association

A brief introduction to the Guadalupe Mountains as well as the National Park that includes a portion of them. The geology, wildlife, and history of the area are included. Available at the Headquarters Visitor Center, Carlsbad Caverns National Park, as well as from the Carlsbad Caverns/Guadalupe Mountains Association at 505-785-2318.

BIRD'S-EYE VIEW

ATOP GUADALUPE PEAK

8,749 feet above sea level

A hell of a hike. The top of Texas is less than five miles from the Pine Springs Visitor Center, and that means views of the Chihuahuan Desert and the mountains of three states: Chihuahua, New Mexico, and Texas. Wear sturdy shoes, bring plenty of sunscreen, and take even more water. Directions, information, and trail maps are all available at the Visitor Center. Allow several hours each way. With breaks, a summit siesta, and fatigue, this haul can easily stretch beyond half a day. On a clear day, vistas of more than 100 miles including the Davis Mountains and Mexico are not uncommon as are views of the Sierra Diablos directly south and the Delaware Mountains to the southeast. Of course, right in front of you is the *El Capitan* escarpment which stands as sentinel for the highlands and is another half-hour hike.

For those of you unwilling, uninterested, or unable to scale massive heights in a single bound, drive south on Highway 62-

180 from the Pine Springs Visitor Center towards Guadalupe Pass and pull over at the scenic viewpoint. El Capitan, the jagged limestone monolith before you, has stood as a beacon to travelers for centuries as it hovers more than a mile above the surrounding flats. Even the accidental tourist can savor this sensation as he drives on Interstate 10 east of Van Horn and spies El Capitan more than 50 miles to the north.

HISTORIC PLACES

Much of the history of this region concerns cultures that hardly left footprints, let alone more substantial remnants. Dating from about 12,000 years ago, pottery shards, projectile points, and other artifacts reveal man's earliest known sojourns through these hills. More identifiable is the presence of the Mescalero Apache. Stone circles several feet in diameter are found in both Guadalupe and Carlsbad Caverns national parks. They were used as roasting pits to prepare agave or mescal. This plant, an integral part of the diet of this band of Apaches, led to the white man's name for this people, the Mescalero.

The U.S. Army came to the Guadalupes looking for a watering hole as early as 1849, but it wasn't until the late 1850s when John Butterfield's Overland Mail Route was established that there was regular traffic. As part of his contract with the government, Butterfield was awarded 320 acres for each of his changing stations (see **The Pinery** below). The Pinery was in use less than a year as the harsh climate and the harsher Mescalero Apaches forced the route south to more plentiful water and less hostile country.

Historic structures are all that remain of the Overland Trail and the early ranches. As you look closely at these buildings (or their remains) and consider life out on this range, keep in mind that the hundreds of thousands of acres that surround Guadalupe National Park's Texas boundary are privately-owned ranches.

THE PINERY
Immediately east of Pine Springs Visitor Center
The Butterfield Overland Mail route ran between St. Louis and San Francisco. Over 2,700 miles long, the three- to four-week delivery actually had two stages: a westbound driver who departed St. Louis and an eastbound one who left San Francisco. Not surprisingly, the Lone Star State occupied the longest segment. The changing station at the Pinery was the halfway mark. The first eastbound stage met its westbound counterpart at the Pinery on September 25, 1858. Though the Butterfield Mail continued till March 1861, the Pinery was abandoned as a changing

station. Guadalupe Pass was the highest point on the entire run, and a lower route via Fort Davis offered better protection and more water.

FRIJOLE RANCH

Follow the Frijole Ranch turnoff (less than two miles north of the Visitor Center) three-quarters of a mile to the ranch house.

Hardy ranchers like the Rader brothers homesteaded the Guadalupes even when the Apache roamed. The Rader brothers' Frijole Ranch headquarters (1876) is now open to the public and is used by the National Park Service as a cultural history museum. Much less accessible is the **Williams Ranch** which can be reached only by four-wheel-drive vehicles over seven miles of rough road. Complete directions and a gate key are available from park personnel at the Visitor Center.

OTHER POINTS OF INTEREST

MCKITTRICK CANYON

Take the McKittrick Canyon turnoff seven miles north of the Visitor Center on Highway 62-180 and drive four miles to the parking lot. • **Open from 8 a.m. to 6 p.m. (summer) or 4:30 p.m. (winter)**

Steep canyon walls and a perennially spring-fed stream keep this relic forest alive thousands of years after a drier climate parched the Chihuahuan Desert. Four miles of self-guided trail along the floor of the canyon offer casual hikers sights commonly seen in many states not including Texas: little leaf walnut, velvet ash, big tooth maple, and the state's only reproducing stock of rainbow trout. The canyon is busiest during the fall when it wears autumn colors. Picnicking is permitted at the parking lot, in the canyon near the Pratt Cabin (2.3 miles from the parking lot), and at the Grotto picnic area (3.4 miles from the parking lot).

SPORTS AND ACTIVITIES

Camping

At the lower campgrounds, Pine Springs and Dog Canyon, it's first-come, first-served. These two areas are accessible by road and are also fee campgrounds ($6 per night per site). Pine Springs lies right off Highway 62-180 adjacent to the Visitor Center. Dog Canyon is on the north side of the park just a mile south of the

New Mexico border and approachable by car only from New Mexico on State Highway 137. Proceed north from Carlsbad approximately 12 miles and then head west to access State Highway 137. By foot, Dog Canyon is a mere 12 miles from Pine Springs via the Tejas Trail through some of the park's most scenic terrain. Both campgrounds can accommodate RVs as well as tents, and each has running water, handicapped-accessible restrooms, and picnic tables.

Due to the natural dryness as well as the limited fuel, *open fires are prohibited*. The reasons for this were quite evident during the spring of 1993 when a fire started by an errant match covered more than 6,500 acres. This was not an isolated incident. A lightning strike on Frijole Peak caused a 6,000-acre burn in 1990. The moral of the story is bring a camp stove if you like your coffee hot. Registration is a must; permits are required for overnight camping and are available at the Pine Springs Visitor Center or at the Dog Canyon Ranger Station.

Hiking

The novice hiker as well as those unfamiliar with the demands of this region are counseled to look elsewhere for introductory remarks on both topics. As wonderful as this park can be, plenty can go wrong: The cactus are sharp, the cliffs are steep, the snakes are poisonous, and the water is scarce. Winds of over 100 mph are not uncommon around Guadalupe Pass, snow accumulation of several feet is typical in protected areas of the high country, and temperatures can reach a high of 100 degrees during the summer and below zero in winter months.

First of all, either stop by a visitor center or phone the Carlsbad Caverns/Guadalupe Mountains Association at 505-785-2318 for a copy of *Trails of the Guadalupes* by Don Kurtz and William D. Goran and the Guadalupe Mountains National Park topo map (*Trails Illustrated* topo map #203). Both are indispensable. The booklet details trails, temperatures, mileage, rainfall, etc. The topo map is tearproof, waterproof, $7.95, and much more practical than purchasing any or all of the 7.5-minute USGS series that apply to Guadalupe Mountains National Park: *Guadalupe Peak, Guadalupe Pass, PX Flat,* and *Patterson Hills.* Whatever your trek, be sure to pack plenty of water. The curse of the Texas hiker strikes again as there are no high country watering holes of any sort. For day hikes, it is generally recommended to carry ½ a gallon per person. Overnight hiking typically requires a gallon per person per day on the trail. At two pounds per quart or eight pounds per gallon, you be the judge. During the hotter summer months, H_2O consumption will increase substantially. Some good day hikes include to Smith Spring—2.3 miles (3.8 km) from the Frijole Ranch House (round trip), and to the top of Texas and back—the 8.4-mile (13.6-km) Guadalupe Peak hike from the Pine Springs Campground (round trip). All longer trails are rewarding hikes. Take the time to discuss your interests and abilities with a park ranger before deciding on longer trails or overnight hikes like the Tejas Trail (11.9 miles/19.2 km).

RESTAURANTS AND ACCOMMODATIONS

See **CARLSBAD CAVERNS NATIONAL PARK** or **VAN HORN.**

LAJITAS

BREWSTER COUNTY   ★   48   ★   (915)

Once the hot Chihuahuan summer cools off and snow birds and tourists arrive, Lajitas comes to life. In centuries past, the onset of autumn brought the Comanches to Lajitas and its San Carlos crossing, known as the best ford across the Río Grande from Del Rio to El Paso.

Historians credit H.W. McGuirk with the founding of the town (1899). McGuirk was a rancher with mining and mercantile interests who eventually sold his holdings and relocated to New Mexico before Lajitas came of age. During the turbulent times of the Mexican Revolution and World War I, Lajitas served the immense Big Bend region as a cavalry post. Border raids by Mexican bandits at Glenn Spring (present-day Big Bend National Park), in nearby Presidio County, and at Columbus, New Mexico, heightened the importance of the garrison. The legacy of this era is the modern re-creation of the Lajitas Cavalry Post as a resort.

HISTORIC PLACES

LAJITAS TRADING POST
1 Clay Henry Rd. • 424-3234 • Daily • 8 a.m. to 8 p.m.
Best known as the home of Clay Henry (deceased) and Clay Henry, Jr., internationally renowned beer-drinking goats, the Trading Post was built during World War I. In its early years, it resupplied the U.S. Cavalry as well as Pancho Villa's followers. Still a general store, it serves tourists as well as locals from both sides of the river with a wide range of merchandise: groceries, picnic supplies, beer, ice, bait, gas, diesel, a fax machine, and a notary public. Around the corner, stop in at **Arrowhead Sotol** (424-3224). Owner Larry Harris gathers and cures the stalk of the century plant, whose length can exceed six feet. He then handcrafts furniture, walking sticks, and even golf clubs using the durable shaft. Collectibles include wind chimes, earrings, and silver jewelry.

SANTA MARIA Y SAN JOSE MISSION
At the west end of Lajitas on the Río Grande
Town father H.W. McGuirk built this 20- by 40-foot Catholic church shortly after he settled in Lajitas. A focal point of the early community, it fell into disrepair and wasn't renovated until 1990. Note the stained glass windows, crafted by Jim Box (1990). Santa Maria y San Jose now hosts weddings and other celebrations as well as weekly Catholic and Episcopal services.

Keep an eye out just east of Lajitas for the town's tiny cemetery. Dating back to the era of founding father McGuirk, the graveyard is worth a visit to view rarely seen, oven-shaped *hornitos* ("little ovens") made of native stone and built over gravesites. The Lajitas Cemetery stands on the north side of FM 170 just down the hill from Lajitas on the Río Grande.

SPORTS AND ACTIVITIES
See also **BIG BEND NATIONAL PARK.**

Golf

LAJITAS GOLF COURSE
Open every day of the year • 424-3211
Right along the Río Grande, this nine-hole course rarely gets crowded (ask Paul Lee). Green fees are $14 all day on weekends and holidays and $10 all day during the week. Carts available.

Horseback Riding

LAJITAS STABLES
Just east of Lajitas • 424-3238
Daily from sunrise to sunset with a siesta in the summer
Unlike Montana or Colorado stables, once winter sets in these wranglers don't close shop. Lajitas Stables offers several packages ranging from a one-hour ride ($15) to multi-day trips or ride/raft packages that run about $100 per person per day. Plenty of gentle, dependable mounts are available for greenhorns.

Rafting

See separate listing under **BIG BEND NATIONAL PARK.**

SIDE TRIPS

SAN CARLOS, CHIHUAHUA, MEXICO
$50 per person (two-person minimum) • 424-3221
San Carlos is a traditional Mexican village of 2,500 south of Lajitas. A little bit of farming, ranching, mining, and a *candelilla* waxworks keep it going. Depart the Lajitas Trading Post at ten in the morning. San Carlos native Kiko Garcia uses a Suburban to traverse the 18 miles of rugged dirt roads in about an hour and a half. Highlights include San Carlos Canyon and its lush springs, lunch at Señora Garcia's house, and an afternoon visit to a second canyon or the ruins of the old Spanish *presidio*, one of five built in the late 1700s to protect Spanish citizens from marauding Apaches and Comanches. Arrive back in Lajitas between 5:30 and 6:00 p.m.

ANNUAL EVENTS

February

CHIHUAHUAN DESERT CHALLENGE MOUNTAIN BIKE RACE AND FESTIVAL
Lajitas on the Rio Grande and surrounding area • 424-3471
Sponsored by the Chihuahuan Desert Riders Mountain Bicycle Club and hosted by Lajitas on the Rio Grande, this four-day event attracts hundreds of amateurs and pros and features fun rides to San Carlos, Chihuahua, and the ghost town of Buena Suerte, as

well as a circuit race, time trials, and a cross-country event for cash prizes and NORBA points.

November

FRANK X. TOLBERT—WICK FOWLER MEMORIAL CHILI COOK-OFF
CASI (Chili Appreciation Society International)
CHILI COOK-OFF
First weekend of November
   See separate listing under **TERLINGUA.**

RESTAURANTS

($ = Under $7.50, $$ = Under $15, $$$ = $15+ plus tax & tip)

BADLANDS RESTAURANT
Lajitas on the Rio Grande • 424-3471 • Daily
Breakfast, lunch, and dinner • Saloon opens at 5 p.m. • $–$$
AE MC V • W
   The family-friendly menu features plenty of appetizers, salads, sandwiches, and side orders. In addition to BLT's, burgers, and barbecue, this eatery just north of the Río Grande offers numerous Mexican food entrées—*burritos, enchiladas, fajitas, tacos,* and an excellent *picadillo* (sauteed beef tips). During the holidays, special Thanksgiving and Christmas buffets are served ($$). Bar.

DOS AMIGOS
Paso Lajitas • Mexico • Daily • Breakfast, lunch, and dinner till 8 p.m. • $ (dollars and pesos)
   Immediately west of Lajitas, a big dry wash cuts two deep dips in FM 170. In the middle of the second one, fork left on a sandy car path and meander about 100 yards towards the river. Parking is plainly visible and safe. A boatman ferries you across at a dollar per person round trip (pay when you return). High water can push market rates up several bucks. A short stroll and you're in front of Dos Amigos. Order the Mexican plate: two *enchiladas,* one *taco,* a *flauta,* a *tostada* (also called a *chalupa*), beans and rice. Mexican beers are a dollar. After you arrive back on the American side, a dollar covers the guy who patrols the parking lot in your absence.

CLUBS AND BARS

BADLANDS SALOON
Lajitas on the Rio Grande • 424-3452 • Nightly till 11 p.m.
There's usually something brewing on weekends during the high season, and count on live music next door at the Pavilion on the last Saturday night of the month. Bands cater to all tastes and play country & western, *tejano*, and rock & roll. Bar.

ACCOMMODATIONS

($ = Under $40, $$ = $40–$75, $$$ = $75–$100, $$$$ = Over $100)

LAJITAS ON THE RIO GRANDE
424-3471 • $$–$$$
A wide range of lodging is available in Lajitas. All units at the Badlands Hotel, the Cavalry Post Motel, La Cuesta Motel, and the Officer's Quarters are air-conditioned. Accommodations include hotel rooms, one- and two-bedroom condos, bunkhouses, and residences with daily, weekly, and monthly rates. Rooms include cable TV and phones (charge for local calls). Rates are typically reduced from June 15 to September 15. The Lajitas RV Park has 75 sites as well as a camping ground complete with restrooms, showers, and picnic tables. Amenities include the Badlands Restaurant and Saloon, the Lajitas Mercantile, the Frontier Drug Company featuring an old-fashioned fountain and gift items, a pool, laundry room, the Lajitas Golf Course, tennis courts, bike rentals, and plenty of free parking. The resort has its own 4,777-foot paved airstrip just east of the property. Bring your own rope for tie-downs. Pets welcome.

LANGTRY

VAL VERDE COUNTY ★ 30 ★ (915)

Though the railroad may have built Langtry, Roy Bean gave it lasting renown. Situated near the rail line that connected the Gulf and West coasts, Langtry first achieved fame for its proximity to Dead Man's Gulch, site of the completion of the Southern Pacific's transcontinental Sunset Route in 1883 (see **Pecos River Bridge Overlook** below). With the construction came much mayhem. This rowdy piece of the Lower Pecos River Valley required a justice of the peace; Bean began his work the week before he was appointed.

As a jurist Roy Bean had no compare, be it ordering the defendant to buy the house a round (at Bean's saloon) or fining a dead man the sum of his worldly possessions. With age came even greater autonomy: Bean defied Governor Culberson and circumvented the state's anti-prizefight law in 1896 by hosting a heavyweight title bout within sight of some Texas Rangers but beyond their domain on a sand bank in the middle of the Río Grande. Peter Maher, fresh from a victory over Gentleman Jim Donnell, lost to Bob Fitzsimmons, but it was Bean who won everlasting fame.

TOURIST SERVICES AND MUSEUM

JUDGE ROY BEAN VISITOR CENTER
Loop 25 one mile south of Highway 90 • 291-3340
Open from 8 a.m. to 5 p.m. except December 24, 25, 26, and New Year's Day • **Free** • **W**

With the exception of the State Capitol, the Judge Roy Bean Visitor Center is the only state-operated travel information center that is not at an entry city like El Paso or Brownsville. Before you visit the Jersey Lilly, pick up a copy of the *Texas State Travel Guide*, plan your vacation with the assistance of Department of Transportation travel counselor, and tour the cactus garden. Most of the 100+ varieties are Chihuahuan Desert natives.

Roy Bean's courtroom and billiard hall stands out back. It was called the Jersey Lilly (Bean was smitten with the English starlet Lillie Langtry and continually invited her out west). When Miss Langtry finally assented to his invitation, His Honor had been dead and buried for several months. Judging from Bean's condition and Langtry's remote desolation, no one in Miss Lillie's party was heard to mutter "better late than never."

SIDE TRIPS

PECOS RIVER BRIDGE OVERLOOK
18 miles east of Langtry
Scenic viewpoint from the south side of the east bank   •   W+
An earlier bridge, constructed in Roy Bean's day (1891), was the highest in the world and stood over this once empty canyon long before Lake Amistad filled up the bottom 80 feet (1969). The present one towers 273 feet above the Pecos.

Just up river and 2½ miles west of the Pecos on private property is Dead Man's Gulch. Much like the celebration at Promontory Point in 1869, speeches and a silver spike commemorated the completion of the Sunset Route across the southern United States here by Irish and Chinese crews in 1883. Even more noteworthy was the route's centennial celebration. Former state senator Don Kennard invited Lieutenant Governor Bill Hobby to join the party planning to overnight under the stars in early January 1983, and the rush was on. A short list of attendees included Majority Leader Jim Wright, historian T.R. Fehrenbach, several Railroad Commissioners, Texas Supreme Court Justice Jim Wallace, and then-state treasurer Ann Richards.

SEMINOLE CANYON STATE HISTORICAL PARK
Park Superintendent   •   Box 820   •   Comstock   •   78837
292-4464   •   *19 miles east of Langtry*   •   *45 miles west of Del Rio*
Daily 8 a.m.–10 p.m.   • $3 per vehicle   •   W+ but not all areas
Located just south of the confluence of the Pecos River and the Río Grande, Seminole Canyon is the site of Fate Bell Shelter which contains some of North America's oldest and most impressive Native American pictographs (rock paintings). Over 200 Pecos River-style sites exist but none like this one. Considered by experts to be among the most important rock art in the New World, Fate Bell is accessible only via guided tours at 10 a.m. and 3 p.m. Wednesday through Sunday (weather permitting). Moderately strenuous hiking is involved. Seminole Canyon Park contains many other activities: campsites with water (23) and with water nearby (8), eight miles of hiking trails, a six-mile mountain biking loop, picnic tables and grills, and plenty of opportunities for wildlife observation and photography. Several ecosystems are present at the park—the Chihuahuan Desert, the Tamaulipan Thorn Scrub, and the western edge of the Texas Hill Country—and provide for an unusual diversity of flora and fauna.

MARATHON

BREWSTER COUNTY   ★   800   ★   (915)

Named for its likeness to the plains where the Athenians defeated the Persians (490 B.C.), Marathon was founded by Captain Albion Shepard (1881), a member of the Southern Pacific Railroad's original surveying party. More important than the railroad was nearby Camp Peña Colorado (see **OTHER POINTS OF INTEREST** below). Peña Colorado was the last of the frontier forts, and its abandonment in 1893 signaled the end of the Indian Wars in Texas. By then, the Marathon area had become prime cattle country with thousands of acres of pasture claimed by enterprising ranchers (see **Gage Hotel** below).

To this day, resupplying and ranching are the town's twin industries. The railroad still passes through; AMTRAK stops in Alpine, a 30-minute drive west. Most visitors to Big Bend National Park (55 miles south via US 385) pass through Brewster County's second largest community, located just over four thousand feet above sea level. Hoteliers, craftsmen, artisans, and shopkeepers have made this tiny town as much a part of any Big Bend visit as the park itself.

TOURIST SERVICES

MARATHON CHAMBER OF COMMERCE
P.O. Box 163 • Marathon • 79842

If you'd like general information, drop a note to the Chamber at the post office box or stop by the Gage Hotel, a designated State Information Site for Big Bend National Park (see **ACCOMMODATIONS**).

OTHER POINTS OF INTEREST

THE POST aka CAMP PEÑA COLORADO
Four miles south of Marathon via Avenue D

Established in 1879 as one of the last posts of the Army's Frontier defense system, by the time Camp Peña ceased operations (1893) the West was won in Texas. Camp Peña was one of many Texas posts garrisoned by buffalo soldiers, former slaves whose regiments pushed the frontier forward. A term first coined by

Native Americans, buffalo soldier was used to describe the fighting spirit and the tight, curly hair of the troops. Nowadays the Post is a rendezvous for dances, weddings, and holiday celebrations. The front desk of the Gage Hotel keeps tabs on upcoming events.

SHOPPING

HALEY'S TRADING POST

Monday–Friday 9–11 and 3–5 • Saturday 9–11 • Closed Sunday
Highway 90, just east of the Gage Hotel • No phone
   This shop is perfect for Marathon—one-of-kind—and is full of antique bridles, chaps, saddles, and spurs along with an amazing assortment of bleached skulls.

JUST TEXAS

Highway 90, just east of the Gage Hotel • 386-4217
   As chauvinistic as Texans are, Just Texas suits this trait or curse (depending on your perspective) with Texas antiques, crafts, collectibles, photographs, and posters.

LOVEGENE'S

21 South First St. • 386-4366
Daily 9–6, closing early on Tuesday and Thursday
   Owners James Evans and Gene Kraft migrated west from Austin several years ago, and their gallery highlights friends and artists from Central and West Texas in a variety of media: photography, watercolor, ceramics, and pottery, as well as jewelry and hand-painted silks. Evans, an accomplished photographer with credits ranging from *The New York Times* to *Texas Highways*, has resurrected the lost art of photographic lamp shades. This Big Bend artistic tradition began with W.D. Smithers and is detailed in his autobiography, *Chronicles of the Big Bend* (Madrona Press: Austin, 1976).

MARATHON EMPORIUM

Highway 90 just east of the Gage Hotel • 386-4384
   After you stroll through the Gage, head over to the Emporium to purchase the furnishings and accessories that you can't live without (and don't feel comfortable walking off with).

ANNUAL EVENTS

March

WORLD CHAMPIONSHIP JACKASS ROPING AND RANCH RODEO
Fussy Flats Arena • 386-4202
Nominal admission to events
Like cow chip tossing and rattlesnake roundups, you've got to see this one to believe it. The festivites kick off with a parade to the arena late Saturday morning featuring riders and mule-drawn wagons. After a barbecue lunch ($) comes the ranch rodeo. Five-member teams compete in categories meant to be as entertaining as trying: jenny milking, jackass dressing, pasture roping, jackass riding, and team penning. Dance Saturday night at the Post. About 200 men and women compete in Sunday's jackass roping.

SPORTS AND ACTIVITIES

SPRING CREEK RANCH
23 miles south of Marathon • 376-2260
See separate listing under **BIG BEND NATIONAL PARK.**

RESTAURANTS

($ = Under $7.50, $$ = Under $15, $$$ = $15+ plus tax & tip)

GLASS MOUNTAIN BAR AND GRILL
Gage Hotel • 386-4205
Daily • Breakfast, lunch, and dinner • $–$$ • MC V • W
The superbly grilled lamb chops with *jalapeño* jelly are mandatory. Other tempting choices include the *chile rellenos* stuffed with goat cheese and any item off the rotisserie. Traditional fare includes chicken-fried steak and hand-cut ribeyes. Domestic and imported beers and Texas wines are featured. Bar.

PHIL'S
Highway 90 East • 386-4558
Daily except Tuesday • Lunch and dinner • $ • W
You probably recognize Marathon's leading celebrity, Phil Thomas, from his stellar performance on *Jeopardy* (a close second). Most locals appreciate him because he keeps regular hours at the

old Southern Route diner. The decor—red checkered tableclothes and Lone Star memorabilia—mirrors the cuisine: wholesome meals served in ample portions. The locals favor the chicken-fried steak, but consider the excellent chili (no beans and plenty hot). Other good calls include the catfish, the *enchiladas*—cheese, chicken, and *barbacoa,* and plenty of fresh cornbread. Bring your own beer or wine.

ACCOMMODATIONS

($ = Under $40, $$ = $40–$75, $$$ = $75–$100, $$$$ = Over $100)

CAPTAIN SHEPARD'S INN
386-4205 or 800-884-4243 • $$$–$$$$
Run as a bed and breakfast, the inn has been Marathon's preeminent address since it was erected in 1899 by the town's founding father, Albion Shepard. The main house, a two-story adobe finished in Greek Revival and furnished in Victorian, has five bedrooms ($$$), all with private baths. The carriage house, let as a two-bedroom suite ($$$$), offers a large common area featuring a fireplace, sitting and dining areas, and a full kitchen.

The staff of the Gage Hotel (see below) handles all details of your stay including reservations and payment. A direct line from the foyer of Captain Shepard's Inn to the front desk at the Gage is available to make dinner reservations, ask travel questions, and handle emergencies. All facilities of the Gage including the pool are at the disposal of inn guests. A generous continental breakfast is served including baked goods, fruit, cereal, juices, and coffee.

GAGE HOTEL
Highway 90 • 386-4205 or 800-884-4243 • $$–$$$
Countless articles in publications like *The New York Times, Condé Nast Traveler,* and *Texas Monthly* have described the allure of this hotel. The site of innumerable weddings, reunions, and Big Bend outings, the Gage continues in its historic role as headquarters for trips out West. Built in the 1920s, it served as headquarters for the 500,000-acre ranch of Alfred Gage, a Vermont native who came to Brewster County to punch cattle in the 1880s and bequeathed one of the state's greatest ranches four decades later.

The recent addition of Los Portales to the west of the original hotel complements the design of Gage's original architect, Henry Trost. The outdoor pool and covered patio offers welcome relief from the West Texas sun. The 37 rooms are appointed with Mexican, Indian, and Anglo artifacts (but not telephones or televisions). The knowledgeable front desk can book rafting on the Río Grande, horseback and bicycle rides locally, hunting on area ranches, or stargazing at McDonald Observatory. The Gage offers packages featuring noted photographers, musicians, and chuckwagon cooks as well.

MARATHON MOTEL & RV PARK
West Highway 90 • 386-4241 • $
Located at the west end of town, there are four inexpensive cabins, each a duplex. For larger parties, a house with a room downstairs and a kitchenette and rooms upstairs is available. Full RV hookups (including cable TV) are available. If you're coming through during hunting season—October, November, December—or during the spring, call Mary or John Hoover in advance to see if any rooms are left.

MARFA

PRESIDIO COUNTY SEAT   ★   2,424   ★   (915)

Collar a video of *Giant* starring Rock Hudson, Liz Taylor, and James Dean, and you'll get a good look at Marfa. The vistas are as grand today as four decades ago when this town was knee-deep in movie stars and everyone was an extra. The name Marfa comes from a Dostoevsky novel that a railroad official's wife was reading when tracks were first laid west. Cattle has been king since Milton Faver founded the Cibolo Creek Ranch south of town before the Civil War. Unlike Alpine with its university and Fort Davis with its fort, observatory, and state park, Marfa keeps to cattle and each November holds one of the top bull sales in America, the Highland Hereford Breeders Association sale.

TOURIST SERVICES

MARFA CHAMBER OF COMMERCE
131 E. San Antonio • P.O. Box 635 • Marfa • 79843
729-4942 • Monday–Friday 10–12 and 1–5
Tourist information, t-shirts, mugs, caps, and books and merchandise on the Marfa Lights is available.

GUIDEBOOKS AND PUBLICATIONS

BIG BEND SENTINEL
Box P • Marfa • 79843 • 729-4342
Annual subscription: $21
The best of the Big Bend's weekly newspapers, the *Sentinel* is full of news about the Big Bend area and covers Marfa, Alpine, Fort Davis, and all the national and state parks.

MARFA LIGHTS
By Judith M. Brueske, Ph.D. • $6.95
Full of eyewitness accounts, this is the most comprehensive work on the Lights available. Pick up a copy at the Marfa Chamber or Ocotillo Enterprises in Alpine (see **ALPINE**).

BIRD'S-EYE VIEW

PRESIDIO COUNTY COURTHOUSE
Weekdays during office hours
The view from the fifth-story perch is more than adequate compensation for the 86 steps you'll climb en route. High among Marfa's many steeples, wrestle with the unwieldy set of binoculars and set your sights on the Big Bend's foremost tabernacle, Cathedral Mountain, clearly visible to the southeast.

MUSEUMS

CHINATI FOUNDATION
Highway 67, half a mile south of Marfa at Fort D.A. Russell
1 Cavalry Road • 729-4362 • Thursday–Saturday 1–5 or by appointment • Free (donations accepted) • W
A not-for-profit arts organization, the Chinati Foundation is so out of place in Marfa that it actually fits in. The first aspect to the *Fundacion Chinati* worth noting is that the buildings that house

the art also form an integral part of the collection. The Chinati Foundation is committed to alternative museum forms, and in Marfa they selected a superb setting. The permanent installations of works by John Chamberlain, Claes Oldenburg, Roni Horn, and Donald Judd are not ensconced in magnificent structures with designer nametags like Johnson, Pei, or Wright, but in a collection of renovated and reinterpreted buildings including abandoned ones in town that the foundation and Judd salvaged and the remnants of Fort D.A. Russell south of Marfa. Secondly, consider that many of the works, particularly Judd's, were created to be integrated into their architectural surroundings, and in some instances—most notably at the Fort—the renovation of the often dilapidated buildings was subsumed into the art. This becomes apparent not on a crowded October day during the foundation's open house (see **ANNUAL EVENTS**) but when you and a few others have the collection to yourselves during the off-season, i.e., the other 51 weeks of the year. Finally, consider the art itself. It is not as intimidating as it first seems. Ask your guide for assistance and explanation. They are quite familiar with the art and often the artist.

Your guided tour begins at Fort D.A. Russell, where the most recent addition to the permanent collection is an installation by Kabakov. Entitled *Shkola No. Shest* (school number six), it's appropriate that the Russian tongue is used not only because of Kabakov's designs but because Marfa was named for a character from Dostoevsky's *The Brothers Karamazov*. Your group and guide will then proceed into town to several other properties. Be sure to take the time to include a stop at the old Wool & Mohair house, which has been renamed the Chamberlain Building. More than 20 works by artist John Chamberlain are displayed; all feature his interpretations of salvaged automobile shells, pieced together and refitted.

OTHER POINTS OF INTEREST

MARFA LIGHTS
At historical marker on Highway 67/90, nine miles east of Marfa
When the sun goes down, the cars pull up. People who need an excuse to go parking late at night in the middle of nowhere have been pretending to look for the Marfa Lights for better than a century. Whereas the rest of the country winks at the mention of submarine races, the locals, tourists, and even accredited scientists have eyeballed this unexplained phenomenon. The first sighting was by Bill Ellison (1883). Since then, the different interpretations

of these nightly apparitions has expanded geometrically, particularly during Prohibition: St. Elmo's Fire, phosphorescent minerals, lanterns of massacred troops, and swamp gas. About the only good rule of thumb is that the more a car's windows are fogged up, the less chance of a confirmed sighting.

PRESIDIO COUNTY COURTHOUSE AND JAIL
Town Square
Presidio County ranks up there with Ellis and Wise counties for the state's most picturesque courthouse. Certainly the setting is more dramatic. Built in Second Empire style for $60,000 (1886), consider that renovation costs a century later totaled $350,000. Until 1993, the adjacent jail was the longest continually operated one in the state.

SPORTS AND ACTIVITIES

Golf

MARFA MUNICIPAL GOLF COURSE
At the end of Golf Course Road • 729-4043
Tuesday through Sunday • Greens fee: $8.50
Welcome to the highest golf course in Texas. At an altitude of 4,882 above sea level, your tee shots will travel appreciably farther due to the thinner air. You may not notice, however, because of the panoramic views. Many a bogey has been overlooked (and gone unrecorded) while taking in views of Cathedral Mountain south of Alpine, Blue Mountain west of Fort Davis, and Chinati Mountain south toward Mexico. Better holes include the par three sixth hole with a water hazard in front of the green and the par five number seven (495 yards) with a dogleg right. Hardest hole on the course is the par four ninth hole, also a dogleg right, at 425 yards.

SIDE TRIPS

SHAFTER, TEXAS
40 miles south of Marfa on US 17
There's more to Texas than just oil and gas. Try silver and gold. What's left of Shafter stands beside Cibolo Creek, beneath *las Tres Hermanas* (three peaks named for sisters Anita, Aurora, and Ida Brooks). From 1883 until 1942, the Shafter Mine produced more

than $23,000,000 in silver ore as well as gold, lead, and zinc. With over 100 miles of tunnels, the mine supported a mill, a smelter, and men's and women's clubs for the more than 200 miners, machinists, and their families. Shafter now boasts less than 50 residents and has a general store, a well-marked pay phone, and an historic cemetery. Drive past the Catholic church through town and across Cibolo Creek. The cemetery is dead ahead as is a chronology of the town courtesy of the Speed family. Movie fans note that portions of the silver screen version of Michael Crichton's *Andromeda Strain* were filmed locally.

ANNUAL EVENTS

April

MARFA OLD TIMERS ROPING
Presidio County Fairgrounds off Golf Course Rd. • 729-4942
Not a fancy, made-for-TV event but an annual tradition among friends, the Old Timers Roping is sponsored by the Marfa Roping Club. This is a roping competition for a variety of age groups but featuring teams with at least one member over forty and a second member over sixty. The minimum combined ages must exceed 100 with some teams in the 115-plus bracket.

September

MARFA LIGHTS FESTIVAL
Presidio County Courthouse • 729-4942 • (Chamber of Commerce) • Labor Day weekend • Free: Courthouse Lawn Festival • Admission: dance & concerts
People may argue about the existence of the Marfa Lights, but no one disputes the popularity of this shindig. Activities begin the Friday evening before Labor Day with a street dance by the Presidio County Courthouse (admission). On Saturday and Sunday a Lawn Festival (no charge) is held at the courthouse from 10 a.m. till 5 p.m. with vendors selling arts and crafts as well as food. Other than the nightly viewing of the Marfa Lights, the highpoints are concerts on Saturday night (admission) and Sunday evening (admission). Both concerts are usually held at the baseball field on the east side of town. Book in advance for this one. Seeing one of the Marfa Lights is probably easier than finding a room in Marfa, Alpine, or Fort Davis over Labor Day weekend.

CIBOLO CREEK RANCH OPEN HOUSE
Cibolo Creek Ranch • 229-3507
Take Highway 17 32 miles south of Marfa and turn right
First week of September • Noon until 5 p.m. • Free
Each year, the historic headquarters of Milton Faver's pioneering nineteenth-century ranch—the first big spread west of the Pecos—welcomes its neighbors throughout the Big Bend to an afternoon celebration along the banks of Cibolo Creek. The detailed renovation of *el Fortin* can be toured including the artifacts, the numerous period furnishings, and room after room of Texana associated with this historic ranch and the settlement of the Trans-Pecos (see **ACCOMMODATIONS**).

October

CHINATI FOUNDATION OPEN HOUSE
Fort D.A. Russell • 729-4362
Second weekend of the month
Local, national, and international friends of the *Fundacion Chinati* gather for art, film, and music as well as dining, drinking, and dancing. Everyone is invited to join in, and in case you'd like to get a better feel for the intent and efforts of the Chinati Foundation, reserve a seat at the benefit dinner (see **MUSEUMS**).

RESTAURANTS

($ = Under $7.50, $$ = Under $15, $$$ = $15+ plus tax & tip)

CARMEN'S CAFE
317 E. San Antonio • 729-3429
Monday–Saturday • Breakfast, lunch, and dinner • $
Enjoy a *gordita* at Carmen's. This West Texas specialty is a deep-fried cornbread patty sliced open and stuffed with meat, lettuce, tomato, and cheese and topped with *guacamole* and sour cream. Don't forget to add *salsa*. Other good choices: the *chile colorado*, the *asado* plate, and the chicken *enchiladas*.

MIKE'S PLACE
120 E. El Paso • 729-8146
Monday–Saturday • Breakfast and lunch • $
Mike's specialty is some of the best chili in West Texas and an equally famous burger. For a Mexican fix, order the *chile verde* or the *menudo*. Since 1952.

THUNDERBIRD RESTAURANT
509 W. San Antonio St. • 729-4891
Daily • Breakfast, lunch, and dinner • $
Some mighty particular Prude Ranch hands gave the Thunderbird a thumbs-up. The salad bar was well stocked with fresh selections, and all the essentials passed muster including the chicken-fried steak, the burgers, the T-Bird Club, and the soup du jour.

ACCOMMODATIONS

($ = Under $40, $$ = $40–$75, $$$ = $75–$100, $$$$ = Over $100)
Room Tax (in Marfa) 13%

CIBOLO CREEK RANCH
34 miles south of Marfa off Hwy 17 • **915-358-4696** • **$$$$**
Tours by appointment only
If you think you've seen it all, come here. The Cibolo Creek Ranch is without compare nationwide, let alone in Texas. With the assistance of the Texas Historical Commission, the ranch has renovated old Fort Cibolo, constructed in 1857 by Milton Faver, and in the process received three National Historic Site designations and five Texas State Historical markers.

By choosing spring-fed Cibolo Creek for his headquarters, Faver took advantage of the ideal climate which the mile-high ranch offers: moderate temperatures, low humidity, and plenty of shade trees. A second Faver outpost, *La Cienaga*, is the main guest lodge on this 25,000-acre working ranch and features an inviting terrace that fronts an enormous grove of cottonwood, ash, and hackberry. The extensive horseback riding program offered at the ranch is based here and ranges from instruction for beginners to overnight trips. All guests are welcome to tour the ranch via open vehicle and view the game—elk, camel, and the ranch's namesake, bison—as well as view (or herd) the ranch's own Antique Longhorns. Other activities on the ranch include birding, hiking, swimming, and photo excursions. Also available to guests is *La Morita*, the third and most secluded camp on the ranch. This hideaway sits on the northern edge of the Big Bend Ranch State Natural Area and offers all the spring-fed, shady solitude two could hope to find.

At all three of the forts, each room is furnished with western and Mexican antiques and features saltillo tile floors and traditional ceilings—cottonwood *vigas* and oak *latillas* and *rajas*. You can't tell by looking, but central air and heat have been masterfully incorporated into the renovation. Most rooms have fireplaces. The ranch kitchen specializes in cowboy cuisine. At Cibo-lo, all snacks, meals, and alcoholic and non-alcoholic beverages are included, and complete banquet and catering facilities are available.

Off-ranch offerings include complimentary transfers to all of the Big Bend's numerous activities and points of interest. Arrangements for day and overnight float trips on the Río Grande, touring the nearby state and national parks, as well as visits to the University of Texas McDonald Observatory are all handled by the ranch staff. The crew at Cibolo Creek will greet and return guests arriving in Alpine via Lone Star Airlines and AMTRAK as well as at the ranch's own 5,000-foot strip. Charter services are available utilizing the ranch's own KingAir.

HOTEL EL PAISANO

207 N. Highland • 729-3145 • $$–$$$$

After entering the cool, dimly lit, tile-floored lobby, notice the black and white stills from the George Stevens production of Edna Ferber's novel *Giant* (1956). El Paisano was the headquarters for the crew. Throughout the lobby, placards and photos remind visitors of the heady days when Elizabeth Taylor, Rock Hudson, and James Dean strolled the streets of Marfa.

El Paisano was built in 1930 and entered into the National Register of Historic Places in 1978. Designed by Henry Trost, master architect for "arid America," El Paisano is a two-story property located on Highland Avenue, Marfa's central boulevard, directly across from the Presidio County Courthouse. The nine units are all suites of various sizes and come with fully equipped kitchenettes, TV (HBO), and coffee makers. Available in the building are a hotel restaurant, an indoor pool and sauna, a game room, gift shop, and beauty salon. No pets allowed. Government rates are available.

HOLIDAY CAPRI INN and MOTEL THUNDERBIRD

Highway 90 West • 729-4326 or 729-4327 • $

Both properties are located across Highway 90 from each other and are run out of the same office at the Trading Post of the South-west. Both phone lines ring here, and it also serves as the front desk for all 52 rooms including singles, doubles, and triples (sleep six). Rooms include cable TV with basic channels only and phones (50¢ charge for local calls). Amenities include the Thun-derbird restaurant, a pool shared by both properties, the Trading Post of the Southwest gift shop, an adjacent barber shop, and free baby beds.

MENTONE

LOVING COUNTY SEAT   ★   107   ★   (915)

You've heard about it, you've read about it; here's your chance to stop by and visit America's wealthiest county. Each year the runners-up jockey for silver and bronze, has-beens like Orange County, California, Westchester County, New York, and Fairfax County, Virginia. Loving County always leads the pack. The last Texas county organized (1931), it has the smallest population of any county or parish nationwide and was named for traildriver Oscar Loving (remember Robert Duvall as Gus in *Lonesome Dove?*). The only church is the former schoolhouse. There was no replacement—kids are bused out of county for their lessons. Loving County has no doctors, no hospitals, and, in fact, only two community organizations: the 4-H Club and the County Historical Society. Stop by the county's lone diner, the A&G Cafe, for breakfast, lunch, or dinner during the week or till 3 p.m. on Saturday. These folks know the meaning of a dollar—the Wednesday lunch special is steak. In a recent federal election, better than 80 percent of the county's 107 citizens participated, which may go to prove that if more of us took the time to vote we might all be as well off as Loving County.

PECOS

REEVES COUNTY SEAT   ★   12,069   ★   (915)

More than any other watering hole in West Texas, Pecos has a lore about it that goes far beyond the state's borders. Besides claiming Pecos Bill and Calamity Jane, locals brag on the world's first rodeo—held in Pecos on July 4, 1883. All the hoopla goes with the word Indians used to describe the crooked river running down from New Mexico: *pecos.* White men used that same word to describe other riparian activity, however, to "pecos" a fellow meant to murder him and throw his body in the same crooked river with a rock overcoat.

Known officially as the Town of Pecos City, Pecos also achieved lasting fame as the source of the Pecos Cantaloupe. Once crops exceeded local demand, farmers began marketing the cantaloupes to the Texas & Pacific Railroad, whose arrival in 1881 put the town on the map. Situated at the intersection of Interstate 20 and US Highway 285, present-day Pecos is an important crossroads for West Texas and serves as a distribution center for far-flung farming, ranching, and oil and gas interests.

TOURIST SERVICES

PECOS CHAMBER OF COMMERCE
111 S. Cedar • P.O. Box 27 • Pecos • 79772 • 445-2406
Located right next to the West of the Pecos Museum off US 285, the Pecos Chamber also serves as the visitor bureau. From the Chamber, it's a short stroll to the West of the Pecos Museum, Clay Allison's grave, and a replica of the Jersey Lilly Saloon.

MUSEUMS

WEST OF THE PECOS MUSEUM
Highway 285 and 1st St. • 445-5076
Monday–Saturday 9–5 • Sunday 2–5
Closed Thanksgiving Day and December 18–25 • Admission
Housed in over thirty rooms of the #11 Saloon (1896) and the adjacent Orient Hotel (1904), this two-story structure is one of the most complete historical museums between San Antonio and El Paso. Established in 1962, the extensive collection of Texana and Western American artifacts is housed in and around an Old West Saloon where a double killing occurred in 1896. Out back stands a replica of the Jersey Lilly and the grave of Clay Allison, the "Gentleman Gunfighter."

ANNUAL EVENTS

July

WEST OF THE PECOS RODEO
Reeves County Rodeo Arena • 800-588-7326
Weekend closest to the 4th of July
The world's oldest rodeo has evolved into a fully sanctioned PRCA event and is the highlight of Western Week. Activities are held all week including the Rodeo Parade downtown, the Old

Timer's Reunion at the West of the Pecos Museum, the Golden Girl Pageant, Fiesta Night in Old Pecos, a Western Art Show and Sale at the Civic Center, and dances nightly.

August

PECOS CANTALOUPE FESTIVAL
Reeves County Civic Center
First weekend • Free
The pride of Pecos is its world-renowned cantaloupe. Pecos celebrates each year's crop with this weekend of cantaloupe eating, seed spitting, and a cantaloupe look-a-like contest. The Cantaloupe Fly-in Breakfast is held at the airport. Also on the agenda are a golf tournament, a softball tourney, and, for the serious athletes, a putt-putt golf competition.

October

REEVES COUNTY FALL FAIR
Reeves County Civic Center • Early October
Thursday–Saturday • Admission fee for concert
The county fair is the biggest time in Pecos and includes a sanctioned World Championship Barbecue Beef Cook-Off at the Sheriff's Posse Arena, the livestock show at the Civic Center, and scores of vendors. Each year, a top *tejano* band performs at the rodeo arena. Past entertainers include Mazz, Emilio Navaira, the Texas Tornadoes, and La Mafia.

ACCOMMODATIONS

($ = Under $40, $$ = $40–$75, $$$ = $75–$100, $$$$ = Over $100)
Room Tax 13%

BEST WESTERN SUNDAY HOUSE
I-20 at Exit 40 • 900 W. Palmer • 447-2215 or 800-528-1234
$$
This single-level motor inn is located on the south end of town and has 104 smoking and non-smoking rooms. Rooms include TV (HBO) and phones (charge for local calls). Amenities include the Alpine Lodge Restaurant, complimentary coffee in the lobby, outdoor pool, same-day valet laundry, and free parking. Pets OK. AAA, AARP, commercial, and military rates are available.

PRESIDIO & OJINAGA

PRESIDIO COUNTY	★	3,072	★	(915)
STATE OF CHIHUAHUA	★	40,000+	★	(011 52 145)

Known nationwide for its scalding temperatures (rare is the summer day without temperatures over 100 degrees), Presidio and Ojinaga are situated on the historic Chihuahua Trail, one of the Southwest's great commercial routes. Both cities share a distinct past and a promising future. *La Junta de los Ríos* is the centuries-old name for this area, site of the confluence of the Río Grande and Mexico's Río Conchos. For thousands of years, Native Americans were drawn to the fertile floodplain; early Spanish accounts (1581) mention some of the later settlements. Over the next century and a half, military men and missionaries attempted to subdue this area and settle *la Junta,* but *Presidio del Norte* (present-day Ojinaga) was too distant a town and too low a priority for long-lasting success.

Commerce, not conquest or converts, led to settlement and is the focus of Presidio and Ojinaga's future. The Chihuahua Trail bypassed El Paso and Santa Fe and led from Chihuahua City across the Big Bend via Presidio del Norte to San Antonio and the gulf port of Indianola. First traversed by the Connelly Expedition (1839), it brought traders and pioneers like Milton Faver (see **Cibolo Creek Ranch** under **MARFA**), John Spencer, John Burgess, and Ben Leaton (see **Fort Leaton State Historical Park** below). The old ruts of the Chihuahua Trail are the future of both cities. The passage of the North American Free Trade Agreement (NAFTA) was critical to this region, and, much like the confluence of *los ríos Grande y Conchos,* the intersection of US 67 and the South Orient Railroad here promises great fortunes to future pioneers.

TOURIST SERVICES

PRESIDIO INFORMATION CENTER and GIFT SHOP
US 67 Business (next to the Post Office) • 229-4478
Daily 9–6

Unlike the Chamber of Commerce, there's always someone here during business hours to take your call and help with directions and other questions. The gift shop stocks gifts crafted by Tarahumara Indians including dolls, clay figurines, wooden bowls, and the ubiquitous Tarahumara drums. Other items include Zapotec folk art, maps, books, and Presidio brand gourmet barbeque sauce.

HISTORIC PLACES

FORT LEATON STATE HISTORICAL PARK
Three miles east of Presidio along FM 170 • 229-3613
Park Superintendent • P.O. Box 1180 • Presidio • 79845
Daily 8–4:30 • Adults $2, children $1 • W

Fort Leaton, the historic outpost of Ben Leaton, serves as the western gateway to the Big Bend Ranch State Natural Area. Three veterans of the Mexican-American War—Ben Leaton, John Spencer, and John Burgess—quit Chihuahua City after the war to seek their fortunes on the recently established Chihuahua Trail. Their arrival in 1848 and the mercantile business they established were the first American inroads in this area. Leaton distinguished himself by acquiring an old Spanish garrison, *el Fortin de San Jose* "the Little Fort of Saint Joseph." *El Fortin* was built in 1773 by Spaniards stationed at *Presidio del Norte* (present-day Ojinaga) and was abandoned in 1810. Leaton traded with friend and foe including Apaches and Comanches who bartered stolen livestock for gunpowder, lead, and arms. Ben Leaton quickly fell out of favor with locals and officials on both sides of the border.

A favorite Leaton boast was that his fort enclosed exactly one acre. The restoration of so large an adobe structure was a major undertaking. Renovation required 77,000 adobe bricks. Craftsmen with such skills—adobe brick making and laying—were found in Mexico. Brought to Fort Leaton, they crafted the bricks and applied the stucco finish using traditional methods. Tours of Fort Leaton include 25 of the fort's 40 rooms with exhibits and programs detailing the history of the Spanish, Mexican, Texan, and American colonizers. Several picnic sites are available.

OTHER POINTS OF INTEREST

BIG BEND RANCH STATE NATURAL AREA
Western entrance at Fort Leaton State Historical Park three miles east of Presidio on FM 170
See separate listing under **BIG BEND RANCH STATE NATURAL AREA.**

SHOPPING

UETA
2403 O'Reilly • 229-3766
Monday–Saturday 10–6 • Sunday 12–5
UETA stores can be found at most major border crossings from Brownsville to San Diego. Originally designed to target Mexican nationals with brand-name, duty-free goods, *norteamericanos* can find bargains too. A quick pass through the Presidio store uncovered Lee jeans, Victorinox Swiss Army knives, Rolex watches, Calvin Klein perfumes and colognes, and Johnny Walker scotch at prices well below retail. For some items, such as a Rolex, alcohol, or cigarettes, you'll have to cross the border to receive your purchase, declare it, and pay a duty or tax before you can bring it back to the States. For the hardened shopper this only adds to the satisfaction of uncovering a bargain.

SIDE TRIPS

CANDELARIA, TEXAS and SAN ANTONIO, CHIHUAHUA
49 miles west of Presidio via FM 170 (paved all the way)
Candelaria Mercantile • 8 a.m. to whenever • 229-3531
Lajitas sits 50 miles east of Presidio along FM 170. Head west on that same road and you'll end up in a town like Lajitas once was ages ago—Candelaria. The site of a World War I U.S. Cavalry post, this unpretentious border village serves area cattle ranches in remote Presidio County and Chihuahua as well as curious tourists. The focal point of the town is the **Candelaria Mercantile,** which houses the all-important **End of the Road Cantina.** Park here and get gasoline, food, snacks, cold drinks, beer, and other sundries. In front of the mercantile you'll notice the local incarceration facility (a fine deterrent only recently removed from its longtime schoolyard home). The Pancho Villa-era cavalry post is a short stroll from the mercantile as is the town of San Antonio.

This clean little cowtown of several hundred *mexicanos* is conveniently reached by a foot bridge across the rio or your own four-wheel-drive vehicle.

COPPER CANYON

For decades, West Texans have kept for themselves and their close friends an unspoiled Mexican getaway, *las Barrancas de Cobre*. Unlike Acapulco or Cancun, commercial development won't tarnish this jewel. The only way to enjoy the six-canyon journey is by train, twisting and winding across 39 bridges and through 86 tunnels during a 400-mile journey from Chihuahua City to Los Mochis on the Gulf of California. Local travel agents are well-versed with the itinerary which can vary slightly. **Alpine Travel** (915- 837-3356) in Alpine quoted a rate of $950 per person, double occupancy, for a professionally escorted Copper Canyon trip including two nights in Chihuahua City, one night en route to the coast, and one more down on the water.

PEGUIS CANYON

About 30 miles west of Ojinaga on the Chihuahua Highway

Imagine viewing Santa Elena Canyon from the top down. That's what this venture is for. Just as the Río Grande slices through several canyons in Big Bend National Park, the Río Conchos carves through the Peguis Mountains west of Ojinaga. No special vehicle permit or visa is required to drive to the overlook which is less than 45 minutes outside of Ojinaga via the Chihuahua Highway (Mexico 16). You'll park at the top of a long incline at the *area de descanso* (rest stop), and hike down a paved trail to spectacular vistas of sheer canyon walls and the Conchos. From OJ, the road narrows to a paved, one-lane highway with speed limits up to 80 kph (less than 50 mph). Daytime forays are recommended.

ANNUAL EVENTS

May

ONION FESTIVAL

Downtown Presidio • 229-3199 (Chamber of Commerce)

Millions of years of rich sedimentary deposits along the Río Grande and the Río Conchos have developed a soil perfect for onion growing (melons, too). Locals celebrate this gift of nature with a parade, a 5K Race, volleyball and softball tournaments, an arts and crafts bazaar, *folklorico* dancing, and dances Friday and Saturday nights featuring entertainers like Freddy Fender.

RESTAURANTS

CAFE ROSE'S
Next to the Three Palms Inn on Business 67 • 229-3998
Daily • Breakfast, lunch, and dinner • $–$$ • W

Ever had an *encharito?* Rose's is your best bet to sample this sliced beef and green *chile* (mild) treat, served in a flour *tortilla* and smothered in cheese. On the lighter side, order a *chalupa: frijoles*, lettuce, tomatoes, and *guacamole* on a corn tortilla. Scrumptious homemade desserts, particularly the pecan pie.

LAS PAMPAS
O'Reilly St. • 299-3552
Daily • Breakfast, lunch, and dinner • $–$$

After a professional soccer career in Argentina, Brazil, and Mexico, Gualberto Laperuta settled in Presidio, where he prepares Argentine, Italian, Mexican, and American specialties. Like Texans, Argentines love a good steak; order yours *churrasco*-style and enjoy this top sirloin cut served with Gualberto's own *chimichurre*. The popular *milanesa* is the choice of chicken-fried steak fans. The *huevos rancheros* are served all day long. Las Pampas and families go together; pizza, burgers, Mexican food, and a salad bar cover most hard-to-please appetites. Beer and wine.

ACCOMMODATIONS

THREE PALMS INN
Highway 67 Business • Presidio • 229-3211 • $–$$

This two-story, 42-room motel is located on what used to be Presidio's principal thoroughfare which has now been circumvented by the new Highway 67. Four non-smoking units are available. Rooms include cable TV (HBO) and phones with no charge for local calls. Ojinaga is not a local call. An outdoor pool and free parking are available. Cafe Rose's is right next door. Pets OK.

SIERRA BLANCA

HUDSPETH COUNTY SEAT   ★   758   ★   (915)

Named for the imposing 6894-foot massif northwest of town, Sierra Blanca offers more than just a welcome break between El Paso and Van Horn. The mountains, canyons, and flats that comprise Hudspeth County have been important crossroads for centuries.

Native Americans venturing to and from Old Mexico regularly stopped at springs 30 miles south of town (as did Pancho Villa, Gene Tunney, and former owner H.L. Hunt). To curb Indian attacks along the Butterfield Overland Mail route, Fort Quitman was established just before the Civil War. Abandoned for the duration of the conflict, it eventually served as headquarters for the final effort to subdue Apaches under Victorio. (No remnants exist of either Fort Quitman or Fort Hancock, a sub-post of Fort Bliss). Indian battles at Quitman Canyon and Rattlesnake Springs were among the state's last (1880), but it was Mexican forces who killed Victorio the following year to end the struggle.

Neither Indian nor soldier participated in Hudspeth County's best known fracas: the El Paso Salt War of the 1870s. Long before there was an El Paso, Mexicans from both sides of the Río Grande led their *caretas* (two-wheeled ox carts) through the desert to salt flats still visible at the foot of the Guadalupe Mountains and the national park, roughly 100 miles east of El Paso. The battle over who should profit from this windfall corrupted El Paso politicians and businessmen as well as the parish priest at San Elizario. In addition to numerous murders and executions, vigilantism, and looting, the Salt War marked the only known surrender by Texas Rangers to a hostile force and the reactivation of Fort Bliss.

Helpful Numbers

Car Trouble: Sierra Blanca Exxon Food Mart (AAA Approved). Open 24 hours. 915-369-2341.

HISTORIC PLACES

RAILROAD DEPOT/HUDSPETH COUNTY MUSEUM
P.O. Box 411 • Sierra Blanca • 79851
Wednesday afternoons from 1 to 5 • Free (donations accepted)
W (ramp around back)

America's second transcontinental railroad was completed in Sierra Blanca (1881), connecting the Texas & Pacific line with the Southern Pacific. The depot that houses the museum was built by the SP a year later (1882). Look out its back door depot towards Sierra Blanca Mountain and you'll see where the tracks merge. Inside you'll learn about the state's only adobe courthouse, the history of the state's third largest county, former residents such as Lt. George Patton (posted here during World War I), and the only known bombing of an American city during World War II.

RESTAURANTS

The **Best Cafe, Michael's,** and **Lina's** are Sierra Blanca's only restaurants, with Lina's taking the honors with its easy-to-find location (by the Chevron station off I-10) and its regular hours (daily from 7 a.m. to 10 p.m.). The Exxon Station in town on Business Loop I-10 is open all night and offers deli sandwiches, snacks and beverages, as well as clean tables.

ACCOMMODATIONS

($ = Under $40, $$ = $40–$75, $$$ = $75–$100, $$$$ = Over $100)

EL CAMINO MOTEL
Business Loop I-10 • 369-3331 • $

There are 13 units at this recently renovated single-story property. All have cable TV (HBO). Pets OK. Group discounts available.

TERLINGUA

BREWSTER COUNTY   ★   50   ★   (915)

In the timeless view of Wick Fowler, Terlingua is "the only place on earth where a disaster would never be noticed, the town itself being a disaster." Since those fateful days in 1967, the choice of Terlingua for World Championship Chili Cook-offs has put this abandoned mining town back on the map (if only for a few days each November). The rest of the year, Terlingua is like scores of other Western mining towns whose boom busted long ago.

Cinnabar—also known as quicksilver ore—was discovered locally in the 1890s. When it was finally proved, the Terlingua quicksilver mining district extended from Study Butte to Lajitas and produced 25% of America's quicksilver. The Chisos Mine at Terlingua was the big producer and the region's largest employer pushing Terlingua's population close to 2,000 at its height. The demand for cinnabar tapered and likewise Terlingua's fortunes. Brown and Root, the Houston-based mine owner, closed the Chisos Mine in 1946 and sold the town to Rex Ivey, whose family is renovating this south Brewster County landmark.

TOURIST SERVICES

TERLINGUA TRADING COMPANY
P.O. Box 362 • Terlingua • 78952 • 371-2234

The knowledgeable staff includes folks who can recall the first chili cook-off. Call or stop by for information on Terlingua, the rest of the Big Bend, and the latest chili cook-off updates.

SPORTS AND ACTIVITIES

Rafting

BIG BEND NATIONAL PARK
See separate listing.

SHOPPING

TERLINGUA TRADING COMPANY
P.O. Box 362 • Terlingua • 79852 • 371-2234
Daily • 8 a.m. to 8 p.m.
You'll find this establishment right in the heart of the ghost town's booming commercial district. In addition to a good selection of books and maps, a wide variety of gifts are available: art, jewelry, and other handcrafted items from the desert Southwest and old Mexico.

ANNUAL EVENTS

November

FRANK X. TOLBERT—WICK FOWLER MEMORIAL CHILI COOK-OFF • CASI (Chili Appreciation Society International) CHILI COOK-OFF
First weekend of November
What began as a culinary challenge over a quarter of a century ago has mushroomed into a Texas tradition. During the early part of cook-off week, travel trailers and RVs from across America arrive in Brewster County to stake a claim before the horde descends. By the weekend, more than 7,000 contestants, spectators, peace officers, and startled tourists show up. Once upon a time, almost 10,000 packed the old ghost town, site of the original cook-offs. Bickering led to the establishment of two contenders. The Tolbert-Fowler Cook-off is held on the east side of the ghost town behind the Terlingua General Store. The CASI Cook-off has its own site on the west side of the ghost town. For purists, the chili competitions are the heart and soul of these events. For everyone else, the top priority is showmanship. A lot of time, effort, and alcohol go into the skits, costumes, and sets for this

category. Champions are crowned Saturday—showmanship in the morning and chili judging around lunch.

Be advised. With so many adults acting like children, neither chili cook-off is recommended for kids or even adults averse to plenty of bare flesh, open drunkenness, and the behavior that accompanies the two. Other caveats: Terlingua is in the heart of the Chihuahuan Desert. Temperatures during the cook-off can range from freezing to sweltering. With plenty of dust and even more rocks, don't dress for success. And if you plan to stay at any area lodge, get on the waiting list now.

RESTAURANTS

($ = Under $7.50, $$ = Under $15, $$$ = $15+ plus tax & tip)

Live music is served à la carte at most Terlingua restaurants. A good number of locals are either musicians or are into music, and almost every time you sit down for dinner, someone is behind a mike singing old favorites or making up new ones. More popular weekends find out-of-town performers on stage for bigger gigs.

LA KIVA RESTAURANT AND BAR

Where Terlingua Creek crosses FM 170 • **371-2250**
Dinner daily • **Sunday brunch 11–2** • **$–$$** • **MC V**
Fred Flintstone was well into his Olmec phase when he put this place together. The bathrooms are worth a pit stop in themselves: big brass pots for basins and urinals. Descend into the dark, cavernous dining room for grilled entrées—fish, fowl, and beef. A welcome addition is the chicken Caesar salad, joining longtime menu mainstay *el Diablo Chili.* Bar.

STARLIGHT THEATER

Terlingua Ghost Town • **371-2326** • **Dinner daily**
$–$$ • **Checks not drawn on Terlingua banks**
This theater was built in the late 1930s for local miners. At the end of World War II, Terlingua was dismantled and the theater sat roofless for almost half a century. Reroofed in October 1990, renovated in 1991, it reopened in 1992 to rave reviews as a restaurant and a club. The latest addition is a 20' x 30' mural by Stylle Read, *The Spirit of Terlingua,* right behind the stage. Happy hour starts at five, dinner is served till 9–9:30, and the bar shuts down at midnight (1:00 a.m. on Saturdays). The nightly specials are always a good bet. Bar.

TERLINGUA CAFE

**Terlingua Ghost Town • 371-2465 • Daily • Breakfast and
lunch (dinner by reservation only) • $–$$ • AE D MC V • W**

The Terlingua Cafe serves authentic West Texas and Northern
Mexico cuisine seven days a week from sunup to sundown. Dinner is served for parties of 12 or more by reservation only including gourmet dutch oven dinners served three nights monthly
during the full moon. Bottled beer and sodas. Fresh pastries daily
including *bolillos,* jalapeño corn bread, hamburger and sandwich
rolls. Salsa hour from 3:00 to 5:00. Beer and wine.

ACCOMMODATIONS

See **BIG BEND NATIONAL PARK** or **LAJITAS.**

VALENTINE

JEFF DAVIS COUNTY   ★   217   ★   (915)

Valentine is the only Texas town to be hit by two earthquakes,
but is better known for amorous reasons. The Texas and New
Orleans Railroad arrived here on Valentine's Day, 1882. Come late
January and early February, over 20,000 Valentine's Day cards
from all 50 states and scores of foreign countries are posted to this
West Texas crossroads to be postmarked with the unique Valentine cancellation. To get yours postmarked and delivered in time
for February 14th, place your stamped, addressed card(s) inside a
larger envelope and mail to:

Valentine Post Office
Valentine, Texas 79854-9998
Attn: Valentine's Day Cancellation

VAN HORN

CULBERSON COUNTY   ★   2,930   ★   (915)

Only a few miles east of the Mountain Time Zone, Van Horn serves as the crossroads of West Texas. Situated on Interstate 10, it's the largest and the last city east of El Paso before Interstate 20 branches off Interstate 10. Consequently, millions of vehicles heading west from Dallas/Fort Worth, Houston, and San Antonio pass through these arid hills en route to the west coast and back. In addition to the extensive east-west traffic, Van Horn sits between three national parks: Guadalupe Mountains and Carlsbad Caverns to the north on Highway 54 and Big Bend to the south on Highway 90. From stagecoaches in the mid-1800s to John Madden's Greyhound each football season (see **Chuy's** below), travelers rest and refuel at this watering hole on the southmost overland route across the U.S. Not surprisingly, it has more motels and gas stations than you'd expect for a town of less than three thousand.

TOURIST SERVICES

**VAN HORN CONVENTION CENTER
AND VISITORS BUREAU**

**1801 W. Broadway • P.O. Box 488 • Van Horn • 79855
283-2682**

Located on the south side of Broadway at the west end of town. Brochures and other literature on nearby points of interest like national and state parks are available as well as a thorough Visitor Guide which lists accommodations and restaurants.

SIDE TRIPS

BIG BEND NATIONAL PARK
See separate listing.

CARLSBAD CAVERNS NATIONAL PARK
See separate listing.

GUADALUPE MOUNTAINS NATIONAL PARK
See separate listing.

RESTAURANTS

($ = Under $7.50, $$ = Under $15, $$$ = $15+ plus tax & tip)

CHUY'S
1200 W. Broadway • 283-2066 • Daily
Breakfast, lunch, and dinner • $–$$ • AE MC V • W
The Garcias have been running a first-class operation since the late 1950s. Ask anyone who is familiar with West Texas or, if you get the chance, John Madden, former head coach of the Oakland Raiders and pro football color commentator. Afraid of flying, Madden travels cross-country by bus. Chuy's ranks in the highest echelon among his preferred stops. Madden has even gone as far as designating one of Chuy's dining rooms "Madden's Haul of Fame," and each season he admits two pros into this elite pantheon based upon their eating prowess. Renowned travel experts David and Karen Lee list Chuy's Lime Freeze as mandatory rations on any trip to the Big Bend. This frozen concoction takes the heat out of a scorching West Texas afternoon and is an ideal palate cleanser prior to Chuy's sizzling *fajitas* plate.

SMOKEHOUSE RESTAURANT AND AUTO MUSEUM
905 W. Broadway (Highway 80) • 283-2453
Monday–Saturday • Breakfast, lunch, and dinner
Closed Sunday–$–$$ • AE D MC V • W
As the name implies, smoked meats are the specialty. One Smokehouse Special ought to be enough for the entire table—smoked brisket, ham, and sausage served with cole slaw, beans, mashed potatoes, and homemade bread. Plenty of other menu choices include smoked turkey and bacon, steaks, and Mexican food as well as rainbow trout, a fruit plate, and the chef's salad. Restaurant owners Mitch and Glenda Van Horn display their extensive automotive collection right off the main dining room.

The display changes every other week and includes cars from the 1920s through the 1960s as well as other automobilia.

ACCOMMODATIONS

($ = Under $40, $$ = $40–$75, $$$ = $75–$100, $$$$ = Over $100)

BEST WESTERN INN OF VAN HORN
1705 W. Broadway (Highway 80)
283-2410 or 800-528-1234 • $
   This single-story motel has 61 smoking and non-smoking units including one suite. Rooms include cable TV (HBO) and phones (no charge for local calls). Amenities include a complimentary continental breakfast, the Westerner and the Iron Rail restaurants, outdoor heated pool, gift shop, convenience store on the property, laundry room, complimentary golf, and free parking. Pets OK. AAA, AARP, corporate, and group rates are available.

PLAZA INN
200 E. Golf Course Dr. • 283-2804 or 800-543-8831 • $
   This two-story motel has 98 smoking and non-smoking units including handicapped-access rooms. Rooms include cable TV (HBO) and phones with free local calls. Amenities include the Chaparral Restaurant, the Sportsman Lounge, an outdoor unheated pool, laundry facilities, complimentary golf, and free parking. Pets OK. AAA, AARP, and commercial discounts are available.

Panhandle-Plains

The Panhandle-Plains extends from the Oklahoma border south to the Permian Basin. *Panhandle* is a simple term and refers to the northernmost twenty-six counties in Texas. *Plains,* however, includes several regions. Like any part of the Great Plains, the Texas portion was created by debris that eroded from the Rocky Mountains. Local designations are numerous. The region around Amarillo, including parts of the Panhandle, is called the High Plains. A second area, with Lubbock as its hub, is known as the South Plains. And a third region, south of the Canadian River and north of the Pecos, has been known for centuries as the *Llano Estacado* (see **Museum of the Llano Estacado**). Decades after the 49ers and the Butterfield Overland Mail plied Texas west of the Pecos, Comanches, *comancheros* (traders from New Mexico), and *ciboleros* (buffalo hunters) traversed these endless grasslands.

After the defeat of the Comanches at their Palo Duro Canyon camp (1874), settlement began. Grasslands once home to huge bison herds became the largest ranches in Texas history (see **DALHART**). Cattlemen, cowboys, and cattle drives quickly followed. Old Mobeetie and Tascosa, ghost towns today, embodied the Wild West with their saloons, bordellos, gunfights, and boot hill cemeteries.

(text continued on page 170)

167

PANHANDLE-PLAINS

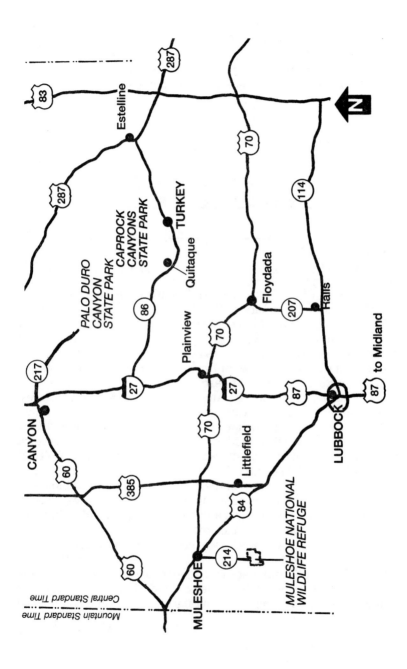

(text continued from page 167)

Far more valuable resources lay underground, ones that shaped the development of this region even more than beef production. The Ogallala aquifer, immense petrochemical reserves, and most of the world's helium are found under the Panhandle-Plains. The bustle above is a tribute to pioneers of both centuries.

AMARILLO

POTTER AND
RANDALL COUNTIES ★ 157,615 ★ (806)

Portions of West Texas such as El Paso were colonized over a century before the American Revolution. Others, most notably the Panhandle, saw no settlement until the end of the Red River War (1875). Within a few years, only one battle remained—to develop Amarillo. James Berry, Abilene's mastermind, settled that score by rigging the election for the county seat. Local cowboys got two lots in return for their vote, and Berry's site won.

During its first decade, Amarillo became America's largest rural shipping point for cattle. Millions of acres of ranch land on the LX, the JA, the T-Anchor, and the XIT gave rise to an industry that manifests itself in modern times at the **Amarillo Livestock Auction,** the world largest's weekly cattle auction (see **OTHER POINTS OF INTEREST** below). Other agricultural interests developed before the turn of the century as the multi-million-acre XIT began large-scale production of forage crops for cattle feed. Soon the enormous Ogallala aquifer was tapped, and millions of acres of cattle country were converted to croplands. The Panhandle Oil and Gas Field was discovered in 1916 and recognized as the world's largest by 1930 (just before oil was discovered in Arabia). Oil and gas, pipelines and refineries, carbon black and the world's largest helium field fueled Amarillo's growth. The city now serves as a regional and national crossroads and commercial center.

AMARILLO

to Dumas

to Lake Meredith and Alibates National Monument

Boys Ranch Ascosa

Cadillac Ranch

Albuquerque

to Pampa

to Okla. City

Tri-State Fairgrounds

Amarillo College

Travel Info. Center

to Canyon and Lubbock

to Palo Duro Canyon State Park

TOURIST SERVICES

AMARILLO CONVENTION AND VISITORS COUNCIL
1000 S. Polk • Amarillo • 79101 • 374-1497 or 800-692-1338
Monday–Friday 8–5 • W

The Bivins home is the headquarters for Amarillo's tourism office. Here the staff offers the latest details on Amarillo activities like trips to area ranches and hunting information.

TEXAS TRAVEL INFORMATION CENTER
Interstate 40 East between Lakeside and Airport exits • 335-1441
Open daily 8–5 except New Year's and Christmas • W

The state-run info centers are staffed by trained travel counselors. Pick up a free copy of the *Texas State Travel Guide,* the best travel value in the state.

GUIDEBOOKS AND PUBLICATIONS

ACCENT WEST
$2.00 • Box 1504 • Amarillo • 79105 • 806-371-8411
This monthly offers a complete listing and accurate descriptions of area restaurants, clubs, and events.

MUSEUMS

AMARILLO ART CENTER
Amarillo College Campus • 2200 S. Van Buren • 371-5050
Tuesday–Friday 10–5 • Weekends 1–5 • Free • W+
Housed in a three-story facility designed by Edward Stone of Kennedy Center fame, the range of exhibits extends from antiquity to the present. The permanent collection emphasizes American moderns, including works by former Panhandle resident Georgia O'Keeffe.

AMERICAN QUARTER HORSE HERITAGE CENTER AND MUSEUM
I-40 East at Quarter Horse Drive • 376-5181
Summer hours: 9–5 Monday–Saturday • 12–5 Sunday
September through April: 10–5 Tuesday–Saturday
Admission • Gift shop • W+
With over three million quarter horses registered, this is the largest horse registry in the world. Designed to appeal to the novice as well as the veteran horseman, hands-on displays range from authentic starting gates to the real McCoy—genuine American quarter horses at the Demonstration Arena. In addition to the orientation show in the 70-seat Theater of America's Horse, two other video mini-theaters feature six programs and allow more select viewing of equine activities.

DON HARRINGTON DISCOVERY CENTER AND PLANETARIUM
Amarillo Medical Center • 1200 Streit • 355-9547
Tuesday–Saturday 10–5 • Sunday 1–5 • Free • W+
Planetarium shows daily in summer and weekends in winter
Admission • Gift shop • W+
Unless a school group is in attendance, most visitors to the Discovery Center are curious adults. Featuring temporary and permanent exhibits, the Discovery Center has several learning centers including an Exploration Gallery, the Construction Zone, and

Kidscovery. Outside by the Discovery Center parking lot is the **Helium Monument**, America's only above-ground time capsule. Erected in 1968, the first of the four columns was opened in 1993 (a 25-year wait). The other three are scheduled for 2018 (50 years), 2068 (a century), and 2968 (a millennium). The smart money says an almost fresh Collin Street Bakery fruitcake will be found in all three. Folks interested in helium, its production and uses in fields like cryogenics, press the button at the base of the monument. Right.

KRITSER AVIATION MUSEUM
Tradewind Airport • 372-6999 • Monday–Friday 1–5
Sponsored by the Texas Aviation Historical Society, this working museum demonstrates aircraft restoration and hosts an air show annually.

HISTORIC PLACES

HARRINGTON HOUSE
1600 S. Polk St. • 374-5490 • April–December
Tuesday and Thursday from 10 a.m. to 12:30 p.m.
This 15,000-square-foot neoclassical mansion was built in 1914 by John and Pat Landergin, local ranchers. Acquired in 1940 by Don and Sybil Harrington, visitors 14 and older are welcome to tour in groups of four or less by appointment only.

OTHER POINTS OF INTEREST

AMARILLO GARDEN CENTER
1400 Streit • 352-6513 • Monday–Friday 9–5
Center closes December 15–31 • Free • W
Covering two acres, the gardens are open year-round and include an iris bed, a rose garden, and a scent garden.

CADILLAC RANCH
Just west of Amarillo's city limits
Few ranches in Texas history rival the Cadillac, where Amarillo native Stanley Marsh rides herd on ten vintage Cadillacs. Rumor has it that their angle of burial is parallel to the sides of the Great Pyramid of Cheops. You be the judge, Pythagoras. If you're driving west, exit Soncy (Exit 64) and drive through the Soncy intersection to Helium where a U-turn under the Interstate leads to the ranch. Those driving in from the west (New Mexico)

should take the Hope Road/Helium Road exit (Exit 62A) and keep their eyes open. A well-worn path leads to the wrecks and perfect pictures every time.

LIVESTOCK AUCTION
Western Stockyards • 100 Manhattan St. • 373-7464
Cattle auctions Tuesday at 9 a.m. except the weeks of July 4th and Christmas
   If you think it stinks out here, remember what the locals say: it smells like money. Each year, by satellite or in person, buyers from across America close on over a quarter million cattle at the state's largest cattle auction. Tours are available daily, but call in advance for one on sale day. Mosey next door to the **Stockyard Cafe** for authentic cowboy fixings. Breakfast and lunch is on Monday through Saturday, and dinner is served Friday and Saturday nights. Prices are fair, the steaks are excellent, and Mastercard and Visa are accepted.

THOMPSON PARK
Just north of Amarillo on US 287
Open around the clock • W
   More than 600 acres of park land include a 36-hole golf course, an Olympic-sized swimming pool, Wonderland Park, and Storyland Zoo.

SPORTS AND ACTIVITIES

Amusement Parks

WONDERLAND AMUSEMENT PARK
Highway 287 north to Thompson Park
April–Sept. weekends only • May–August daily 7 a.m.–10 p.m. Admission • W
   The highlight is the Texas Tornado, which has been voted the best double loop, steel roller coaster in America. Other attractions include a 19-hole miniature golf course and the Rattlesnake River Raft Ride.

Chuckwagons/Guest Ranches

   Each of these outfits offers a different way to see the Old West. All have toll free numbers. Call in advance for reservations and accurate prices.

BAR-H DUDE RANCH
Take US 287 south 54 miles to FM 3257 (three miles west of Clarendon) • *North two miles to the Bar-H Dude Ranch on the left* • **874-2634 or 800-627-9871**

Guest ranches serve up vittles, herd cattle, or perhaps put on a show. A dude ranch such as the Bar-H takes guests overnight, puts them up (in climate-controlled bunkhouses), serves meals prepared by a chuckwagon crew, and offers a variety of daytime activities like working cattle, feeding livestock, or mending fences. If you came to play, try horseback riding, fishing, horseshoes, or relaxing poolside.

COWBOY MORNING
Take Interstate 40 east to Exit 77 • *Head 27 miles south on FM 1258 to Cowboy Morning* • **944-5562 or 800-658-2613**

Originally part of the million-acre JA Ranch, the Figure 3 is run by the Christian family. Several generations ago, they helped settle the High Plains and even worked cattle for Charles Goodnight. Plan to arrive at the Figure 3 by 8:30 a.m. for the two-hour venture. Everyone piles into mule-drawn wagons to ride to the rim of Palo Duro Canyon where ranch hands serve up stunning scenery, steaming coffee, orange juice, fresh sourdough biscuits, sausage, gravy, and eggs. Steak is served at the dinner excursion where you'll sample the same panoramas enjoyed by millions of moviegoers who watched Harrison Ford and Sean Connery in *Indiana Jones and the Last Crusade.*

CREEKWOOD RANCH OLD WEST SHOW AND CHUCKWAGON SUPPER
From Interstate 40 downtown, take Washington Street (FM 1541) 12 miles south to the Creekwood Ranch **356-9256 or 800-658-6673**

Take a step back into the 1880s at the Creekwood Ranch. Reservations are requested for the popular Old West Show which gets underway after a wagon ride across the ranch and back through history to the early days of the Panhandle. After dinner and dessert, enjoy the Old West Show. Ask about the overnight Tepee and Breakfast excursion.

Golf

AMARILLO GOLF COURSE
Texas State College Campus • 335-1142 • 18-hole course
Mon.–Tues.: $3 • Wed.–Fri.: $5 • Weekends: $7

COMANCHE TRAILS GOLF COURSE
4200 South Grand • 378-4281
18-hole course • Weekdays: $7 • Weekends: $9

ROGERS GOLF COURSE
Adjacent to Thompson Park • 378-3086
36-hole course • Weekdays: $7 • Weekends: $9

SOUTHWEST GOLF CLUB
Hollywood Rd. off Canyon Expressway • 355-7161
18-hole course • Weekdays: $7 • Weekends: $9

Hunting

The Panhandle offers excellent bird hunting including golden pheasant, duck, and sandhill crane. Most property is privately owned, and a wide variety of native game and birds as well as exotics are available in an area covering over 300,000 acres. Unless you already have a particular ranch or lease in mind, contact the visitor bureau at 800-692-1338.

Tennis

MUNICIPAL TENNIS CENTER
Austin Middle School • Elmwood and 26th • 378-4213
Eleven hardcourts and a pro shop with concessions and lessons.

COLLEGES AND UNIVERSITIES

AMARILLO COLLEGE
2201 S. Washington • 371-5000
A state and locally supported two-year institution with an enrollment of more than 5,000, the curriculum at AC ranges from vocational to academic. One of the highlights on campus is the Amarillo Arts Center (see **MUSEUMS** above), which is part of a three-building, Edward Stone-designed complex that also includes indoor and outdoor theaters and a sculpture court.

Prominent AC alumni include G. William Miller, Secretary of the Treasury under Jimmy Carter, and Ben Sargent, Pulitzer Prize-winning editorial cartoonist for the *Austin American-Statesman.*

PERFORMING ARTS

AMARILLO CIVIC CENTER
3rd and Buchanan • 359-5491 • W+
   This 270,000-square-foot facility hosts everything from ice capades to rodeo to Broadway as well as the Amarillo Symphony and other concerts.

AMARILLO LITTLE THEATRE
2019 Civic Circle • 355-9991 • Admission • W
   The longest continually performing little theatre in the United States. Four productions are scheduled each year, including a drama, a musical, and a children's show.

AMARILLO SYMPHONY
Civic Center Music Hall • 376-8782
Admission varies • W+
   An Amarillo tradition since 1924. The season runs from September to April featuring half a dozen concerts, including a holiday production of *The Nutcracker* with the Lone Star Ballet.

LONE STAR BALLET
Civic Center Auditorium • 372-2463
Admission varies • W+
   What do those performers from the musical *TEXAS* do when summer ends? They band together and perform *The Nutcracker* with students from West Texas A&M and the Amarillo Symphony. Call for a complete schedule of performances and prices.

SHOPPING

OLD SAN JACINTO ANTIQUES AND CRAFTS ON HISTORIC ROUTE 66
6th Street between Georgia and Western • 374-0459
Most shops open Monday–Saturday 10–5:30 and Sunday 1–5
   Not too long ago, this section of town was a rundown historic district. Only two miles west of downtown (just stay on Sixth), it has some of Amarillo's best antique shopping as well as several

enjoyable watering holes and eateries including the **Garden Light Cafe** and the **Neon Grill.**

WESTGATE MALL
Interstate 40 West at Coulter or Soncy • 358-7221
Monday–Saturday 10–9 • Sunday 12:30–5:30
Right off I-40 on the city's western edge, Westgate has over a hundred stores and a six-screen theater. Major department stores include Sears, Dillard's, Mervyn's, Beall's, and J.C. Penney.

SIDE TRIPS

ALIBATES FLINT QUARRIES NATIONAL MONUMENT
LAKE MEREDITH NATIONAL RECREATION AREA
Go 40 miles northeast of Amarillo on Texas 136 and follow signs
Superintendent • Lake Meredith National Recreation Area
P.O. Box 1460 • Fritch • 79036 • 857-3151
The Panhandle town of Fritch serves as the headquarters for the region's most visited attraction—Lake Meredith—as well as Alibates Flint Quarries National Monument and the Lake Meredith Aquatic and Wildlife Museum. Activities on the lake include boating, waterskiing, fishing, and swimming. Boat ramps and a full service marina are available, including boat rentals. Fish for large-mouth, smallmouth, and white bass, carp, catfish, white crappie, sunfish, and walleye.

Alibates Flint Quarries National Monument preserves a site of human habitation that dates back at least 12,000 years. The flint quarries were a natural draw for prehistoric man. Flint from Alibates was crafted into tools and used for trade for thousands of years until 1870. The quarries and flint mining villages can be viewed only by free guided tours. Contact the superintendent's office for schedules and information.

Run by the City of Fritch, the Lake Meredith Aquatic and Wildlife Museum has five aquariums, including the Panhandle's largest, and six dioramas featuring area wildlife.

CAL FARLEY'S BOYS RANCH
JULIAN BIVINS MUSEUM • OLD TASCOSA
Take Tascosa Road (RR 1061) 34 miles northwest from Amarillo to US 385 • The Boys Ranch entrance is two miles north off
U.S. 385 • 372-2341 • Open daily 8–5 • Free • Gift shop
Tascosa was the cowboy capital of the western Panhandle. Established in 1876 near the Canadian River by Hispanic *pastores* (shepherds), it was the seat of Oldham County as well as the judi-

cial center for the western Panhandle's numerous unorganized counties. In addition to serving ranches like the XIT, the LIT, LX, and the LS, Tascosa was the starting point for cattle drives to Kansas, Colorado, and Montana. Proof of the town's notoriety is its boot hill cemetery. Take your first right after entering the Boys Ranch and you'll find it atop the passable dirt to the right of the Boys Ranch Cemetery. The 20-odd occupants include plenty of gunslingers. In some cases the cause of death was accidental or even natural, but a March 26, 1886, shootout claimed four *hombres*.

Before the 1880s were up, the Fort Worth and Denver Railroad had bypassed Tascosa by a mere two miles; the town's days were numbered. Vega (24 miles south by US 385) eventually became county seat. The original Oldham county courthouse, the Panhandle's second, still stands at Boys Ranch; it houses the Bivins Museum. The world famous Boys Ranch was founded in 1939 by Mr. Farley. More than 4,000 boys ages four to eighteen have been schooled along the Canadian Breaks on this 10,000-acre ranch.

CANADIAN, TEXAS
100 miles northeast of Amarillo via US 60 east (93 miles) and US 60/83 north (7 miles) • **806-323-6234** • **(Chamber of Commerce)**
    Named for the nearby Canadian River, the county seat of Hemphill County is renowned for its autumn colors. Since the 1950s, a Fall Foliage Festival has been held in and around Canadian, Lake Marvin, and the Black Kettle National Grassland featuring driving and walking tours, a sanctioned rodeo and chili cook-off, and historic home tours. The **River Valley Pioneer Museum** (806-323-6548) houses dinosaur bones, Indian artifacts, and plenty of more recent Panhandle history.

PALO DURO CANYON STATE PARK
Highway 217 • **Canyon** • **488-2227**
    A scenic shortcut via South Washington Street (FM 1541) goes directly to Highway 217 and the park and shaves several miles off the usual 20-minute drive. The foolproof method is to follow I-27 south to Canyon and the Palo Duro Canyon State Park exit. See separate listing under **CANYON**.

ANNUAL EVENTS

September

TRI-STATE FAIR
Bell and 10th at the Fairgrounds • 376-7767
Third week of the month • Admission • Parking • W
The Panhandle is closer for many out-of-staters than their own state fairs. More than 250,000 participants and spectators visit the Tri-State Fair to compete in the livestock show, to listen to nationally-known entertainers, and to enjoy the midweek carnival.

November

NATIONAL OLD TIMERS RODEO
Amarillo Civic Center • 359-4777
Admission • W+ but not all areas
Cowboys at competitions like the Old Timers Rodeo in Marfa earn points to become eligible for this one, the national championship held annually at Amarillo's Civic Center.

RESTAURANTS

($ = Under $7.50, $$ = Under $15, $$$ = $15+ plus tax & tip)

For up-to-date reviews, refer to *Accent West* magazine.

BIG TEXAN STEAK RANCH
I-40 East at Lakeside Exit • 372-7000 or 800-657-7177
Daily • Lunch and dinner • Cr • $–$$ • W+
Tens of thousands have taken the challenge: Finish the Big Texan in less than an hour and the $40 tab is on the house. Before you place your order, consider your chances—less than 20%—and your portion—a 72-ounce side of beef as well as a baked potato, a shrimp cocktail, salad, and a roll. No leaving the table and no barfing. Try instead the rattlesnake, rabbit, Rocky Mountain oysters, or a buffalo burger. Dinner shows run nightly and include musicals, cowboy poetry, a melodrama, and the opry. Bar.

CALICO COUNTY
2410 Paramount • 358-7664
Daily • Lunch and dinner • Cr • W
If it can be dragged through the door, they'll chicken-fry it at Calico County: steak, pork chops, chicken livers, chicken giz-

zards, corn on the cob, even catfish or cod. On a healthier note, both fishes are served grilled, and there are plenty of salads—grilled chicken, chef's, and, of course, chicken-fried chicken salad. Shakes, malts, chocolate and vanilla Cokes, and fresh-squeezed lemonade at the full bar. Bar.

LA FRONTERA

1401 S. Arthur • 372-4593
Tues.–Sat. late breakfast, lunch, and dinner
Sunday breakfast and lunch • Closed Monday • $ • Cr
The old Cuellar Grocery (1939-1975) has new life now that one of Juan Cuellar's grandsons, Greg Martinez, and his wife Mary have opened *La Frontera*. Try a *burrito*; it's made with beef tips, not ground beef. Or choose from other plates that Greg himself cooks: the soft *tacos*, the *enchiladas*, the *tostadas*, and the *carne guisada* served either regular or spicy. Located just east of downtown in the heart of Amarillo's *barrio*, the kitchen uses fresh meats, horns of Colby cheese, and homemade *tortillas*. You bring the beer.

OHMS GALLERY CAFE

619 S. Tyler (Atrium Plaza) • 373-3233
Monday–Friday lunch • Friday–Saturday dinner
Closed Sunday • $–$$ • MC V • W
A cafeteria-style eatery. Signature dishes include pork loin and chicken breast with cornbread stuffing. There are always several vegetarian dishes to choose from. Be sure to go with several friends—the kitchen has its own fudge kettle and serves slabs by the pound. Specialty teas, beer, and wine.

SCOTT'S OYSTER BAR

4150 Paramount • 354-9110 • Monday dinner
Tues.–Sat. lunch and dinner • Closed Sunday • $
"If you're in a big hurry, Long John Silver's is down the street." Get the picture? The Oyster Bar is a popular Amarillo night spot with favorites like boiled shrimp, fried oysters, po-boys, and oysters on the half shell. Shrimp creole, crawfish etouffée, and other specials are served regularly. Beer and wine coolers.

VAN DYKE'S

210 W. 6th just west of Polk St. • 373-1441
Monday–Saturday breakfast and lunch • Closed Sunday • $
It seems like forever to most natives, but it was only the late 1950s when Red Van Dyke first started serving some of the best breakfasts in the Panhandle smack dab in the heart of downtown Amarillo. Norma Murphy spent three years working for Mr. Van Dyke and has owned Van Dyke's for over a decade since then.

Breakfast is the busiest part of the day (particularly Saturdays). Real ham, homemade sausage, and omelettes have made Van Dyke's an Amarillo institution. Though breakfast steals the thunder, the lunch menu has plenty of good home cooking: meatloaf, chicken-fried steak, and daily specials. Just north of the tallest building in town.

CLUBS AND BARS

HUMMER'S SPORTS CAFE

2600 Paramount • 353-0723 • Bar stays open till 2 a.m. except Sundays till 12 a.m. • Kitchen is open during the week till 11 p.m. • Friday & Saturday till 12 a.m. • Sunday till 10 p.m.

Unlike most sports bars—crowded with potbellied wannabees clad in coaching shorts—Hummer's attracts all ages and all physiques. Families enjoy the casual menu and laid-back atmosphere, fans head right to the photos of championship teams from years gone by, and the dozen TVs cover all sports. Over 50 different beers are served at the full bar.

ACCOMMODATIONS

($ = Under $40, $$ = $40–$75, $$$ = $75–$100, $$$$ = Over $100) Room Tax 13%

AMARILLO HOLIDAY INN

1911 Interstate 40 at Ross Rd.
372-8741 or 800-HOLIDAY • $$–$$$

This four-story hotel has 247 units including one suite and non-smoking rooms with cable TV (Showtime) and pay-per-view movies, room phones (charge for local calls), fire sprinklers, smoke detectors, and visual alert systems in all rooms. Amenities include a hotel restaurant and lounge, an indoor pool with sauna, jacuzzi, and whirlpool as well as an outdoor deck, exercise room, game room, billiards, gift shop, courtesy shuttle to Amarillo Airport, complimentary breakfast with the Best Breaks rate, free parking, and truck parking. Pets OK. Kennels available with advance notice. AAA, AARP, corporate, government, and military rates available.

BIG TEXAN MOTEL

I-40 East at Lakeside Exit • 372-5000 or 800-657-7177 • $–$$

Follow the billboards to the world-famous Big Texan Steak Ranch (see **RESTAURANTS**) and you'll be across the parking lot from this two-story motel. Inexpensive and clean, the Big Texan has 52 smoking and non-smoking rooms; all have big brass beds. Rooms include cable TV (HBO) and pay-per-view movies and phones with free local calls. Amenities include a complimentary continental breakfast, an outdoor Texas-shaped pool (closed in the winter), and plenty of free parking. Small pets are OK.

FIFTH SEASON EAST

I-40 East at Nelson Street Exit • 379-6555 or 800-245-5525 • $$

This three-story hotel is located right next to the American Quarter Horse Heritage Center and Museum on the north frontage road along I-40 East. It has 185 smoking and non-smoking rooms including 24 suites. Rooms include cable TV (Showtime), phones with free local calls, and coffee makers in all atrium rooms. Amenities include a complimentary American breakfast, complimentary happy hour from 5:30 to 7:00, the Atrium Restaurant, the Western Horseman lounge, an indoor heated pool and sauna, game room, same-day valet laundry, courtesy shuttle to and from the airport, and free parking. No pets. AAA and AARP rates are available.

FIFTH SEASON WEST

I-40 West at Coulter Exit • 358-7881 or 800-858-2223 • $$

This three-story property is right next to the UA Six Cinema at Westgate Mall and half a mile from the mall itself along the south frontage road of Interstate 40. It has 242 rooms including smoking and non-smoking rooms and 24 suites which include cable TV (Showtime), free local calls, and coffee makers in all atrium rooms. Amenities include a complimentary American breakfast, complimentary happy hour from 5:30 to 7:00 p.m., the Atrium Restaurant, the Fifth Season Club and cocktail lounge, an indoor heated pool and sauna, exercise room, game room, same-day valet laundry, laundry room, courtesy shuttle to the airport, and free parking. No pets. AAA and AARP rates are available.

HARVEY HOTEL

3100 I-40 at Ross • 372-8741 or 800-922-9222 • $$–$$$$

This highrise hotel is one of Amarillo's tallest buildings and has 265 rooms including six suites ($$$$), non-smoking rooms with cable TV, pay-per-view movies and room phones with a charge for local calls. Amenities include complimentary continental breakfast for all guests, complimentary happy hour for Concierge Level guests, the Canyon Rose restaurant, the Atrium bar, and Bailey's dance club. Also at the hotel are an indoor heated pool, exercise room with weights, complimentary airport shuttles, and free parking. The policy for pets requires a $125 deposit of which only $100 is refundable.

LA QUINTA—MEDICAL CENTER
I-40 West at Coulter exit • 352-6311 or 800-531-5900 • $$

This three-story motor inn has 129 rooms including suites and non-smoking rooms with cable TV (Showtime) and pay-per-view movies and room phones (free local calls). Amenities include complimentary continental breakfast from 6:30 to 9:30, complimentary coffee in the lobby, a Waffle House restaurant next door, outdoor heated pool open from May through September, and free parking. Pets under 25 pounds welcome.

RADISSON INN AMARILLO AIRPORT
Interstate 40 at Lakeside Dr
373-3303 or 800-333-3333 • $$–$$$

A two-story hotel, the Radisson is right by the airport and has 207 smoking and non-smoking units including suites and handicap rooms. All rooms have cable TV, pay-per-view movies, and phones with free local calls. Amenities include the Steakery restaurant, the Garden Cafe, the Silver Dollar Piano Bar, the Krystal Palace Night Club, exercise facilities, an indoor atrium pool with hot tub, game room, gift shop, same-day valet laundry, laundry room, complimentary airport transportation, and free parking. No pets. AAA rates available.

Bed & Breakfasts

GALBRAITH HOUSE BED & BREAKFAST INN
1710 S. Polk St. • 374-0237 • $$

It's hard to imagine that a B&B could be so centrally located, but Galbraith House is about a block from the intersection of Interstate 27 and Interstate 40. The 1912 two-story prairie-style home was built for H.W. Galbraith, co-founder of the Foxworth Galbraith Lumber Company, and was constructed with three-inch-thick doors, parquet floors, and scores of handcrafted details. The owners, internationally renowned soprano Mary Jane Johnson and her husband David, have furnished the five bedrooms (each with private bath) much like when their family lived here. Autographed posters from Mary Jane's performances in the

U.S., Canada, and Europe line the halls. Breakfast is served in the dining room or the solarium. Limited smoking area.

PARKVIEW HOUSE
1311 S. Jefferson • 373-9464 • $$–$$$
Parkview offers two rooms with private baths and three with shared baths. In addition, a hot tub and sauna can be enjoyed while sampling complimentary beverages. Breakfast is served in the kitchen, out in the dining room, or on the porch. Ask about children. No smoking. No pets.

CANYON

RANDALL COUNTY SEAT   ★   11,365   ★   (806)

The combination of West Texas A&M, Palo Duro Canyon State Park, and the *TEXAS* musical makes Canyon an unusual Texas town—small enough to stay friendly yet with enough diversity to be enjoyable. Canyon is known as much for its role in Texas history as for attractions like the park and the university. Quanah Parker's band of Comanches wintered in Palo Duro Canyon, and their defeat by the U.S. Cavalry under Colonel Ranald Mackenzie (1874) was the last major Indian battle in the Lone Star State. Two years later, Charles Goodnight stocked the JA Ranch with 1600 cattle trailed south from Colorado and brought large-scale ranching to the Panhandle. Stop by the Panhandle-Plains Historical Museum to view the T-Anchor Ranch headquarters (1877). Built by Leigh Dyer, a brother-in-law of Goodnight's, it's the oldest surviving structure in the Panhandle and formed the nucleus for this High Plains university town.

TOURIST SERVICES

SAD MONKEY RAILROAD
P.O. Box 952 • Canyon • 79015 • 488-2222
Weekends year-round • Daily April through September • W
Admission $2.50
The Sad Monkey is a narrow-gauge railroad and follows a 30-minute, two-mile loop to areas not accessible by cars. The tour includes a concise presentation on the park's history.

MUSEUMS

PANHANDLE-PLAINS HISTORICAL MUSEUM

West Texas A&M Campus • 656-2244 • Monday–Saturday 9–5 (till 6 p.m. June–August) • Sundays 2–5 • Free Gift shop • W+

Budget plenty of time for the state's oldest (1933) and largest museum. An art deco masterpiece, the main building anchors the south boundary of West Texas A&M and houses more than three million artifacts. Look above the entrance doors and note the brands of pioneer ranches. Inside, the collection is grouped into five specialties: dinosaurs, western heritage, fine art, vintage autos, and the Don Harrington Petroleum Wing which features an informative film on one of the state's greatest boom towns, Borger. Outside, the original T-Anchor Ranch House stands reconstructed with windmill and outbuildings.

OTHER POINTS OF INTEREST

PALO DURO CANYON STATE PARK

Highway 217 • *12 miles east to Park Rd. 5* • 488-2227 Summer: 6 a.m. to 10 p.m. • Winter: 8 a.m. to 10 p.m. Admission: $2 per vehicle • W

Visually attractive and historically significant, the name Palo Duro is Spanish for "hard wood," a reference to the plentiful junipers in this 100-mile-long canyon. Hundreds of millions of years are exposed in the red-stained rocks, and many picturesque formations are visible within the park's 16,000 acres including the famous Lighthouse Formation. Spanish explorers camped here in 1541, as did generations of Comanches. You can tour it best by car or by taking a ride on the Sad Monkey Railroad (See **TOURIST SERVICES** above). Picnic sites, hiking trails, mountain bike trails, riding stables, and over 100 campsites are available ranging from primitive to RV.

SIDE TRIPS

MUSEUM OF THE LLANO ESTACADO

1900 W. 8th St. • Plainview • 79072 • 806-296-4735 *Take I-27 60 miles south from Canyon to Plainview*

9–5 weekdays • **1–5 on weekends (March–November only)**
Free • **W+**

If your trip south from Canyon or Amarillo includes Plainview, take a breather at this first-rate facility featuring 20th century *llano* history as well as its formation over 200 million years ago. See separate listing under **LUBBOCK.**

COLLEGES AND UNIVERSITIES

WEST TEXAS A&M UNIVERSITY

2501 Fourth Ave. • **656-2000**

Founded in 1910, WTAMU is the only institution within 150 miles to grant bachelor and master degrees. Enrollment is over 6,600, with three-quarters of the student body from the 26-county Panhandle region. The curriculum includes more than 140 undergraduate majors and 40 master's programs from five different colleges. Two WTAMU institutes have developed national reputations: the Dryland Agriculture Institute and the Alternative Energy Institute, the state's principal center for wind research.

PERFORMING ARTS

TEXAS MUSICAL

Pioneer Amphitheatre in Palo Duro Canyon State Park
***TEXAS* Tickets** • **Box 268** • **Canyon** • **79015** • **655-2181**
Nightly except Sunday from mid-June to late August
Barbecue buffet begins at 6:00 p.m. • **Admission**
Performance begins at 8:30 p.m. • **Admission**
Free parking • **Snack bar** • **Gift shop** • **No credit cards**

With 30 seasons and more than two million spectators to its credit, the Official Play of the State of Texas is alive and well in Palo Duro Canyon. Acknowledged as the best attended outdoor drama in the nation, *TEXAS* was written by Pulitzer prize winner Paul Green, is set in the 1880s, and comes complete with cowboys, Indians, and early settlers. The Pioneer Amphitheater, a natural stage with its 600-foot backdrop, showcases the presentation.

RESTAURANTS

($ = Under $7.50, $$ = Under $15, $$$ = $15+ plus tax & tip)

COPE'S CONEY ISLAND

2201 Fourth Ave. (just west of WTAMU) • **655-1184**
Monday–Saturday • **Breakfast, lunch, and dinner**
$ • Checks • W

With less than three dozen seats, this Canyon eatery defines downhome. Hope that you stop by Tuesday (all-you-can-eat fried chicken) or Saturday (all-you-can-eat fried fish). Otherwise, enjoy a club steak ($). Cope's homemade pies are a local favorite. Choose from half a dozen, fresh from the oven, including the rare opportunity to sample a slice of Jeff Davis Pie.

DOS CABALLEROS

711 23rd Street • **655-7734**
Tuesday–Sunday • **Lunch and dinner**
$ • AE D V MC • W

Stop in for delicious *fajitas* (chicken or beef) or the *enchiladas*. For a taste of everything, try the combination plates, particularly #2 and #3.

CLUBS AND BARS

Get out of town. This precinct is dry.

BED & BREAKFASTS

HISTORICAL HUDSPETH HOUSE

1905 4th Ave. • **$$** • **Cr** • **655-9800**

Dave and Sally Haynie have brought new life to Mary Hudspeth's famed home. Miss Hudspeth, longtime faculty member and a former dean at West Texas Normal College, was a prominent Canyon hostess who set a celebrated table. Among the invitees was Georgia O'Keeffe, one of West Texas Normal's early instructors. The two-story Victorian has five rooms, three with private baths. Seven fireplaces, a jacuzzi, spacious common areas, and the Georgia O'Keeffe Dining Room round out the 1909 home. A full breakfast is served either in the dining room or in guest rooms; other meals are available by reservation. Well-behaved children are welcome.

DALHART

DALLAM COUNTY SEAT   ★   6,246   ★   (806)

Dalhart's history includes chapters on the largest ranch in Texas—the XIT, the largest state capitol in America—down in Austin, and the largest free barbecue in the world—the XIT Reunion each August. Most of the rest of the year, residents tend their crops, graze their cattle, and cater to truckers and tourists crossing Texas to and from New Mexico, Colorado, and Oklahoma.

MUSEUMS

XIT MUSEUM

108 E. Fifth • 249-5646 • (Chamber)
Tuesday through Saturday 2–5 • 9–5 during the XIT Reunion
Closed December 24th through January 2nd • Free • W

A visit to the XIT Museum is an opportunity to learn about the largest ranch in Texas history. At its height, the 3,000,000-acre XIT Ranch had nine divisions, 94 fenced pastures, 335 water wells, and 500 windmills. The XIT came about because the cash-poor state, worn thin by Reconstruction, swapped three million acres of the public domain for construction of the present state capitol. Bailey, Castro, Cochran, Dallam, Deaf Smith, Hartley, Hockley, Lamb, Oldham, and Parmer counties—ten in all—combined to form this tract, hence the name XIT (ten in Texas). The deal was a bargain for the state, whose vast holdings were slightly diminished at a value more than twice the market rate of 50¢ an acre.

OTHER POINTS OF INTEREST

EMPTY SADDLE MONUMENT

Highways 87 North and 285 on the north side of town

Traditionally, a riderless horse symbolizes a fallen soldier. This monument honors deceased XIT cowboys and was erected to memorialize one widow's wish that her husband not be forgotten.

ANNUAL EVENTS

August

XIT RODEO AND REUNION
Rita Blanca Park • 249-5646
First Thursday, Friday, and Saturday
Admission to rodeo and dances
   The world's largest amateur rodeo is combined with the world's largest barbecue to celebrate the largest ranch in Texas history (see **MUSEUMS** above). A Reunion Parade, a children's rodeo, Pony Express races, and the XIT Arts and Crafts Show are also held.

LUBBOCK

LUBBOCK COUNTY SEAT ★ 186,206 ★ (806)

   Here's a simple geography lesson that can save lives. Most Texans (and plenty of other fine folks) know that if the Lone Star State were a pan, then the top 26 counties would form its handle. What people don't realize is the price you can pay for mistakenly including Lubbock County and Lubbock, Texas, in that grouping. It is true that Lubbock is situated on the southern reaches of the Great Plains, which also includes the Panhandle. However, the Panhandle does not extend as far south as Lubbock County, and Lubbock is proudly known as the Hub City of the Plains, not the Panhandle.
   Lubbock was named for Thomas Lubbock, who commanded Terry's Texas Rangers. Situated atop the huge Ogalalla aquifer, the Lubbock area quickly evolved into one of America's foremost farming regions. Tiny O'Donnell, Texas, home to Dan Blocker of *Bonanza* fame, was the world's leading cotton baler in 1961. Over 20 percent of America's cotton is produced locally, and the Lubbock area leads Texas in grapes under cultivation. Though agribusiness is an enormous part of the local economy, Lubbock is a diverse city offering educational opportunities like Texas Tech and Lubbock Christian and some of the best medical care between Dallas and the west coast, with half a dozen hospitals and research centers.

LUBBOCK

TOURIST SERVICES

LUBBOCK CONVENTION AND VISITORS BUREAU
14th and Avenue K • P.O. Box 561 • Lubbock • 79408
763-4666 or 800-692-4035 • Weekdays 8–5 • W
   In addition to brochures and other literature, miniature cotton
bales produced on local farms are for sale.

CITIBUS TROLLEYS

Daily throughout downtown • 767-3062
(schedule and routes) • W

Lubbock has one of the better urban acronyms for this transit system, COLT, which stands for City of Lubbock Trolley. You've probably seen these superbly crafted brass and mahogany vehicles in Austin, Brownsville, or San Antonio, and Lubbock's have the same function: short, highly touristed routes in the heart of downtown.

GUIDEBOOKS AND PUBLICATIONS

LUBBOCK TRAVEL GUIDE

Lubbock Convention & Visitors Bureau
747-5232 or 800-692-4035

Give the folks at the CVB a call, and they'll be glad to send out a handy 20-page publication featuring where and when to go, what to do for fun and food, and where to stay.

MUSEUMS

FINE ARTS CENTER

2600 Avenue P • 767-2686
Monday–Friday 9–5 • Saturday 10–4 • Free

Visual arts such as painting, photography, and sculpture are displayed on a rotating basis. Cultural programs ranging from dance to music are also regularly presented.

LUBBOCK LAKE LANDMARK STATE HISTORICAL PARK

Off Loop 289 on the northwest edge of Lubbock • 765-0737
Tuesday–Saturday 9–5 • Sunday 1–5
Admission: Adults $2, children $1

This 307-acre park is the only known continually inhabited site in the South Plains region over the past 12,000 years. Life on the South Plains from prehistoric times up to its settlement is presented via self-guided and guided tours.

MOODY PLANETARIUM

4th and Indiana • **742-2490** • **Shows begin at 2 p.m.
Tuesday–Friday and 3:30 on weekends** • **Admission: Adults
$1, children 50¢**

Daily programs and special outer space exhibits are featured in
the Stardome located between the Museum of Texas Tech University and the Ranching Heritage Center.

MUSEUM OF TEXAS TECH UNIVERSITY

4th and Indiana • **742-2490**
Tuesday–Saturday 10–5 • **Thursday till 8:30** • **Sunday 1–5**
Free admission to main museum

The collections of the Museum of Texas Tech include more than
1,500,000 objects. The full extent of the Museum is apparent when
you consider that it also includes the adjacent **Moody Planetarium** (see below), the **Ranching Heritage Center** next door (see
below), and educational and research programs at the **Lubbock
Lake Landmark** (see below), as well as the **Natural Science
Research Laboratory.** Self-guided tours of the main museum, the
Ranching Heritage Center, and the Lubbock Lake Landmark are
available, as well as guided tours at the Lubbock Lake Landmark
and daily shows at the Moody Planetarium.

RANCHING HERITAGE CENTER

4th and Indiana • **742-2498**
Monday–Saturday 10–5 • **Sunday 2–5** • **Free** • **W+**

Historic structures dating back to the Republic of Texas have
been relocated to Lubbock to form this monument to ranching in
the Lone Star state. Stop by the Orientation Building and pick up
a guide to the 30-plus buildings that have been moved to this 14-
acre site next to the Museum of Texas Tech.

A sampling of what you'll find outside includes the *El Capote*
Cabin (ca. 1838), the Waggoner Ranch Commissary (1870), and
King Ranch Cattle Shipping Pens (1934), ranch offices, carriage
houses, bunkhouses, a milk and meat house, even a locomotive.
Note the two-story, white limestone *Las Escarbadas,* one of the
XIT's nine division headquarters.

SCIENCE SPECTRUM

South Loop 289 • **745-2525**
Monday–Friday 10–5:30 • **Saturday 10–6** • **Sunday 1–5:30**
Admission: Seniors $3, adults $5.50, students $4.50, children $3

Technology and science are this museum's focus with topics
like light, sound, and energy explored for visitors young and old.

A hands-on approach is taken giving kids the opportunity to work with computers, make their own bubbles, as well as gawk at the over 100 demonstrations, films, and exhibits available. Special attention is given to preschoolers. An excellent stop in conjunction with a visit to neighboring Omnimax Theatre. (see **OTHER POINTS OF INTEREST** below).

SOUTHWEST COLLECTION
Texas Tech University • 742-3749
Monday–Friday 9–5 • Tuesday 9–7 • Saturday 9–1
The research center's collection and the scholars who study it are concerned with the historical aspect of the Southwest and its cultures. The Southwest Collection contains a rare cache of manuscripts, books, maps, and other materials pertinent to the American Southwest.

HISTORIC PLACES

LUBBOCK LAKE LANDMARK STATE HISTORICAL PARK
Take US 84 to Loop 289 • 765-0737
Operated by the Texas Parks & Wildlife Department, this archaeological site evidences man and animal dating back approximately 12,000 years. The Museum of Texas Tech University (see above) also operates a Learning Center. Other activities include self-guided tours, a one-mile archaeological trail, a four-mile nature trail through the 366-acre park, and picnic areas.

OTHER POINTS OF INTEREST

BUDDY HOLLY STATUE AND WALK OF FAME
8th and Avenue Q at Civic Center entrance • 767-2236
Bigger than life and above the crowd stands this bronze Buddy Holly minus the Crickets, who were back in New York with his wife when he perished in an Iowa plane crash with Ritchy Valens and the Big Bopper. Other West Texans from the music and entertainment world honored here include Bob Wills, Waylon Jennings, Joe Ely, Tanya Tucker, Mac Davis, Bob "the Bopper" Murphy, and Wink's own Roy Orbison.

More of the spirit of Buddy Holly can be found at the **Lubbock City Cemetery,** where Buddy and his parents are interred. Though it's listed on 34th Street, don't expect to drive straight from the downtown area east on 34th and get there. You'll have better luck by finding 19th Street, heading east through Yellow-house Canyon Lakes Park, and taking a right (south) on Quirt Road. Just before you start up the huge overpass that spans the railroad tracks, take a left on 34th. The cemetery is straight ahead. Pass through the gates and immediately fork right. Their head-stones are on the left across from the tire ruts. Buddy's marker is bolted down. Note the different spelling of the Holley name. On Buddy's first record contract, his name was listed incorrectly and was printed on record labels minus the "e."

MACKENZIE PARK

Enter from Avenue A or East Broadway • Free • 765-6679

In addition to Joyland Amusement Park and Meadowbrook Golf Course (see **SPORTS AND ACTIVITIES**), Mackenzie Park is the home of one of America's last prairie dog colonies—Prairie Dog Town.

MUNICIPAL GARDEN AND ART CENTER

4215 University Avenue • 767-3724

Tour the gardens and consider attending or participating in one of the many lectures or workshops.

OMNIMAX THEATRE

2579 South Loop 289 • 745-6299
Admission: Adults $5.50, students $4.50

The projector in this facility stands over six feet tall and weighs two thousand pounds. The image that emerges is so crisp (and so large) that the screen is actually a dome with a diameter of 80 feet. Ten clusters of speakers—72 in all—are positioned to master the six-track sound. Combined admission with the Science Spectrum is available.

REESE AIR FORCE BASE

4th St. and War Highway • 885-3843

Tours of this jet pilot training facility are available if scheduled in advance.

SPORTS AND ACTIVITIES

Amusement Parks

JOYLAND AMUSEMENT PARK
Mackenzie Park • 763-2719
March 15–September 15: Saturday–Sunday 2–10
June through Labor Day: weekdays till 7 p.m. • Admission
With over 20 rides, Joyland caters to families. Bumper cars, merry-go-rounds, and skyrides are all included in the single admission price with snacks, fast food, and drinks also available.

TEXAS WATER RAMPAGE
Brownfield Highway • 796-0701
June–August: Sunday–Friday 12–7 • Saturday 11–7
May and October weekends only • Admission
Plenty of ways to get wet: a wave pool, slides, and an adult pool. For the landlubbers who tag along, there is a children's activity center, horseshoes, go-carts, and volleyball.

Basketball

TEXAS TECH RED RAIDERS AND LADY RAIDERS
Lubbock Municipal Coliseum • Admission • W+
The Texas Tech basketball program—men's and women's—has attracted some well-deserved attention lately. The men won the 1993 Southwest Conference tournament in Dallas to earn a bid to the NCAAs, and the women brought home the 1993 NCAA championship with a decisive victory in the Final 4 over Ohio State.

Football

TEXAS TECH RED RAIDERS
Jones Stadium • Texas Tech University Campus at University and 4th • Ticket Office: 742-3341 • Admission • W+
A lot of West Texans call the Red Raiders their team. In addition to longtime rivals Texas and Texas A&M, Tech typically plays grueling non-conference opponents like Red River foe Oklahoma, perennial national champion Miami, and Big 10 powerhouse Ohio State.

Golf

MEADOWBROOK GOLF COURSE
Mackenzie Park • 765-6679
Weekdays: $12 • Weekends: $15 • Cart: $16.50

PINE VALLEY GOLF COURSE
111th and Indiana • 748-1448
Weekdays: $8.50 • Weekends: $11 • Cart: $7

SHADOW HILLS GOLF COURSE
6002 3rd • 793-9700
Weekdays: $9 • Weekends: $12 • Cart: $10

TREASURE ISLAND GOLF CENTER
501 Frankford • 795-9311
Weekdays: $8 • Weekends: $9 • Cart: $12

Tennis

LUBBOCK MUNICIPAL TENNIS CENTER
3030 66th at Indiana • 767-3727
Open daily • $2 per person per 90 minutes
  Twelve outdoor lighted hard courts and a pro shop. Reasonably priced lessons are available by the hour and half-hour.

COLLEGES AND UNIVERSITIES

LUBBOCK CHRISTIAN UNIVERSITY
5601 19th St. • 792-3221 • W
  An independent liberal arts school with 35 degree programs, LCU was founded in 1957 and is affiliated with the Church of Christ. Enrollment on the 120-acre campus is over 1,000, and numerous sporting and theatrical events are open to the public.

TEXAS TECH UNIVERSITY
University and Broadway • 742-2011 • W
  It's hard to think of Lubbock without including Texas Tech. The fifth largest university in Texas is situated on an 1,837-acre campus in the heart of downtown Lubbock. Texas Technological College opened in 1925, and was designated a university by the legislature in 1969. Economically, the expenditures of the 25,000

students and the employee payroll combine to make the university a substantial factor in the South Plains economy, but Tech's impact is obvious in many other ways. Red Raider athletics are big news, Texas Tech's museums, archives, and collections are highly respected, and South Plains residents regularly enjoy Tech's cultural events. Noteworthy programs include the Advanced Technological Learning Center, the Seismological Observatory, and commitment to fostering grape growing and wine production atop the caprock formation.

PERFORMING ARTS

BALLET LUBBOCK
Civic Center Theater • 741-1899
   Contact the ticket office for performances in addition to the annual production of *The Nutcracker* with the Lubbock Symphony (see below).

LUBBOCK SYMPHONY ORCHESTRA
8200 Nashville • 794-7175
Call for program, dates, prices, and venue
   From its first performance nearly half a century ago, the Lubbock Symphony has progressed from a volunteer organization to one recognized and rated by the American Symphony Orchestra League. Performances range from outdoor concerts on the Fourth of July to an annual performance of *The Nutcracker* in conjunction with Ballet Lubbock at the Civic Center.

TEXAS TECH UNIVERSITY THEATER
University Theater Building • 742-3601 • Admission • W
   Site of several productions each semester by Tech players.

SHOPPING

ANTIQUE MALL OF LUBBOCK
Three miles west of Loop 289 at 7907 W. 19th St. • **796-2166**
Daily 10–6 • W
   With more than 50 booths and 24,000 square feet of display space, the Antique Mall is Lubbock's largest and is limited to just antiques and collectibles. Arts and crafts are not exhibited. Antique and reproduction signage, jukeboxes, glassware, and furniture are featured at different vendors. Weekends are busiest. Cokes and coffee available up front.

BUFFALO BEANO COMPANY

801 University Avenue • 762-8553 or 800-788-2326
Monday–Saturday 10–6 • Sunday 1–5

The list of hand-held contraptions available at Buffalo Beano is amazing: boomerangs, darts, and frisbees in addition to one-of-a-kind, all-leather "Texas Ripstop" kites. Probably the only leather kites on the market (no one else has stepped forward to fight for the honor), they are handcrafted, numbered, and actually do fly. As of late 1994 they cost $500, and there's a waiting list. Others include indoor kites, sport kites, dual control stunt kites, and a full range of single-line kites—boxes, deltas, diamonds, and parafoils (see **ANNUAL EVENTS**).

SOUTH PLAINS MALL

6002 Slide Rd. • 792-4653
Monday–Saturday 10–9 • Sunday 1–6

Lubbock approaches major metropolitan status with this immense mall, the largest in the region. Anchored by national giants Sears, J.C. Penney, Mervyn's, and Dillard's, smaller shops include Eddie Bauer, the Gap, and Victoria's Secret.

SIDE TRIPS

BUFFALO SPRINGS LAKE RECREATIONAL AREA

50th Street (becomes FM 835) five miles southeast of Lubbock
747-3353 • Admission: Adults $1.50, children 75¢ • W

Buffalo Springs Lake sits in Yellowhouse Canyon on a fork of the Brazos River—the same Brazos River that runs clear across Texas through Waco down to the Gulf of Mexico. Spring fed and big enough for any water sport, this county park offers full and electric hookups, tent camping, archery, fishing, hiking, picnicking, volleyball, and a new beach area with waterslides. Buffalo Springs also hosts its own triathlon. There is an Audobon Society Nature Trail as well as nationally famous horseshoe pits. On the lake, take a sightseeing tour, rent a paddleboat, go tubing, or put your water skis on. With its own marina and two concrete launching pads, any craft can be accommodated. As a finishing touch, there is a restaurant by the lake.

CAP*ROCK WINERY

Less than a mile east of US 87 south of Lubbock on Woodrow Rd.
863-2704 or 800-546-9463 • Monday–Saturday 10–5
Sunday 12–5

Cap*Rock Winery is one of the most picturesque wineries nationwide and worth a look even if you're not a wine connoisseur. Once inside, Cap*Rock treats visitors lavishly with its gorgeous tasting room and tours of its state-of-the-art production facility.

HERITAGE FARM

Ten miles west on Hwy 84 to Shallowater • *Exit FM 179*
832-4294

Stop in on Elleine and Dana Woodward and step back half a century to a typical West Texas farm. Complete with barn, windmill, and a two-hole crapper, you kind of expect to bump into Auntie Em on the porch.

LLANO ESTACADO WINERY

3 miles east of Hwy 87 south of Lubbock on FM 1585 • 745-2258
Tours and tastings Monday–Saturday 10–5 • Sunday 12–5

Perhaps the state's most prestigious winery, Llano Estacado has a well-deserved reputation for excellence. With only ten acres under cultivation at the winery itself, Llano purchases all of its grapes from within a 60-mile radius. These South Plains grapes and Llano's winemaking skills produce *vinos* that have garnered a host of awards.

MUSEUM OF THE LLANO ESTACADO

1900 W. 8th St. • Plainview • 79072 • 806-296-4735
Take I-27 50 miles north from Lubbock to the 5th Street exit in Plainview • *Drive east (right) to Quincy St. and take a left. The museum is just north of W. 8th Street* • 9–5 on weekdays 1–5 on weekends (March-November only) • Free • W+

The Museum of the Llano Estacado stands adjacent to the campus of Wayland Baptist University. The centuries old term *Llano Estacado* describes the plain south of the Canadian River and north of the Pecos River. The museum collection includes geologic, biologic, and historic exhibits pertaining to this rich region. Artifacts range from a 20,000- to 25,000-year-old Imperial mammoth skull and tusks to the uniform and equipment of Buffalo Soldiers. Also on display are many items from Native American cultures like Pueblo and Comanche Indians as well as *ciboleros* (buffalo hunters) who hunted the herds to near extinction while satisfying fashion-conscious American markets.

PHEASANT RIDGE WINERY

Two miles east and one mile south of New Deal off I-27 and FM 1729 • **885-3843** • **Tours by appointment only**

Unlike Cap*Rock and Llano Estacado, Pheasant Ridge buys no grapes and uses only those produced at the winery. This European-style operation is much less commercialized to the point that it doesn't have a tasting room. A tour of Pheasant Ridge offers visitors a hands-on trek through the vineyards including discussion of the varietals, wine production, and the rich soil of the South Plains.

ANNUAL EVENTS

February

TASTE OF LUBBOCK

Call 797-6150 for venue, events, and admission

A Taste of Lubbock marries the cooking of dozens of members of the Lubbock Restaurant Association with wines from over 20 different Texas Wine and Grape Growers. Attend the second serving. The restaurateurs serve and the vintners pour till the lights go out. For the aficionado, lectures and seminars on wine characteristics and pairing food and wine are also offered.

EASTER EGG HUNT

Buffalo Springs Lake • **747-3353**

The Easter Bunny really has taken to Buffalo Springs Lake. Last few years, he's cached more than twenty thousand eggs at a time along the shore of this south Lubbock oasis for area kids (and ones passing through).

April

BUFFALO BEANO KITE FLY AND FRISBEE FLING

Berl Huffman Soccer Complex • **762-8553 or 800-788-2326**
Last Sunday of the month

This extravaganza includes Sport Kite Conference competitions and several different frisbee categories: adult, canine, and kids. The *rokkaku* event is based on traditional Japanese kite fighting.

September

LITTLEFIELD DENIM FESTIVAL

40 miles west of Lubbock via Highway 84 to Littlefield
The week following Labor Day • 385-5331 (Littlefield Chamber)
The self-proclaimed Denim Capital of America mushrooms from 7,400 residents to almost 50,000 during this week-long event. Many show up to enjoy the free street dance hosted by Littlefield native Waylon Jennings, but a host of other activities are always slated (call the Chamber for a complete list). A few include Waylon's West Texas Bar-B-Que Cook-Off (a sanctioned event), a radio-controlled airplane fly-in, sewing and photo contests, and tours of the American Cotton Growers plant.

NATIONAL COWBOY SYMPOSIUM AND CELEBRATION

Lubbock Memorial Civic Center • 1501 6th St. • 742-2498
Adults $5, children $2.50 • Meals and events extra
A full-blown, four-day fandango dedicated to exploring and extolling life on the range. Artisans, cowboys, and scholars gather to demonstrate, ruminate, and pontificate on matters close to their hearts. About twenty different wagons vie in the chuckwagon cook-off, and there are ones for chili and brisket too. Each night features a different entertainment program. Additional events are held at the South Plains Fairgrounds including a cutting horse competition, team roping, team penning, trick roping, and sheepdog demonstrations. Call the Ranching Heritage Association (806-742-2498) for dates, times, and details.

September/October

PANHANDLE SOUTH PLAINS FAIR

Fair Park • 105 E. Broadway • 763-2833
Last week of the month
Even with the horse and livestock shows, flower festival, and other activities, this is not just a carnival. Each year the Fair brings in top-dollar talent to highlight the event. Mickey Gilley, Charlie Pride, Barbara Mandrell, Reba McEntire, Marty Robbins, and Mel Tillis have all performed. Call for schedule and prices.

October

FLOYDADA PUNKIN DAYS
Less than an hour east via US 82 and Hwy 207 to Floydada
Weekend closest to Halloween • **800-288-3619**
(Floydada Chamber)
   More than a million pumpkins are harvested each fall in fields surrounding Floydada, America's Pumpkin Capital, and once the crop is in locals celebrate with two days of activities and contests. Try your hand at pumpkin carving, cow-patty bingo, Pumpkin Pie Relays, a wheelbarrow race, and a not-too-serious Pumpkin Queen Contest, or enjoy plenty of pumpkin pie, pumpkin ice cream, pumpkin cake, and other pumpkin products.

FOURTH CAVALRY OLYMPICS
East Airport District • **799-0054**
First weekend of the month
   Recognized as the Governor's Own Cavalry, the Fourth Cavalry preserves the heritage of one of America's most distinguished military units. Each October, the Fourth hosts a competition that highlights the skills and techniques essential for mounted combat.

RESTAURANTS

($ = Under $7.50, $$ = Under $15, $$$ = $15+ plus tax & tip)

COUNTY LINE
FM 2641 west of I-27 N. and the airport • **763-6001**
Daily dinner • **$–$$** • **AE MC V** • **W call ahead**
   Patrons argue over favorite entrées, but everyone enjoys the Escondido Canyon views at County Line. Though à la carte dinners are available, most order platters and get the extra homemade potato salad, cole slaw, and beans. County Line is not all beef and pork (though the ribs are outstanding). Try the grilled chicken, smoked chicken or turkey. Call ahead to avoid a lengthy wait. Bar.

THE DEPOT RESTAURANT & BAR
19th and G Street • **747-1646** • **Daily** • **Lunch and dinner (closed Saturday lunch)** • **$$** • **AE D MC V** • **W call ahead**
   The heart of the Depot District is anchored by the historic 1928 Fort Worth and Denver Depot, now a restaurant and bar. Period antiques and the depot's original blueprints line the walls as

attorneys, cowboys, and Tech faculty and students fill up the tables. The prime rib is a mainstay, but consider ordering it smoked. An old baggage cart has been converted into the salad cart for fixings with dinner or à la carte. Plenty of Southwestern flair can be found throughout both the lunch and dinner menus, but the big draw during the hot summer months is some of Lubbock's best live music in the Depot's beer garden. Bar.

LLANO LAND AND CATTLE COMPANY
Lubbock Plaza Hotel • 797-3241
Daily dinner • $–$$ • Cr • W+
Formerly Beethoven's, Llano Land and Cattle Company features lower prices, regional Texas cuisine, and the same high quality. Nice accents like chalkboard menus and the house dressing—a green chile ranch—won't prepare you for the Armadillo Egg, a deep-fried avocado stuffed with jalapeño jack cheese and served on a nest of fried onion strips. Order the Taste of Texas ($$) and keep in mind it serves two. Beef and chicken fajitas, baby back ribs, brisket, sausage, and pinto beans make dessert a chore. The Symphony Room, which seats ten, is available for fans of Beethoven. Bar.

STUBB'S BAR-B-Q
620 19th St. • 747-4777
Daily • Lunch and dinner • $ • AE MC V • W
For decades, Stubb's has been a Lubbock landmark, and they're still serving great barbecue in their new location on 19th right behind the Depot. The pork ribs, the sliced beef, the homemade biscuits, and the barbecue sauce are as good as ever. Stubb's Major ($$) is an order for two that covers all the bases: sliced beef, chopped beef, pork and beef ribs, sausage, chicken, and all the fixings. All their meats and side orders are available by the pound and the pint, and Stubb's Regular and Spicy Barbecue Sauce is on sale at the restaurant and in local grocery stores. Bar.

CLUBS AND BARS

LONE STAR OYSTER BAR
3040 34th Street and Flint • 796-0101
Though you can order a dozen oysters on the half shell or boiled shrimp, most locals come to the original Oyster Bar to enjoy the happy hour from 4 to 7 p.m. Young professionals hang around till dinner, and the Tech crowd starts to show up after 10 p.m.; Thursday, Friday, and Saturday nights are a zoo. Bar.

MIDNIGHT RODEO

7301 S. University Ave. at Loop 289 • 745-2813
Cover varies • **21 and over only**

This country and western club offers a comfortable, upscale atmosphere full of sofas, nice furniture, and a signature circular dance floor. A DJ spins records most nights, but top talent like Jerry Jeff Walker, David Alan Coe, and Brooks & Dunn is brought in at least once month. Rock & rollers and Top 40 fans head to a separate back room. The award-winning fajita buffet is Sunday from 7 to 9 p.m. for a paltry $2 cover. Bar.

ACCOMMODATIONS

($ = Under $40, $$ = $40–$75, $$$ = $75–$100, $$$$ = Over $100)
Room Tax 13%

BARCELONA COURT

5215 S. Loop 289 • **794-5353 or 800-222-1122** • **$$**

Located adjacent to South Plains Mall, this three-story all-suite hotel has 161 two-room units and non-smoking suites with cable TV and room phones (charge for local calls). Amenities include complimentary cooked-to-order breakfast, complimentary afternoon cocktails, room service from the Olive Garden, indoor pool, jacuzzi, exercise room, game room, gift shop, barber shop, beauty salon, laundry, courtesy shuttle to airport and shopping, guest memberships available at local club for tennis and racquetball, and free parking. No pets and no tipping allowed.

HOLIDAY INN CIVIC CENTER

801 Avenue Q • **763-1200 or 800-HOLIDAY** • **$$–$$$**

Adjacent to the Lubbock Memorial Civic Center, this six-story Holiday Inn has 295 rooms including suites and non-smoking rooms with cable TV (Showtime) and pay-per-view movies, room phones (charge for local calls), and fire sprinklers and smoke detectors in all rooms. Amenities include the Greenery restaurant, the Brass Banjo Dance Club, a heated indoor pool with sauna and whirlpool, game room, complimentary airport shuttle, complimentary breakfast with Best Breaks rate, and free parking. Pets OK. AAA, AARP, corporate, government, and military rates offered.

LA QUINTA INN
601 Avenue Q • 763-9441 or 800-531-5900 • $$

This two-story motor inn across from Texas Tech and next to the Civic Center has 137 units including suites and non-smoking rooms with cable TV (Showtime), room phones (no charge for local calls), microwaves upon request, and fire alarms for the hearing impaired in all rooms. Denny's is right next door, and amenities include a complimentary continental breakfast, complimentary coffee in the lobby, an outdoor pool, and free parking. Small pets are allowed. AAA, Sam's Wholesale Club, and government rates available.

SHERATON INN LUBBOCK
505 Avenue Q • 747-0171 or 800-325-3535 • $$$

This six-story hotel is right by the Civic Center and has 145 units including suites and non-smoking rooms with cable TV and pay-per-view movies, room phones (charge for local calls), coffee makers, and fire sprinklers in all rooms. Amenities include Vintages restaurant, the Atrium Lounge, heated indoor pool, fitness center privileges at a health club, courtesy shuttle to the airport, complimentary breakfast, complimentary newspaper, and free parking. No pets. A variety of discount rates are available.

MULESHOE

BAILEY COUNTY SEAT ★ 4,571 ★ 806

The town was named for the muleshoe brand of one of the many ranches carved from the famed XIT Ranch (see **DALHART**) and is still a High Plains hub. For more information contact the **Muleshoe Chamber of Commerce** at 806-272-4248 or write to P.O. Box 356, Muleshoe, Texas 79347.

OTHER POINTS OF INTEREST

NATIONAL MULE MEMORIAL
Downtown at the intersection of US 70/84 and Main Street

This fiberglass testimonial to an America trailblazer stands fifteen hands tall and has been a Muleshoe monument since 1965.

SIDE TRIPS

MULESHOE NATIONAL WILDLIFE REFUGE

20 miles south of Muleshoe on Texas 214 • 1-946-3341
Monday–Friday 8–4:30 • **Free** • **W**

No state in the Union hosts a wider variety of birds than Texas, and one of the most important flyways extends from Canada to Mexico through the Panhandle. The Muleshoe National Wildlife Refuge was established for these migratory birds, particularly waterfowl, and is the oldest in the state (1935). The 5,809-acre preserve is mainly native gramma grasses and shrubs surrounded by caliche rock outcroppings, but sorghum, wheat, and rainwater lakes (a rarity on the High Plains) attract thousands of duck, geese, and sandhill cranes during the winter months. The small visitor center is open during the week only. Photography, not hunting, is permitted. Notable year-round residents include a prairie dog colony along the entrance road.

TURKEY

HALL COUNTY SEAT ★ 2,348 ★ (806)

Combine western dance music and big band jazz—sometimes called swing—and the offshoot is western swing. In a career spanning five decades, Turkey's own Bob Wills and his Texas Playboys were western swing at its finest. Born in East Texas, Wills grew up in Turkey. He quit his chair at Ham's Barber Shop in 1929, moved to Fort Worth, and two years later put together the best known band in Texas political history: the Light Crust Doughboys who later propelled W. Lee "Pappy" O'Daniel into the governor's mansion and eventually a Senate seat. It was only after Wills and the Doughboys went their separate ways that he put together his most signature band, the Playboys (1933).

The town of Turkey and thousands of Bob's fans pay homage to the King of Western Swing the last weekend of April, but there's plenty to see and do year-round now that nearby Caprock Canyons State Park has opened a 64-mile Rail-Trail addition.

SIDE TRIPS

CAPROCK CANYONS STATE PARK
Superintendent • Box 204 • Quitaque • 79255 • 455-1492
Hwy 86 14 miles west to Quitaque and FM 1065 three miles north
Situated on the eastern edge of the High Plains, Caprock Canyons is one of the best multi-use parks in the state. It's roughly 100 miles northeast of Lubbock and 100 miles southeast of Amarillo. Nearly 14,000 acres of activities, animals, and vistas are located at the main park site. Lake Theo has a designated swimming area, a playground, a fishing pier, and plenty of hungry bass, catfish, crappie, and perch. Campers can choose from primitive, tent, sheltered, or equestrian camps. Eighteen miles of hiking and equestrian trails exist at the main park, but head to the recently opened 64-mile Caprock Canyons State Park Rail-Trail for plenty more. Built as the Fort Worth and Denver South Plains Railroad in 1927-28, it achieved record profits during its heyday before the advent of the modern highway system. Burlington-Northern closed the line in 1989, and with the assistance of the Rails-to-Trails Conservancy it was donated to the Texas Parks & Wildlife Department. Recently opened as the Rail-Trail, it extends from Estelline (east of Turkey on Highway 86) to South Plains (20-plus miles southwest of the state park). This new right-of-way offers hikers, mountain bikers, and trail riders access to the second longest trail in Texas and is the nation's fourth longest rail conversion.

ANNUAL EVENTS

April

BOB WILLS DAY
Last Saturday of April
People always had a great time when Bob Wills brought them together, and this day is no exception. With its parade, arts and crafts show, fiddlers contest, and outdoor concert, Turkey takes off. A special treat is the dance. Of course breakfast is served afterwards. As much as you'll do and see this weekend, don't forget to stop in at the Bob Wills Museum at Sixth and Lyons featuring music and memorabilia relating to Wills and his Texas Playboys. Keep in mind that Bob Wills Day organizers book the Hotel Turkey for the entire weekend.

BED & BREAKFASTS

HOTEL TURKEY
Alexander and 3rd • 423-1151 or 800-657-7110 • $$

This two-story brick building was built in 1927 and has been open for business without exception every day since. The State of Texas recognizes the hotel as a Living Museum, i.e., all furnishings and furniture are museum quality and used daily. Each of the twenty bedrooms is appointed with antiques, linens, and other unique furnishings. Four share baths (all have sinks). Owners Jane and Scott Johnson serve a full American breakfast including flapjacks, breakfast meats, their trademark sweet potato pancakes, fresh fruit, pastries, cereal, toast, orange juice, and coffee. Special diets and dinner service can be accommodated with advance notice. Out back, an arbor shades the summer breakfast service and leads to a duck pond and petting barnyard including llamas, miniature goats, a pot-bellied pig, and Gobbler, a black steed who pulls a 1918 Amish surrey. Swimming and tennis are available on the property, and the Hotel Turkey is adjacent to the 64-mile Rail-Trail which offers hiking, biking, and horseback riding. Group rates available.

West Texas

The Edwards Plateau sits at the center of Texas. Its eastern, eroded edge is known as the Hill Country and enjoys plentiful streams, occasional rivers, and almost 30 inches of rain a year. Follow the setting sun, and crops give way to cowboys as rainfall drops and creek beds run dry. This is where West Texas begins—on the western reaches of the Edwards Plateau and along the prairie to the north.

Closer to the Gulf Coast than either the Trans-Pecos or the Panhandle-Plains, West Texas wasn't easier to settle nor was it settled earlier. Credit the Comanches for the slow start. For over a century America's greatest horsemen hunted, inhabitated, and traversed the Edwards Plateau and the Hill Country as well as the Big Bend and the Plains. Technology and the times ended their reign: The combination of the Colt revolver and the close of the Civil War focused too much firepower and too many soldiers on the outmatched natives.

Note the diverse biologic and geologic zones including the Permian Basin, the Chihuahuan Desert, and the Edwards Plateau. Local economies fluctuate with changes in geography and geology and include most of America's wool and mohair production and the nation's largest inland petrochemical complex. As with any portion of Texas, federal installations are abundant and include three Air Force bases—Dyess, Goodfellow, and Laughlin—and a B-1B Bomber Wing.

WEST TEXAS

ABILENE

TAYLOR COUNTY SEAT ★ 106,654 ★ (915)

In 1880, the county seat of Taylor County, named to honor two brothers who fell at the Alamo, was the prosperous community of Buffalo Gap. Abilene was a city in Kansas. The present site of Abilene, Texas, was Milepost 407 on the telegraph route from Marshall to El Paso. The future of Buffalo Gap was derailed (and its historic nature preserved) when area ranchers finally convinced the Texas & Pacific Railroad to set up a shipping point for their cattle operations north and east of the rolling hills around Buffalo Gap. Not even an intersection, Abilene was a true railroad town with the first post office as well as the railroad's ticket office housed in boxcars. James T. Berry organized the sale of the original townsite which became the county seat and the commercial center for Taylor County.

Buffalo Gap is doing fine these days (see **SIDE TRIPS** below), and so is Abilene whose greatest resource is and has always been the ingenuity and drive of its citizens. Home to three institutions of higher learning and a United States Air Force base, extensive community support has also resulted in the preservation of civic monuments like the Paramount Theatre and the T&P Depot and the creation of cultural centers, museums, and annual events that make this city and its neighbors well worth a visit.

TOURIST SERVICES

ABILENE CONVENTION AND VISITORS COUNCIL

Texas & Pacific Railroad Depot • 676-2556 or 800-727-7704
Open weekdays 9–5 • Weekend afternoons • W+

Housed in the renovated T&P Depot, the Convention and Visitors Council offers brochures and coupons from area hotels, motels, restaurants, and attractions.

MUSEUMS

MUSEUMS OF ABILENE at GRACE CULTURAL CENTER

102 Cypress Street • 673-4587
Thursday 10–8:30 • Sunday 1–5 • Closed Monday
All others 10–5 • Admission: Adults $2, children $1

The classic Mission Revival styling of the Texas & Pacific Depot, the Elks Building, and the Grace Hotel (1909) manifest Abilene's rise. This portion of the downtown district served as Abilene's hub for decades, with the Grace Hotel the site of countless volumes of local fact and fiction. Located across from the T&P Depot, the Grace has been converted into the home of three of Abilene's cultural institutions and has again become a focal point for Abilene. All follow the same schedule and fee structure.

The Art Museum displays exhibitions from many sources in addition to the museum's permanent collection of paintings by American regionalists from 1900 to 1950.

The Historical Museum focuses on Abilene in the twentieth century. Period rooms from pre-World War I, the Roaring Twenties, and post-World War II are presented along with a re-created hotel room from the Grace circa 1928.

The Children's Museum encourages kids and adults to do exactly what museums abhor: touch the merchandise. Kids two and older welcome.

HISTORIC PLACES

In addition to the Paramount, Abilene has several distinct historic districts: the **Parramore** district north of North Sixth Street and west of Hickory Street; **Sayles Boulevard** with its distinctive landscaped esplanade; the **Abilene State Epileptic Colony,** once the largest in Texas; and the **Commercial** district centered on the Texas & Pacific Depot and the Grace Hotel (now the Grace Cultural Center). Contact the City's Planning Department at 676-6237 for a list of historic properties.

PARAMOUNT THEATRE

352 Cypress St. • Business hours daily 1–5 • 676-9620
Call for event schedule and prices

Before the rise of TV and long before the advent of VCRs, there were movie houses where America went for entertainment. The Paramount was built in 1930 under the auspices of the Paramount Motion Picture Company for more than $400,000. Restored in 1985, nothing on HBO can quite compare to this jewel with its two grand staircases, floor-to-mezzanine arched columns, and glass chandeliers.

OTHER POINTS OF INTEREST

ABILENE ZOOLOGICAL GARDENS AND DISCOVERY CENTER

State Highway 36 at Loop 322 in Nelson Park • 672-9771
Memorial Day–Labor Day: 9–5 weekdays and 9–7 weekends
9–5 all other times • Closed Thanksgiving, Christmas, New

Year's • **Admission: Adults $2, seniors/children $1**
Gift shop • **Picnic area**
Abilene's top attraction is also the only zoo between Fort Worth and El Paso. The zoo's design enables different animals to live together in groups similar to their natural habitats. Spread over 13 acres, more than 500 species of mammals, reptiles, amphibians, and invertebrates are represented in a unique comparison of animal and plant life from the American Southwest with their counterparts from the African *veldt* (plains).

LINEAR AIR PARK at DYESS AIR FORCE BASE
Open during daylight hours • **Free** • **696-0212**
Ranging from Korea to Vietnam, nearly thirty different craft are on display at the Air Park. Though Dyess is a closed base with restricted access, a temporary pass is available at the main gate. Dyess is the home of the B-1B's sole crew training center, an Air Command Wing of B-1B bombers, a KC-135 Stratotanker squadron, and an Air Mobility Command Wing with two squadrons of C-130 Hercules transport planes.

SPORTS AND ACTIVITIES

Golf

MAXWELL GOLF COURSE
South 32nd St. • **692-2737**
Weekdays: $9.75 • **Weekends: $12.45**

WILLOW CREEK GOLF CENTER
1166 Ben Richey Dr. • **691-0909**
Weekdays: $5.75 • **Weekends: $8.75**

Outdoor Activities

ABILENE STATE RECREATION AREA
Park Rd. 32, 15 miles southeast of Abilene off FM 89 • **Park Superintendent** • **Route 1** • **Tuscola** • **79562** • **572-3204**
Memorial Day through Labor Day from 12 to 9
Admission: $2 per vehicle or 50¢ per pedestrian or cyclist
This recreational area is a welcome wet spot near semi-arid Abilene. Swim in the spring-fed pool, hike nature trails, picnic

under pecan trees, or spend the night—campsites and screened shelters are available.

Tennis

ROSE PARK TENNIS CENTER

South 7th and Mockingbird • 673-8396
Monday–Thursday 9–8 • Friday 9–5 • Weekends 1–5
   All 13 hardcourts have lights, but only six stay lit after the pro shop closes. Fees are $2 per person per 90-minute session. Pro shop with stringing, concessions, and lessons available.

COLLEGES AND UNIVERSITIES

ABILENE CHRISTIAN UNIVERSITY

1600 Campus Court • 674-2000 • W+ but not all areas
   Founded in 1906, granted senior college status in 1919 and university status in 1969, ACU has an enrollment of about 4,000 students and includes graduate programs. Exchange programs with Hardin-Simmons and McMurry expand the broad curriculum, and campus facilities present a wide variety of athletic, theatrical, and cultural programs. Affiliated with the Church of Christ, the 208-acre campus is located right in the heart of town.

HARDIN-SIMMONS UNIVERSITY

2200 Hickory • 670-1000 • W+ but not all areas
   Founded in 1891 and affiliated with the Southern Baptist Church, Hardin-Simmons has an enrollment of approximately 2,000 and is an active member of the Abilene community. Performances at the Van Ellis Theatre like *The Man Who Came to Dinner* and *The Taming of the Shrew,* concerts at the Woodward-Dellis Recital Hall, and regular art exhibits keep a steady stream of visitors on the 40-acre campus.

McMURRY UNIVERSITY

Sayles and 14th • 691-6200 • W+ but not all areas
   A third institution of higher learning in Abilene, McMurry also has a church affiliation, the United Methodist Church. Offering associate's degrees as well as bachelor's, McMurry's athletic teams compete in the TIAA versus other non-scholarship schools like Tarleton and Sul Ross.

PERFORMING ARTS

ABILENE CIVIC CENTER
1100 N. 6th • 676-6211
Rodeos and big concerts head to the Taylor County Exposition Center. The Civic Center hosts events like the Taste of Abilene, auto shows, arts and crafts fairs, gun and knife shows, and performances by the Abilene Philharmonic. Several gift shows and the Abilene Tree Lighting Ceremony are scheduled in November.

ABILENE COMMUNITY THEATER
801 S. Mockingbird Lane • 673-6271 for schedule and tickets
Recent productions include *Father of the Bride, The Lion in Winter, A Few Good Men,* and *Little Shop of Horrors.*

ABILENE PHILHARMONIC ORCHESTRA
Civic Center • 677-6710 for schedule and tickets
The concert season runs from September through April with programs ranging from classical to pop to patriotic.

ABILENE REPERTORY THEATRE
825 N. Second St. • 672-9991 for schedule and tickets
Recent performances include *One Flew Over the Cuckoo's Nest, On Golden Pond,* and *The Tempest.*

PARAMOUNT THEATRE
352 Cypress St. • Business hours daily 1–5 • 676-9620
The Paramount, also listed under **HISTORIC PLACES,** regularly runs American and foreign classics. Christmas favorites are scheduled in December. The theatre is also home to the Paramount Performing Arts Series, which has a long tradition of productions like *Oklahoma* and *The Nutcracker.*

ROCOCO DINNER THEATRE
670-0149 for schedule and tickets
Dial M for Murder, Hope for the Best, and *Once Upon A Mattress* are some of the recent performances at this popular local dinner theatre.

TAYLOR COUNTY EXPOSITION CENTER
Texas Highway 36 • 677-4376
George Strait plays the Expo Center when he comes to town. Also the site of the Western Heritage Classic, the Taylor County

Livestock Show, the West Texas Fair, the Farm and Ranch Show, barrel racing, cutting shows and clinics, and team ropings.

SHOPPING

ART REED CUSTOM SADDLES
904 Ambler • 677-4572 • W
Right down the street from James Leddy Boots, Art Reed's reputation as a first-rate saddlemaker goes back three decades. Reed's saddlery is a rarity because his saddle trees are crafted at the shop. Most saddle shops buy the trees these days (and some don't even make the saddle). Tack and chaps along with other hand tooled leather items are also available.

JAMES LEDDY BOOTS
926 Ambler • 677-7811
In a state full of bootmakers, James Leddy stands tall. Custom-made boots, matching belts, and billfolds can set a dandy (or a lady) back thousands of dollars. This shop is not just for show. Repairs and boots for working hands keep work benches busy.

MALL OF ABILENE
4310 Buffalo Gap Rd. • 698-4351 • W
In addition to Sears, Dillard's, J.C. Penney and 100 other stores, the Mall of Abilene schedules a variety of programs like antique, art, bridal, and home shows. Six-screen cinema.

SIDE TRIPS

BUFFALO GAP HISTORIC VILLAGE
FM 89 (Buffalo Gap Rd.) 14 miles southwest of Abilene
572-3365 • Summer: 10–7 daily • Winter: 10–6 weekends only • Admission: Adults $4, seniors $3, children $1.75
This complex of 19 buildings, many over a century old, preserves pioneer structures from the earliest days of Taylor County. The town got its name from migrating herds of buffalo that used to pass through nearby Callahan Divide. Buffalo Gap lost out when cattlemen lured the Texas & Pacific Railroad to Abilene. It gradually became the historical curiosity it is today, with half the population of more than a century ago. The original county courthouse and jail are here, as is the oldest log cabin in the area and one of the oldest churches in the region, the Buffalo Gap Chapel.

The self-guided tour includes a brief video and a visit to the Buffalo Gap Historic Museum.

FORT PHANTOM HILL
FM 600 14 miles north of Abilene
676-2556 (Visitors Council) • **Free**
Privately owned, the ruins are well maintained and graciously shared with the public. Though never officially named, this garrison was founded (1851) along with Forts Belknap, Chadbourne, and McKavett to protect 49ers en route to West Texas and California. The post never stood a chance: Timber was scarce, reliable water was never discovered, and, worst of all, the companies assigned to corral the Comanches were infantry units. Almost no contact was ever made with these superb horsemen, and the post was abandoned in 1854. The charred ruins were used as a changing station on the Butterfield Overland Mail Route (1858), as a post for the Texas Rangers and the Confederates during the Civil War, and as a sub-post of Fort Griffin during the Indian Wars (1871-1872).

ANNUAL EVENTS

March

SWEETWATER JAYCEES RATTLESNAKE ROUNDUP
Nolan County Coliseum • **Sweetwater** • **235-5488**
40 miles west of Abilene on Interstate 20 • **Admission** • **W**
Thousands of wild rattlesnakes are stalked and caught, milked for their venom, cleaned for their skins, and served up for vittles at the largest rattlesnake roundup in Texas. Ranch outings, plenty of rattlesnake snacks, a 10-K, and a variety of contests fill this March weekend. Sweetwater is also home to Lake Sweetwater and several public golf courses.

May

WESTERN HERITAGE CLASSIC
Taylor County Exposition Center • **677-4376**
Second weekend
Tickets to each night's ranch rodeo also include admission to the dance and breakfast that follow. During the day enjoy the world's largest bit and spur show, held at the Expo Center. Other

activities include sheep dog trials, cowboy horse races, readings by the Cowboy Poets Society, and a chuckwagon cook-off.

WEST TEXAS FILM FESTIVAL
Paramount Theatre • 676-9630 • Middle of the month

Great films in the quintessential movie house. Movies Featuring a different Hollywood legend are featured each year, with past honorees including James Dean and the Duke. A movie memorabilia show and sale are also held at the Civic Center.

July

TEXAS COWBOY REUNION
Stamford Rodeo and Reunion Grounds • Stamford
38 miles north of Abilene on US 277 **• Fourth of July weekend**

Stamford hosts a rodeo and reunion known far and wide. Things get going bright and early with the slack roping contests followed by the Cowboy Reunion parade and a memorial service for deceased members of the Texas Cowboy Oldtimers Association. By the time lunch rolls around, the cook-offs are underway. There's one for chuckwagons and another for brisket as well as a fiddler's contest and a spur and bit show. Barbecue lunches and dinners are served, and the rodeo begins nightly at 8 p.m. followed by the dance.

RESTAURANTS

($ = Under $7.50, $$ = Under $15, $$$ = $15+ plus tax & tip)

CASA HERRERA
4109 Ridgemont Dr. • 692-7065
Monday–Saturday lunch and dinner • Sunday lunch only
$–$$ • AE MC V • W

After almost twenty years, Casa Herrera has a new location and the same delicious food. Their new Santa Fe style (down to the saltillo tiles) hasn't changed the popular luncheon buffet Featuring spicy *enchiladas rancheras* on flour tortillas, cheese and beef enchiladas, tacos, beans and rice. Always a treat off the salad bar is the cabbage, lemon, and vinegar salad—the perfect complement to any Mexican plate. Order the excellent *chile rellenos* at dinner. Bar.

HICKORY STREET CAFE

**644 Hickory • 675-0465 Monday–Friday • Lunch • $ MC V
W call ahead**

This tea room is located in one of Abilene's many historic homes and also features a Victorian gift shop upstairs. The cafe is on the first floor and is popular with the downtown crowd as well as for birthday parties and luncheons. Enjoy the chicken salad which comes with a wonderful zucchini bread. Other good bets include the quiche and the soup de jour. Plenty of homemade chocolate dessert items.

JOE ALLEN'S PIT BAR-B-QUE

**1233 S. Treadaway • 672-6082 • Monday–Saturday
Lunch and dinner • $–$$$ • AE MC V • W**

When was the last time you ordered steak by the inch? At Joe Allen's you not only pick how well you want your beef mesquite-grilled but you also choose the thickness of your cut of beef. Inch to inch-and-a-quarter ribeyes are the house favorite ($$), but cuts can be pared down to three-quarters of an inch ($$) or up to two inches ($$$) at your request. Plenty of mesquite also goes into smoking and grilling Joe Allen's brisket, sausage, ham, chicken, and pork ribs. Beer and wine.

PERINI RANCH STEAK HOUSE

FM 89 seven-tenths of a mile southwest of Buffalo Gap
**572-3339 • Wednesday–Thursday dinner
Friday–Sunday lunch and dinner • $–$$ • MC V • W**

When in Buffalo Gap, stop by the Perini Ranch for an order of delicious pork ribs and a side of Zuccini Perini or Mexican hominy. Wrap things up with their bread pudding, made with sourdough bread and with pecans instead of raisins. Most entrées are cooked over a mesquite fire, and in addition to ribs they serve plenty of steaks, chicken, and fish. Summer nights are spent out on the patio listening or dancing to live country and western music. Bar.

TURNERHILL'S HOUSE OF BARBECUE

**1881 N. Treadaway • 675-0401 • Monday–Saturday
Lunch and dinner • $ • AE D MC V • W**

Turnerhill's picnic-style service is as popular as it is filling. Prices are inexpensive and vary with the choice of meats, including pit-smoked brisket. Plates come with your choice of vegetable and salad. For a tasty change, try the fried catfish which is battered with a special seasoning. If you have room for dessert, get the old-fashioned butter roll. Beer and wine.

CLUBS AND BARS

PONDEROSA BALLROOM
3881 Vine • 698-2102
Daily • 7 p.m. to midnight (1 a.m. on Saturday nights)
The patrons and the bands come from across West Texas to this Abilene institution. The Ponderosa is home to country & western music and those who like to play it, dance to it, and listen to it. No gimmicks, no bucking broncs, just plenty of dance floor. A DJ spins country classics Monday through Thursday nights (no cover). Weekends have live music with four and five dollar cover charges. Special events may cost more. From famous—Ray Price, B.J. Thomas, Moe Bandy, Radney Foster—to favorites—Jody Nix and the Texas Cowboys (Big Spring), Southern Cross (Coleman), Perfect Stranger (Palestine)—the Ponderosa is what a Texas dance hall is all about. Bar.

ACCOMMODATIONS

($ = Under $40, $$ = $40–$75, $$$ = $75–$100, $$$$ = Over $100)
Room Tax 13%

EMBASSY SUITES HOTEL
4250 Ridgemont Drive • 698-1234 or 800-362-2779 • $$–$$$
This property has only suites—170 of them. The standard suite includes a separate living room and bedroom, satellite TV, microwave, coffee maker, and free local calls. In addition, a full breakfast is included daily as well as a complimentary two-hour manager's reception. Connections to and from the airport are available. For relaxation, they have a heated indoor pool, jacuzzi, sauna, and steam bath, and live entertainment in the lounge of Remington's Steakhouse.

HOLIDAY INN EXPRESS
Highway 351 at Interstate 20 • 673-5271 or 800-465-4329 • $–$$
Winner of a 1992 Quality of Excellence service award within the Holiday Inn organization, this hotel is better than average with some nice amenities. Most of the usual applies: complimentary continental breakfast, free local phone calls, satellite TV, outdoor pool, and free coffee and newspapers in the lobby. A nice

plus is the 12 p.m. check-in/check-out time. A full service restaurant is not located on the premises.

LA QUINTA INN

3501 West Lake Rd. • **676-1676 or 800-531-5900** • **$$**

This two-story inn next to Interstate 20 at FM 600 has 106 rooms including non-smoking rooms with cable TV (Showtime), pay-per-view movies, and room phones (free local calls). Amenities include complimentary continental breakfast, complimentary coffee in the lobby, an adjacent Denny's restaurant open 24 hours, an outdoor unheated pool open April through October, and free parking. One pet per room is allowed, and it must weigh less than 25 pounds. Discounted rates available include AAA, AARP, Sam's Wholesale Club, and active military personnel.

Bed & Breakfasts

BOLIN'S PRAIRIE HOUSE BED & BREAKFAST

508 Mulberry • **675-5855** • **$–$$**

Abilene is barely a century old, and this renovated 1902 Frank Lloyd Wright prairie-style has seen most of those years. Four bedrooms share two baths, and everyone shares breakfast in the dining room (special menus available). It's right next to downtown; if you're coming in from Interstate 20, take the Grape Street Exit, head north to North 5th, and go east one block to Mulberry. Children over 12. No smoking. No pets.

ARCHER CITY

ARCHER COUNTY SEAT ★ **1,748** ★ **(817)**

If Archer City looks familiar, you either grew up here or watched *The Last Picture Show* (1972) written by Archer City native Larry McMurtry. A better way to catch up on this part-time local's work is at his bookstore, the **Blue Pig Book Shop.**

SHOPPING

BLUE PIG BOOK SHOP
216 S. Center (a block past the courthouse on Hwy 79)
574-4245 • Tuesday–Saturday 10–5
Housed in five different buildings along Center Street, over 100,000 books are displayed in the former settings of the Archer County Housing Authority, a car dealership, and the Archer County Tax Office. Phone orders from Houston, Dallas, and across the Southwest are the main source of sales. Most books are antiquarian—rare, out-of-print, or hard-to-find. Prices range from as little as five dollars to thousands per volume. The Blue Pig's specialty is Americana; it also has strong Texana and Southwest sections. New books are limited to McMurtry's and occasional author signings.

RESTAURANTS

($ = Under $7.50, $$ = Under $15, $$$ = $15+ plus tax & tip)

THE COTTAGE TEA AND ANTIQUES
105 N. Ash • 574-4016 • Lunch Monday–Friday
Private parties by appointment • $
Soups, sandwiches, teas, and coffees were the intent, but the locals won't let Bertie Beekman stop there. Favorites include marinated chicken breast, Yankee pot roast, chicken and dumplings, and the meatloaf. Whatever your order, enjoy a serving of Bertie's chocolate meringue pie.

ACCOMMODATIONS

($ = Under $40, $$ = $40–$75, $$$ = $75–$100, $$$$ = Over $100)

SPUR HOTEL
110 N. Center • 574-2501 • $$
With eleven rooms and a complimentary continental breakfast, the Spur has more in common with a bed and breakfast than a hotel. Built in the late 1920s and renovated in 1990-1991, numerous design accents make the Spur a wonderful stop: the Texas sandstone Fireplace, the solid mesquite mantle, Afghani, Iraqi, and Native American rugs, and refinished antiques. Unlike a B&B, however, each room has its own bath, central heat, and air. No pets.

DEL RIO & ACUÑA

VAL VERDE COUNTY SEAT	★	30,705	★ (210)
STATE OF COAHUILA	★	120,000	★ (011 52 877)

Del Rio, the largest city between San Antonio and El Paso, was initially named San Felipe del Río (St. Phillip of the River). Some say it was named by Spanish explorers after their monarch, King Phillip, and others say it was named by Spanish missionaries who arrived here on St. Phillip's Day in the early 1600s. Either way, the name survived more than two centuries until the 1880s when the Post Office suggested shortening it to Del Rio to avoid confusion with another town named San Felipe de Austin.

There are some 400 archaeological sites in Val Verde County, many giving evidence to the presence of Indians in this area thousands of years ago. For example, pictographs painted on the walls of area caves have been dated back some 8,000 years.

Like most towns in semi-arid regions, Del Rio came into being because it was an oasis. The San Felipe Springs, just off US 90 East, gush forth from a subterranean river at a rate of more than 90 million gallons a day. In the early days, the springs were an important watering stop on the historic Chihuahua Road that connected Mexico's Chihuahua City with the bustling Texas port of Indianola. Later they also served as a watering stop for stage coaches on the San Antonio to San Diego trail. But the first real settlement grew up here after the Civil War when a group of ranchers moved in and dug an irrigation system based on the springs.

Irrigated farming is still important; however, farmers soon discovered that sheep and goats could thrive on the sparse vegetation in the surrounding hills. Today, Del Rio claims to be the wool and mohair capital of the world. Other Texas cities, like San Angelo, contest that claim, but there's no doubt that Val Verde County is among the top producers in the state of sheep, lamb, wool, and mohair.

The author wishes to gratefully acknowledge Robert R. Rafferty, author of the Texas Monthly Guidebook to the Texas Coast and Rio Grande Valley, Second Edition *and the* Texas Monthly Guidebook to Texas, Third Edition *(both published by Gulf Publishing Co., Houston) for contributing the* **Del Rio & Acuña** *section of this guidebook.*

An outstanding feature of downtown Del Rio is the number of native limestone buildings. These were constructed by Italian stonemasons who came to build the infant city after the construction of Fort Clark at Brackettville and the stone embankments for the Galveston, Harrisburg and San Antonio Railroad that reached Del Rio in 1882. Some of the Italians also planted vineyards and built a winery that is now called the Val Verde Winery, the oldest winery in Texas.

To the northwest is Amistad Lake, an international reservoir that is located partially in Texas and partially in Mexico. About three miles south, across the Río Grande, is the Mexican city of Acuña with a population of roughly 120,000.

TOURIST SERVICES

DEL RIO CHAMBER OF COMMERCE

1915 Avenue F • Del Rio • 78840 • Behind the Civic Center
775-3551 • W

Among things you can get here are a free city map, a walking
tour brochure, and information on going into Mexico.

AMISTAD TOURS

US 90 West • HCR 3, Box 44 • Del Rio • 78840 • 775-6484
or 800-525-3386

They provide boat tours of Amistad Lake and the Pecos and
Río Grande Rivers on launches. Sights include the Indian pic-
tographs on the canyon walls, the dam, and the high bridges.
Most tours last about four hours. They also offer land tours of Del
Rio and Ciudad Acuña and into Mexico.

HIGH BRIDGE ADVENTURES

Box 816 • Comstock • 78837 • 292-4462

Tours are on a pontoon boat holding six passengers that cruis-
es the Pecos and Río Grande Rivers to see the Indian pictographs
and the highest bridge in Texas. Tours last three to four hours.

MUSEUMS

FIREHOUSE ART GALLERY

120 E. Garfield • 775-0888
Monday–Friday 8:30–5:30 • Saturday 10–4 in November
and December • Free • W (side door)

Traveling art exhibitions in a variety of media are usually rotated about once a month. In May there's the annual juried "Western Art Show and Sale." The building is a 1932 structure that
served as Del Rio's city hall and fire station. The gallery is in the
old City Hall area with the rest of the building occupied by the
gallery's parent organization, the Del Rio Council for the Arts. In
November and December, the gallery becomes a Christmas shop
with art and handcrafted items for sale.

WHITEHEAD MEMORIAL MUSEUM

1308 S. Main at Wallen • 774-7568 ext. 244
Tuesday–Saturday 9–11:30 and 1–4:30
Adults $1, children 50¢ • W

In 1962, the old Perry Mercantile Building, dating from the 1870s and once the largest store between San Antonio and El Paso, was given to the city for a museum by the Whiteheads, a local ranching family. Since that time, the museum has grown to include nine buildings on several landscaped acres. The entrance to the grounds is through the Hacienda. In addition to the small visitor center and gift shop, this building houses the Chapel, which is dedicated to the memory of the Spaniards who brought Christianity to the region. The Perry Store is now an exhibition area for pioneer history. The Hal Patton Office, built in 1905, features both African-American history and the story of the Seminole Scouts (see **SIDE TRIPS** below). A replica of the Jersey Lilly, the saloon/court operated by the famous Judge Roy Bean, is also on the grounds and behind it are the graves of the Judge and his son, Sam. The original Jersey Lilly saloon is located in Langtry, about 60 miles west of Del Rio and was named by Bean after his theater idol, English actress Lillie Langtry. It was in the Jersey Lilly that Bean dispensed his own brand of justice that made him a legend as "the Law West of the Pecos." Other buildings on the grounds include the Log Cabin, which was built by local Boy Scouts in 1924 and contains exhibits about the early settlers; the Barn, which houses exhibits about prehistoric man and the Indians who lived in the area; and the most recent addition, the Cadena Nativity Scene, which depicts Bethlehem on the night of Christ's birth. For this Nativity scene, over 600 figurines and more than 1,200 items were assembled to form this 32-foot long exhibit.

HISTORIC PLACES

A brochure guide to Historic Del Rio is available from the Chamber of Commerce. This includes a walking tour of the downtown Courthouse Square area as well as a map locating the historic buildings in the rest of the city.

COURTHOUSE SQUARE AREA

The oldest building here is the Old Jail, on the northeast corner of the Square, which was built in 1885. Nearby, at 400 Pecan, is the Courthouse, built in 1887, which is listed in the National Register of Historic Places. The old Sacred Heart Church (1892) is at 310 Mills. The original French stained glass windows from this church are now in the new church immediately north.

OTHER AREAS OF THE CITY

There are a number of other historic buildings scattered throughout the city. The ones listed here were all built in the late nineteenth century: Tardy-Borroum Home (1883), 703 Losoya; Brodbent-Hamilton Home (1895), 404 Spring; Chris Qualia Home (1898), 901 S. Main; Tagliabue Home (1881), 609 Pecan; Taylor-Rivers Home (1870), 100 Hudson, built by one of the founders of Del Rio and now the oldest existing house in town; Mason-Foster House (1887), 123 Hudson; and the Val Verde Winery (1883), 139 Hudson (see **OTHER POINTS OF INTEREST**).

OTHER POINTS OF INTEREST

AMISTAD NATIONAL RECREATION AREA

Take US 90 west about 10 miles to the entrances • **775-7491**
Open at all times • **No admission fee** • **W**

The eagle is a symbol of both the United States and Mexico, so it's appropriate that seven-foot-high bronze U.S. and Mexican eagles stand at the border between the two countries in the center of the joint U.S.-Mexican Amistad Dam across the Río Grande. It was at this site that the presidents of the two countries, Richard Nixon and Gustavo Diaz Ordaz, dedicated the dam on September 8, 1969. You can drive into Mexico across the toll-free road atop the six-mile long dam from 10 a.m. to 4 p.m. daily. A visitor center, near the customs station on the dam, is operated daily from 10 a.m. to 6 p.m. during the summer by the National Park Service.

The dam impounds an international lake that reaches 74 miles up the Río Grande, 25 miles up the Devil's River, and 14 miles up the Pecos River with more than 67,000 water surface acres (44,000 acres are in Texas) and 850 miles of shoreline (540 in Texas).

More than a million visitors come to the U.S. recreation area every year. There are facilities for boating and houseboating (rentals available), swimming, waterskiing and other water sports, fishing, limited hunting, nature study, primitive camping, and picnicking. Park facilities are mostly on the east end of the lake; however, the Pecos River Area (44 miles west of Del Rio) has a boat ramp and picnic tables. You can fish on both sides of the international boundary that runs through the lake, and there is no closed season, but a Texas fishing license is required in U.S. waters and a Mexican license in Mexican waters. Check with the park headquarters or the Chamber of Commerce for places where you can get these licenses on the American side. The Chamber can also provide a list of fishing guides. The phenomenal visibility of the water in fall, winter, and spring makes this lake a choice place for scuba shops across the state to bring their students for check-out dives. There are also several commercial campgrounds along the shoreline. On the Mexican side are a swimming beach, picnic facilities, and a marina with launching ramp. However, the president of Mexico has announced "top priority" plans to build a $50 million resort on the lake including a "five-star" resort hotel and a golf course.

In addition to a map/brochure of the area, the National Park Service offers a brochure outlining a self-guided tour of the major attractions in the Pecos River District including the Indian pictographs at the Panther and Parida Caves. For information, contact Superintendent, Amistad National Recreation Area, P.O. Box 420367, Del Rio, Texas, 78842-0367.

BRINKLEY MANSION
512 Qualia Drive • Not open to the public
During the Depression, Dr. John R. Brinkley built this mansion with the profits from his controversial goat gland implants for men that were supposed to restore youthful vigor. To sell his services he built radio station XERF across the border in Acuña. At that time, this station had 500,000 watts of output—which could reach radio sets as far away as Canada—making it one of the most powerful radio stations in the world.

CIUDAD ACUÑA
*Take Garfield Ave. (Spur 239) west three miles to the
International Bridge* • **Area Code 011-52-877**
This city of about 120,000 is named for Manuel Acuña, a romantic poet of the Mexican Revolution. The central plaza, called **Plaza Benjamin Canales** after another revolutionary hero, is worth a visit. On this tree-lined plaza is the *Palacio Municipal* (City Hall). In 1960, Presidents Eisenhower and Lopez Mateo addressed the people from its balcony when they met to conclude the agreement to build Amistad Dam. Most of the tourist shopping is near the bridge, especially along Avenida Hidalgo. The shops here offer a variety of Mexican handicrafts, gifts, souvenirs, and curios. Most shopkeepers speak English and deal in American dollars. As in many tourist shops, there's a lot of junk for sale, but there are also genuine bargains if you know what you're looking for and what it would cost in the States. There are also several restaurants and nightclubs in Acuña that are popular with American visitors. You can drive your car over, but if you do it's suggested you pick up Mexican auto insurance at one of the insurance agencies in Del Rio (see **Driving in Mexico** in the **INTRODUCTION**). If you don't wish to drive, you can park near the bridge and walk across (it's about ¾ mile to the shopping area) or take a taxi or bus. You can also pick up the bus

to Acuña in downtown Del Rio. Del Rio and Ciudad Acuña jointly celebrate Fiesta de Amistad in October each year.

LAUGHLIN AIR FORCE BASE

US 90 six miles east of Del Rio • **298-5201 (Public Affairs)**

An Air Force jet pilot training base, tours are available for groups only. However, you can call, and if there is a tour group scheduled and there's space, you may be able to join it.

VAL VERDE WINERY

100 Qualia Drive • **Monday–Saturday 9–5** • **Free tour**

This is the oldest winery in Texas. Started in 1883 by Frank Qualia, an immigrant from Milan, Italy, it is still operated by the Qualia family more than 100 years later. For years it was the only licensed winery in the state. The tour takes about 20 minutes and covers all the steps in winemaking from growing the grapes to bottling. You will see the vineyard (look for the geese that are used for weeding), storage vats, aging room, and other facilities. Eight different wines are produced here, including the *Lenoir* that was the first wine produced by the winery in the 1880s, and all are usually available for tasting (and sale) during the tour. Diagonally across the street at 100 Hudson is the Taylor-Rivers Home (1870), the oldest existing house in Del Rio, and further down Hudson at 512 is the Brinkley Mansion (see above).

SPORTS AND ACTIVITIES

Fishing

AMISTAD NATIONAL RECREATIONAL AREA

See separate listing.

Golf

SAN FELIPE COUNTRY CLUB GOLF COURSE

US 90 E. at San Felipe Springs Rd. • **775-3953**
Nine-hole course • **Weekdays $10** • **Weekends $15**

Houseboating

LAKE AMISTAD RESORT AND MARINA
US 90 W. at Diablo East Recreation Area • 774-4157
Houseboats are available for rent at this Amistad National Recreation Area concession. Each one accommodates up to ten people and is equipped with bunk beds, stove, oven, refrigerator and ice chest, barbecue grill, cooking and eating utensils, and a shower. You must provide your own bedding, linens, towels, and food. No special boat license is required, but you must take instruction on the safe operation of the boat and its equipment from the concessionaire before setting out. From June 8 to September 2, rates run from about $220 for one night to $1,095 for seven nights.

From September 3 through June 7, rates run from about $135 for one night to $665 for seven nights. There is also a damage deposit required, and you pay for your own gas.

Hunting

Limited free hunting is available at Amistad National Recreational Area (see **OTHER POINTS OF INTEREST** above). A listing of member ranches offering hunting is available from the Chamber of Commerce. The following is an example of one of these.

DOLAN CREEK RANCHES
P.O. Box 420069 • Del Rio • 78842 • 775-3129 or 775-6163
Hunters are picked up at local motels and led on guided hunts for white-tailed deer and wild turkey. A three-day hunting package runs about $1,400. This includes some meals and a good chance of coming out with a buck, two does, and a turkey.

PERFORMING ARTS

PAUL POAG THEATRE
746 S. Main • 774-3277 • Admission varies • W call ahead
A 1940s-era movie theater has been renovated by the Del Rio Council of the Arts and turned into a 726-seat performing arts theater with a proscenium stage. The calendar includes popular musicals, mysteries, and comedies performed by the community theater group, and the community concert and entertainment series that brings in outside talent.

SHOPPING

(To call from Del Rio to Acuña dial 011-52-877 and the number.)

LA RUEDA (THE WHEEL)

215 Hidalgo East • Ciudad Acuña • 2-1260

The wagon wheel that hangs over the shop entrance is old, but inside much of the stock is modern Mexican designer clothes for women, priced from about $50 to $200, and designer jewelry.

LA VILLITA SHOPPING CENTER

2400 Avenue F • Del Rio • Daily

Shops include Dollar Crafts, the 50% Off Store, Eden's Flower Shop, and several restaurants.

LANDO CURIOS

290 Hidalgo • Ciudad Acuña • 2-1269

Mexican crafts, liquor, jewelry, and brass items are just a few of the things you'll find here. Free parking with purchase.

PANCHO'S MARKET

299 Hidalgo East • Ciudad Acuña • 2-0466

If you get weary of shopping this store for leather goods, liquor, jewelry, clothes, etc., you can take a break in Pancho's Lounge in the rear. They also advertise prompt curb service.

PLAZA DEL SOL MALL

2205 Avenue F (US 90) near Garner • Del Rio • 774-3634 • W

Beall's, K-Mart, and J.C. Penney anchor this small mall that includes a three-screen cinema, a cafeteria, and a couple dozen stores and fast food shops.

ROSS EMPORIUM

800 S. Main St. • Del Rio • 774-0962

This turn-of-the-century drugstore has been converted into an old-fashioned soda fountain complete with sodas, sundaes, and coffee drinks including cappucino. A gift shop full of collectibles also offers a surprising array of coffee beans.

SIDE TRIPS

ALAMO VILLAGE MOVIELAND
Take US 90 29 miles east to Brackettville • Take a left on RR 674 and proceed seven miles north • **210-563-2580**
Site of John Wayne's epic film *The Alamo*. This western version of the San Antonio original still stands, battered and bruised, as it was at the end of the filming when the battle was over. There is also an Old West town which is used quite frequently as a set for movies and commercials. Lunch, souvenirs, and a wide variety of entertainment is always on hand as is owner Happy Shahan and his longhorn herd.

SEMINOLE CANYON STATE HISTORICAL PARK
See **LANGTRY.**

ANNUAL EVENTS

May

GEORGE PAUL MEMORIAL BULL RIDING COMPETITION
Val Verde County Fairgrounds • 2001 N. Main
775-3551 (Chamber) • First weekend for the competition with other events the preceding week • $8–$15 • W
Top-ranked bullriders are matched against top-ranked bulls in a competition that offers one of the biggest bullriding purses in the world.

October

FIESTA DE AMISTAD
Downtown Del Rio • 775-3551 (Chamber)
Week nearest October 24th • Most events are free
This bi-national fiesta commemorates the visit of Presidents Eisenhower and Lopez Mateo to Del Rio and Ciudad Acuña on October 24, 1960. A highlight of the fiesta is the International Parade From Del Rio to Ciudad Acuña, reportedly the only parade in the world that starts in one country and ends in another. Other activities during the week include a Battle of the Bands, the Miss Del Rio and *Senorita Amistad* pageants to choose the American and Mexican ladies who will reign over the Fiesta, the *Abrazo* ("friend-ship embrace") Ceremony, an open house and air show at Laugh-

lin Air Force Base, an arts and crafts show, a bicycle race and a 10K International Run. The grand finale is a PRCA Pro Rodeo.

RESTAURANTS

($ = Under $7.50, $$ = Under $15, $$$ = $15+ plus tax & tip)

ASADERO LA POSTA
348 Allende • Ciudad Acuña • 2-2327
Daily • Breakfast, lunch, and dinner • $–$$ • MC V
Roasted and grilled steaks, beef ribs, and other meats are the house specialty in this cozy, brick-walled restaurant. A special *fajita* plate with onions, *quesadilla,* and *guacamole* goes for about $5. Organ music on Friday and Saturday nights. Bar.

CRIPPLE CREEK SALOON
US 90 about one mile west of the "Y" with US 277/377
775-0153 • Monday–Saturday • Dinner • $$ • MC V • W
Outside the log cabin style building there's a small animal farm to entertain the kids. Inside, while owner George Aubrey plays barrel house piano and occasionally leads sing-alongs, the kitchen dishes up entrées that include a variety of mesquite-grilled steaks, swordfish steaks, and chicken, plus prime rib, lobster, shrimp, king crab, catfish, frog legs, and quail. Bar.

CROSBY'S
195 Hidalgo • Ciudad Acuña • 2-2020
Daily • Breakfast, lunch, and dinner • $$ • MC V • W
It started back in the 1930s and, even though the owners have changed, it's still going strong and holding on to its reputation of being one of the best places to eat in Acuña. Inside the etched glass entrance, old photos from the Mexican Revolution and masks from Oaxaca decorate the walls. The menu includes both continental and Mexican entrées ranging from *cabrito* and *fajitas* to seafood, quail, and a house specialty: Portuguese Chicken. Bar and piano bar.

LANDO'S RESTAURANT AND BAR
270 Hidalgo • Ciudad Acuña • 7-1205
Daily • Lunch and dinner • Reservations recommended on weekends • $$ • MC V • W • Secure parking
The walls are covered with elegant wallpaper, the ceiling is mirrored, and there's a chandelier to round out the plush atmosphere. The menu features both Mexican and Continental entrées. Disco Thursday through Saturday nights. Bar.

LA PALAPA DE LANDO'S

1190 S. Guerrero Blvd. • **Ciudad Acuña** • **2-3982**
Daily • **Lunch and dinner** • **$** • **MC V** • **W** • **Secure parking**

While the downtown Lando's is elegant and cozy, this walled restaurant is bright and wide open. Dining on the patio is a big attraction. The menu offers a variety of Mexican dishes, including *tampiqueña* and broiled steaks. A little out of the way, it's still not hard to get to. Two blocks past the bridge, turn left on Iturbide, go nine blocks to Guerrero, and turn left again—or take a taxi. Bar.

MEMO'S

804 E. Losoya • **Del Rio** • **775-8104**
Monday–Saturday lunch and dinner • **Sunday dinner only**
Reservations suggested for Tuesday night jam sessions
$–$$ • **Cr** • **W**

One of the people in the many celebrity photos that line the walls of this Mexican restaurant is always Moises (Blondie) Calderon. Blondie (whose hair is now black but was blonde when he was young) runs the family restaurant when he's in town. He's also the bandleader and piano player for country & western singer Ray Price, which makes him a celebrity in his own right. When he's not on the road, Blondie and his local band play and have jam sessions on Tuesday nights. The food? Well, the family has been serving up Tex-Mex and American dishes since 1936, so it must be pleasing the customers. The menu runs from *chalupas*, *tacos*, *enchiladas*, and *fajitas* to T-bone and chicken-fried steaks. The dining room overlooks the San Felipe Creek. Bar.

ACCOMMODATIONS

($ = Under $40, $$ = $40–$75, $$$ = $75–$100, $$$$ = Over $100)
Room Tax 13%

AMISTAD LODGE

US 90 W. near Amistad Lake, 1/2 mile east of Diablo East Marina • **HCR 3, Box 29** • **Del Rio 78840** • **775-8591** • **$** • **W**

Overlooking the lake, some of the 40 rooms include kitchenettes. Children under 12 stay free in room with parents. Cable TV. Room phones (local calls free). Restaurant, room service, lounge open seven nights. Outdoor pool. Free airport transportation. Boat parking. Fish cleaning house. Texas and Mexican fishing licenses for sale. Pets OK.

BEST WESTERN INN OF DEL RIO

810 Avenue F (US 90 W.) • **775-7511 or 800-528-1234** • **$$** • **W**
This two-story Best Western has 62 rooms including six non-smoking. Cable TV with HBO. Room phones (local calls free). Outdoor pool and whirlpool. Free airport transportation. Free coffee in lobby, free cocktail hour, and free full breakfast. Self-service laundry and same-day dry cleaning. Boat parking. Pets OK (charge of $3/day). Senior discount.

HOTEL SAN ANTONIO

Hidalgo St. • **Ciudad Acuña** • **011 528 77 2 5535 or 2 5108 $-$$**
With a total of 65 units in two wings, the Hotel San Antonio is located on the right-hand side of the fourth block of Hidalgo Street. Amenities include a hotel restaurant, the Amadeus Video Bar, and private parking behind the hotel.

LA QUINTA INN

2005 Avenue F (US 90 W.) • **775-7591 or 800-621-2915 $-$$** • **W+**
The two-story inn has 101 units that include one suite ($$$$) and 11 non-smoking rooms. Children under 18 stay free in the same room with their parents. Cable TV featuring the Movie Channel and free local phones. Restaurant, room service, and lounge open Monday–Saturday. Outdoor pool. Free airport transportation. Free coffee in lobby in morning. Self-service laundry and same-day dry cleaning. Boat parking. No pets. Senior discount.

LAGUNA DIABLO RESORT

Sanders Point Rd. on Devil's River Arm of Lake Amistad 774-2422 • **$$-$$$** • **W**
The ten units in this resort consist of six two-bedroom and four one-bedroom apartments with full kitchen, bath, and living and dining area. Two-night minimum for reservations. Call or write for directions to this hideaway on the lake. No pets.

RAMADA INN

2101 Avenue F (US 90 W.) • **775-1511 or 800-272-6232 $$-$$$$** • **W**
A two-story Ramada with 127 units including one suite with jacuzzi ($$$$) and 27 non-smoking rooms. Children under 18 stay free in room with parents. Cable TV with HBO and VCR rentals. Room phones (local calls free). Restaurant, room service, lounge open seven nights with occasional entertainment on weekends.

Outdoor heated pool, whirlpool, and exercise room. Free transportation to airport and bridge. Self-service laundry and same-day dry cleaning. Boat parking. Pets OK (pet deposit required). Package plans available, senior discount, and weekend rates.

MIDLAND

MIDLAND COUNTY SEAT ★ 89,443 ★ (915)

You'll find Midland halfway between Fort Worth and El Paso. Midway was its chosen name, but the postal service turned down the request: To this day Midway is still in Madison County, not far from North Zulch. For almost half a century after its founding in 1881, Midland prospered as a regional shipping center for area ranchers. Then Santa Rita No. 1 blew in at 6:00 a.m. on May 27, 1923, and the immense petroleum reserves known as the Permian Basin were discovered. Though Midland wasn't the site of much drilling initially, it became the headquarters for many of the locally owned companies that drilled or serviced the petroleum industry as well as regional headquarters for the majors. From the town's perspective, oil brought a new way of life. This region, often referred to as the Permian Basin, developed into America's largest inland petrochemical complex, and royalties from state leases bankrolled the Permanent University Fund, i.e., the University of Texas and Texas A&M University systems. For a town of less than 100,000, Midland has the trappings of a much larger city, including its own symphony, a professional baseball team, Midland College, and numerous museums and attractions.

TOURIST SERVICES

See MIDLAND map on page 246.

MIDLAND INTERNATIONAL AIRPORT
Information Booth • 560-2200

This is a good first stop after you debark and before your luggage hits the carousel. While at the airport, have a look at the Pliska Aircraft. It's hanging from the ceiling of the main terminal now but was one of the first flying machines in the Lone Star State over 90 years ago.

MIDLAND CONVENTION AND VISITORS BUREAU

109 N. Main • 683-1910 or 800-624-6435 • W

Midland emphasizes its convenient access to an immense region of West Texas and New Mexico. The Midland CVB offers plenty of advice and information on local attractions as well as destinations like the Big Bend, the Davis Mountains, and Carlsbad Caverns.

MUSEUMS

AMERICAN AIRPOWER HERITAGE MUSEUM

Midland Air Field • 563-1000
Monday–Saturday 9–5 • Sunday and holidays 12–5
Adults $4, seniors and teens $3, children $2 • W+

Specializing in World War II aircraft, the Ghost Squadron boasts war birds from the U.S. Army Air Force, the Royal Air Force, the Imperial Japanese Navy, and the Luftwaffe. The planes are rotated quarterly and fly to nearly 100 different squadrons and wings internationally. Almost all gather in Midland each October for the CAF AIRSHO (see **ANNUAL EVENTS**). Many of the planes are rare or unique including "FIFI," the last of the great B-29 Superfortresses. Also displayed are uniforms, weapons, armament, and other equipment. The museum also has a research library and archives featuring oral histories, photographs, and films.

FREDDA TURNER DURHAM CHILDREN'S MUSEUM

1705 W. Missouri • 683-2882
Tuesday–Saturday 10–5 • Sunday 2–5 • Free • W

What's more interesting here—the eleven-foot armadillo or the 80-foot photographic mural of the Big Bend? A good interactive exhibit for teaching kids (and adults) about the world around them is *Under Starry Skies*. Designed for hands-on contact, it explores the myths and history of Midland, West Texas, and the Southwest and is presented in conjunction with a second component at the Museum of the Southwest.

MIDLAND COUNTY HISTORICAL MUSEUM

310 W. Missouri Ave. • 688-8991 • Monday–Thursday
11:30–4:30 • Saturday 9–12 and 1–4 • Free • W

From prehistoric Midland Man to modern times, the history of Midland and Midland County is on display in the basement of the Midland County Library in hundreds of photographs, artifacts, and files.

MUSEUM OF THE SOUTHWEST

1705 W. Missouri • 683-2882
Tuesday–Saturday 10–5 • Sunday 2–5 • Free • W
   An entire city block, this 1934 mansion contains both permanent and rotating collections of Southwestern art and archaeologic artifacts as well as the Hogan collection, a permanent exhibit of works by the founding members of the Taos Society of Artists. Both the Fredda Turner Durham Children's Museum and the Marian Blakemore Planetarium are on the premises.

PERMIAN BASIN PETROLEUM MUSEUM

1500 Interstate 20 West • 683-4403 • Monday–Saturday 9–5
Sunday 2–5 • Adults $3, children $1.50 • W
   This museum features the making of Midland—OIL. Special effects enable visitors to feel the force of bringing a well in, to walk under an ancient sea, and to stroll through Boomtown. From the early days of wildcatting to modern technology, explanations, diagrams, and exhibits convey the essence of the oil patch, including the world's largest collection of antique oil field equipment.

OTHER POINTS OF INTEREST

MARIAN BLAKEMORE PLANETARIUM

1705 W. Missouri • 683-2882
Public shows Tuesdays 7:30 p.m. and Sundays 2 and 3:30 p.m.
Adults $2, children $1 • W+
   An assortment of materials from NASA are displayed, but everyone heads straight to the one-third scale replica of the Apollo capsule. In addition to the public shows offered each week, groups, clubs, and organizations can call in advance to schedule private ones. Monthly stargazing is also offered next door at Haley Park. Call for the most up-to-date schedule.

NITA STEWART HALEY LIBRARY

1805 W. Indiana Avenue • 682-5785
Monday–Friday • 9–5 • Free • W
   Though many visitors come to learn more about cattlemen and their industry, one of the most extensive collections on the Lincoln County War featuring William Bonney aka Billy the Kid is housed in this library. The entire collection, including the Lincoln County portion, exceeds 16,000 items and includes materials on the exploration of the western United States, the development of ranching, railroads, mining, and the oil patch.

SPORTS AND ACTIVITIES

Athletic Clubs

THE MIDLANDER
225 Corporate Drive • 682-0813
Daily • $5 guest fee for nonmembers
The Midlander offers a full fitness program for visitors. Facilities include four indoor lighted tennis courts and eight outdoor ones, eight racquetball courts, an indoor Olympic-size lap pool, a jogging track around the pool, a sand volleyball pit, free weights, nautilus, and daily aerobic classes. Other features include a nursery, saunas, a steam room, a snack bar, and a restaurant that serves lunch during the week.

Baseball

MIDLAND ANGELS
3600 N. Fairgrounds Rd. • 683-4251
Call for schedule and ticket information
A member of the California Angels organization, the Angels play in the Texas League against Western Division foes El Paso, San Antonio, and Wichita as well as interdivision rivals from Jackson, Shreveport, Arkansas, and Tulsa. The guys playing today just might turn out to be baseball legends like Fernando Valenzuela, Darryl Strawberry, and Bert Blyleven—all of whom played locally.

Golf

HOGAN PARK GOLF COURSE
3600 N. Fairgrounds Rd. • 685-7360
Weekdays: $10 • Weekends: $12

COLLEGES AND UNIVERSITIES

MIDLAND COLLEGE
3600 N. Garfield • 685-4500 • W+ but not all areas
Founded in 1969, Midland College offers a two-year degree plan and has more than 4,000 students enrolled. Majors are available in numerous disciplines ranging from accounting to welding technology on the 100-acre campus. A member of the NJCAA, the college fields a variety of men's and women's teams.

PERFORMING ARTS

CENTENNIAL PLAZA AND AMPHITHEATER
105 N. Main • 683-3381
With its cascading water fountain and water wall, Centennial Plaza offers welcome and wet relief from the West Texas sun. A 300-seat amphitheater hosts a variety of different performances, and just a stroll away is a bronze plaque commemorating the rescue of Jessica McClure from an abandoned water well in October 1987.

MIDLAND/ODESSA SYMPHONY & CHORALE
3100 LaForce Blvd. • 563-0921 • Call for schedule and ticketing
The largest orchestra in West Texas, the Symphony is home of the Thouvenel String Quartet and the Lone Star Brass Quintet.

SIDE TRIPS

BIG SPRING, TEXAS
40 miles east on Interstate 20 • **263-7641 (Chamber)**
An important watering hole throughout the centuries for Comanches, Forty-Niners, and the railroad, the location of the town's namesake big spring is now a 479-acre city park. Big Spring also boasts 370-acre Big Spring State Park (915-263-4931). Take the Business 20 exit eastbound from I-20 and turn right on F.M. 700 For plenty of picnic sites, a prairie dog town, and nature walks on Scenic Mountain, site of century old rock carvings.

ANNUAL EVENTS

October

CONFEDERATE AIR FORCE AIRSHO
Midland International Airport • 563-1000
Admission • Parking fee • W+
Step back in time to the Battle of Britain or Pearl Harbor on December 7, 1941, as hundreds of vintage aircraft from the Ghost Squadron of the Confederate Air Force relive some of history's greatest moments. More than 100 planes comprise the CAF collection of flyable World War II planes, and many of them are on hand for this two-day event including the world's only remaining flyable Boeing B-29 Superfortress and replicas of Japanese fighters.

Flying demonstrations get underway at noon, but gates are open from 7:30 a.m. till 5:00 p.m.

RESTAURANTS

($ = Under $7.50, $$ = Under $15, $$$ = $15+ plus tax & tip)

American

WALL STREET BAR AND GRILL
115 W. Wall St. • 684-8686 • Mon.–Sat. lunch and dinner Sunday brunch only • Cr • W
For many Midlanders and certainly the downtown crowd, Wall Street is as good as Midland gets. Originally a saddle shop (1916), it still boasts the original pressed tin ceiling and an 1867 Brunswick bar. On the high tech side, diehard tape watchers can peruse up-to-the minute quotes from the floor of the New York Stock Exchange above the entrance. The house salad is mandatory—by itself, at lunch with the soup du jour, or with an entrée selection. The filet and charbroiled shrimp ($$) marries two Wall Street specialties, or try the salmon *Mexicana*. First grilled, it's served topped with *pico de gallo*. Charbroiled, Jamaican, and a honey dijon chicken are menu mainstays. If your timing is right and your shoes are scuffed, stop in next door at the **Lone Star Barber Shop** for a shine. Bar.

Italian

LUIGI'S
111 N. Big Spring • 683-6363
Mon.–Sat. lunch and dinner • Sunday dinner only • Cr • W
Good *trattoria* cooking in the middle of West Texas? Stranger things have happened. The *antipasto* salad is a good start. The large is a meal in itself; the small makes for good beginnings. Entrée suggestions? The eggplant *parmigiana*. It never misses. Families devour pizza (available in whole or half sizes), sandwiches, or items off the children's menu. Everything is available to go. Moderately priced wine list. Bar.

VENEZIA

20 Plaza Center • Intersection of Wadley & Garfield
687-0900 • Monday–Friday lunch and dinner
Saturday dinner only • Closed Sunday • Cr • W
Definitely worth the time spent to find its out-of-the-way location. Off by itself in the southeast corner of a neighborhood shopping center (right behind El Patio), the upscale ambience is deceptive. Prices are moderate, service is excellent, and the food is better. The pepper steak is the best in town. Several small details make dining at Venezia complete. Get the *bruschetta* (garlic bread with olive oil), indulge in the cheese soup, and end the meal with the rum cake. Beer and a good wine list.

Mexican

ABUELO'S

4610 N. Garfield • 685-3335
Daily • Lunch and dinner • $–$$ • Cr • W
Most of the entrées at Abuelo's were sampled in Mexico and brought back to Midland. *Alambre de camaron* features bacon-wrapped jumbo shrimp, accented with a slice of *jalapeño*, charbroiled, and served with a hint of Monterrey Jack cheese. Need a Mexican fix? Abuelo's Grande Combination comes with a beef *enchilada*, a cheese *enchilada*, a beef *chile relleno*, a *taco*, a *tamale*, a small side of *guacamole*. Pass on the rice and choose the *papas con chile*. Bar.

LA BODEGA

2700 N. Big Spring • 684-5594
Sunday–Thursday lunch and dinner • Cr • W
Top shelf *margaritas*. Start with an order of stuffed *jalapeño*s or the *nachos*. For dinner try the *chile relleno*s, the chicken *fajitas*, and Midland's best *jalapeño* burger. Bar.

ACCOMMODATIONS

($ = Under $40, $$ = $40–$75, $$$ = $75–$100, $$$$ = Over $100)
Room Tax 13%

LA QUINTA

4130 W. Wall • 697-9900 or 800-531-5900 • $$ • W
This two-story La Quinta located about six miles from the Midland airport has 146 units including non-smoking rooms with cable TV (Showtime), pay-per-view movies, and room phones (free local

calls). Amenities include a complimentary continental breakfast from 6:30 to 10 a.m., complimentary coffee in the lobby, a nearby Kettle restaurant, outdoor unheated pool open from May to September, and free parking. Small pets, 25 pounds or less, are welcome too. AAA, AARP, government, and military rates available.

LEXINGTON HOTEL SUITES
1003 S. Midkiff • 687-3155 or 800-927-8483 • $$
This three-story, all-suite property has 211 units including studio and one-bedroom suites with non-smoking ones available. Cable TV (Showtime), pay-per-view movies, room phones (charge for local calls), a full-sized refrigerator, and a complete kitchen are included. Amenities include complimentary continental breakfast, outdoor heated pool, complimentary shuttle to the Midland Airport, and free parking. Smaller pets are welcome, but the hotel requires a refundable $100 deposit. AAA and AARP rates are available, and better rates are offered on weekends.

MIDLAND HILTON
117 W. Wall at Loraine • 800-445-8667 or 683-6131 • $$$–$$$$
This 22-story Hilton is located right in the center of downtown Midland and has 249 units including suites and non-smoking rooms. Each room comes with pay-per-view movies and two room phones (charge for local calls). Amenities include complimentary continental breakfast for weekend guests with the Bounce Back package, two hotel restaurants—the Santa Fe Cafe and the Santa Fe Grill, an outdoor pool, jacuzzi, fitness center, flower shop, gift shop, valet laundry service, complimentary 24-hour shuttle to the Midland Airport, valet, and free parking. No pets. Government rates available to federal and state employees only.

ODESSA

ECTOR COUNTY SEAT ★ 89,699 ★ (915)

Founded as a railroad stop for the Texas & Pacific Railroad (1881), the similarity of the Odessa area to the Russian steppes led to the city's being named for a port city on the Black Sea. It wasn't until oil was struck in Ector County (1926) that Odessa took off.

Production spread to the farthest reaches of the Permian Basin and made this area the world's largest inland petrochemical complex. Homage to this industry and that age is found throughout Odessa, for instance, Permian Mall, Permian Playhouse, Permian High School (home of the perennially playoff-bound Permian Panthers), and the Permian Basin Oil Show, held every other year.

TOURIST SERVICES

ODESSA CHAMBER OF COMMERCE

P.O. Box 3626 • Odessa • 79760 • 332-8189 or 800-583-6400

Visitor packets, moving packets, economic developments packets, and plenty of other information is available at the second floor office of the Odessa Chamber, located at 700 N. Grant.

MUSEUMS

PRESIDENTIAL MUSEUM

622 N. Lee (7th and Lee) • 332-7123
Tuesday–Saturday 10–5 • Free (donations accepted) • W+

Documents, campaign memorabilia, photographs, and original cartoons covering the Presidency from Washington to Clinton are on display at the only museum in the United States that focuses on the Chief Executive. In addition, other permanent exhibits include the Dishong Collection of First Lady Dolls which documents colorful designs seen at inaugural balls through the centuries.

WHITE-POOL HOUSE

112 E. Murphy • 333-4072
Hours vary • Call for schedule and/or appointment
Free (donations accepted) • W downstairs only

Lured to Odessa by Texas & Pacific ads promoting cheap dirt and a bright future, the Charles White family relocated from Indiana to Ector County and acquired this tract in 1887. The house, Odessa's oldest structure, was up within a year, and the Whites stayed through 1906. Acquired by Oso Pool in 1923, it stayed in the Pool Family until 1978 when it was donated to the county.

OTHER POINTS OF INTEREST

ART INSTITUTE FOR THE PERMIAN BASIN
4909 E. University • 368-7222 • Tuesday–Saturday 10–5
Sunday 2–5 • Donations accepted • W+

Grand Striptease by Giacomo Manzu stands in front of the Art Institute, a facility that emphasizes visual arts and integrates other art forms such as music with imaginative exhibits. Each exhibition is presented for about a month, and ranges from sculpture, painting, or photography to quilting and juried shows. Lectures, workshops, videos, and other activities are offered in conjunction.

WORLD'S LARGEST JACKRABBIT
Corner of Sam Houston and 8th

From the same mutant gene pool as Paisano Pete in Fort Stockton (the world's largest roadrunner), this bunny stands eight feet tall and doesn't flinch at oncoming pickup trucks.

SPORTS AND ACTIVITIES

Amusement Parks

WATER WONDERLAND ENTERTAINMENT COMPLEX
11013 E. Business Loop 20 • 563-2200
Open early May to Labor Day

Over twenty acres of water slides, wading pools, tubing, and other activities. A 36-hole miniature golf course and a driving range adjoin the park (separate fee). Concession stands serve drinks and snacks, and a cafeteria-style restaurant serves lunch.

COLLEGES AND UNIVERSITIES

ODESSA COLLEGE
201 W. University • 335-6400 • W+ but not all areas

In addition to highly competitive athletic squads, Odessa College is best known as the home of the Globe of the Great Southwest Theater (see **PERFORMING ARTS** below). OC was founded in 1946 and has an enrollment of about 5,000. Students, visitors, and locals often frequent the many cultural, athletic, and educational events on the 87-acre campus.

UNIVERSITY OF TEXAS OF THE PERMIAN BASIN

4901 E. University • 367-2011 • W+ but not all areas

One of the youngest components of the immense University of Texas system was authorized by the Texas Legislature in 1969 as a two-year upper division and graduate school. Home of the Center For Energy and Economic Development, UTPB recently expanded to a four-year university (1991). UT Permian Basin has an enrollment of more than 2,300 students and offers bachelors and masters degrees in the arts, business administration, and science.

PERFORMING ARTS

ECTOR COUNTY COLISEUM

42nd and Andrews Highway • 366-3541

If there's going to be a crowd—rock & roll, country & western bands, *tejano*, or large shows—chances are it's at the coliseum.

GLOBE OF THE GREAT SOUTHWEST THEATRE

Odessa College • 2308 Shakespeare Rd. • 332-1586 • W+

A replica of the London original, the octagonal Globe of the Great Southwest seats 410 and hosts the annual Shakespeare Festival, numerous other theatre productions, a Renaissance Madrigal Feast, and live country & western revues courtesy of the Odessa Brand New Opree. Tours are available but please call in advance.

MIDLAND/ODESSA SYMPHONY & CHORALE

3100 LaForce Blvd. • 563-0921 • Call for schedule and ticketing

The largest orchestra in West Texas is based out of both of the Permian Basin's leading communities. Regular performances by the Symphony and Chorale, the Thouvenel String Quartet and the Lone Star Brass Quintet are scheduled.

PERMIAN PLAYHOUSE

310 W. 42nd St. • 362-2329 • Admission varies • W

For over 40 years, the playhouse has been the stage for dance, drama, music, and mysteries. Productions by children and young adults are also featured. Located near the Ector County Coliseum.

SHOPPING

BRASS LAMP

701 N. Grant • 332-9875 • Monday–Saturday 9 a.m. to 6 p.m.

A 35,000-square-foot gallery full of antiques, objets d'art, and fine art. Because so much is bought and sold, there is a constantly changing inventory of original art, limited edition prints, bronzes, furniture, and furnishings. Vintage autos including an original Ford (1903), an Overland, a Saxon, and a Flanders are showcased in a museum setting (fee).

PERMIAN MALL

4101 E. 42nd St. • 367-6048
Monday–Saturday 10–9 • Sunday 1–6 • W+

With Sears, Dillard's, J.C. Penney, and Mervyn's, this mall has more than 80 different stores in addition to a four-screen cinema.

SIDE TRIPS

MONAHANS SANDHILLS STATE PARK

Interstate 20 about 20 miles west of Odessa at exit 86
943-2092 • Daily 8–10 p.m. (office closes at 5 p.m.)
$3 per vehicle • W+ but not all areas

An enormous dune field more than 200 miles wide stretches from southeast New Mexico into West Texas. Over 3,000 acres of it form this state park right off the Interstate. Where did it come from? New Mexico. During the dry spell that followed the last Ice Age, winds blew portions of the dune field into Texas. Learn more at the interpretive center. Other activities at the park include wildlife viewing and sandsurfing. Boards and disks can be rented. For overnight excursions, showers, restrooms, and trailer sites with hookups are available.

ANNUAL EVENTS

April

ODESSA SHAKESPEARE FESTIVAL
Globe of the Great Southwest Theater • Odessa College
Campus • 332-1586 • The latter portion of the month
Admission • W call ahead
   Shakespearean productions have been showcased at this near-perfect replica of the site of the Bard's original performances. Call the Globe of the Great Southwest for information on schedule and ticket information.

May

RENAISSANCE FAIR
Globe of the Great Southwest Theater • Odessa College
Campus • 332-1586 • First week of the month
Admission • W call ahead
   No better place for a Renaissance Fair. The Globe of the Great Southwest Theater, its Great Hall, and all the furnishings are as much a part of this Renaissance Fair as the participants.

October

CONFEDERATE AIR FORCE AIR SHOW
Midland International Airport • 563-1000 • Admission • W+
   See separate listing under **MIDLAND**.

RESTAURANTS

($ = Under $7.50, $$ = Under $15, $$$ = $15+ plus tax & tip)

BARN DOOR
2140 N. Grant • 337-4142
Monday–Saturday • Lunch and dinner • $–$$$ • AE MC V
   This local favorite sits in the old Pecos City Depot, purchased from the Panhandle and Santa Fe Railroad when the station closed in 1972. Decorated with turn-of-the-century antiques and artifacts, the centerpiece is a 20-foot mahogany, maple, and cher-

rywood bar. Ribeyes, sirloins, tenderloins, and T-Bones are grilled over charcoal, and the prime rib is served in seven-ounce, ten-ounce, and 15-ounce cuts. Other menu items include seafood, poultry, and Mexican food. Bar.

DOS AMIGOS
47th and Golder • 368-7556
Tuesday–Saturday • Lunch and dinner • $ • AE MC V • W
Located right across from the Ector County Coliseum, Dos Amigos draws a crowd of regulars because of the good food, great setting, and the Sunday bullriding. Green chicken *enchiladas*, the *fajita* plate, and nightly specials make this a popular dinner spot. The Tuesday night special is a 10-ounce ribeye served with a baked potato and salad. Cook it yourself over a bed of mesquite coals. Thursday night is seafood—loads of oysters, shrimp, lobster, or catfish at inexpensive prices. The big draw from March to November is the bullriding competition, held every other Sunday. For more than a decade, amateurs and professional cowboys have vied for honors including a $5,000 added purse at the season finale Stan Ham Memorial Bull Ride and Bullfight. Beer and wine.

TEJAS TACOS AND BURGERS
1407 N. Grant • 335-0166 • Monday–Friday lunch
Closed Saturday and Sunday • $ • W
Great prices, good food, and they're happy to accommodate special requests like low-fat or oil-free cooking. Don't plan on dinner and don't bring a lot of money. Tejas is only open for lunch on weekdays, and prices are inexpensive. Where else can you find a *fajita* plate—chicken, beef, or combination—for less than five bucks? Mexican food, the burgers, and the grilled chicken sandwich all passed muster. Beer and wine.

ACCOMMODATIONS

($ = Under $40, $$ = $40–$75, $$$ = $75–$100, $$$$ = Over $100)
Room Tax 13%

LA QUINTA INN
5001 E. Business Highway 20 • 333-2820 or 800-531-5900 • $$
This two-story inn located near the Globe of the Great Southwest has 122 smoking and non-smoking rooms with cable TV (Showtime), pay-per-view movies, and room phones (free local calls). Amenities include complimentary continental breakfast

from 6:30 to 10 a.m., free coffee in the lobby, an adjacent Denny's and nearby Steak and Ale restaurant, an unheated outdoor pool open from April 15 to September 15, courtesy car from the Midland Airport, and free parking. Pets under 25 pounds welcome. AAA, AARP, government and military rates available.

ODESSA HILTON

5200 University at Loop 338 • 368-5885 or 800-445-8667 • $$–$$$

This eight-story hotel is close to UTPB and the Permian Basin Petroleum Museum and has 194 units, including three suites and non-smoking rooms, featuring cable TV (HBO & Showtime) and room phones (charge for local calls). Amenities include complimentary continental breakfast on weekends with the Bounce Back package, Legends restaurant on-site, Spirits bar and lounge, an outdoor pool and jacuzzi, a jogging track two blocks from the property, gift shop, same-day valet laundry service, complimentary van service to and from the Midland Airport from 6 a.m. till 11 p.m., guest privileges at Neal's Fitness Center one mile west of the hotel, and free parking. Small pets OK. A variety of different rates are offered based upon availability.

OZONA

CROCKETT COUNTY SEAT   ★   3,500   ★   (915)

Billing itself as "The Biggest Little Town in the World," Ozona exudes a charm that comes from its historic past and fortunate circumstances. Ozona is one of the few towns in Texas that has an entire county to itself, but it wasn't always a loner. Crockett County was formed in 1875, and a spirited race for the county seat pitted Ozona versus Emerald. Ozona was declared the winner in 1891. Emerald's citizens and merchants packed up and relocated to Ozona. As the older of the two communities, Emerald's legacy was welcome, and today Emerald House, Crockett County's oldest home, stands in Ozona's Memorial Fair Park east of town. Sheep and cattle ruled until oil and gas were discovered. Take a moment to drive Ozona's genteel boulevard, tree-lined and half a mile long, with its shady boughs and stately homes. For more information on the biggest little town in the Lone Star State, contact the **Ozona Chamber of Commerce (915-392-3737).**

OTHER POINTS OF INTEREST

DAVID CROCKETT MONUMENT
Town Square
Of all the defenders of the Alamo, none were more numerous than those from the Volunteer State and none more conspicuous than former U.S. Congressman David Crockett, namesake of Crockett County.

SIDE TRIPS

FORT LANCASTER
Take I-10 30 miles west to exit 343 • *Follow US 290 8 miles east* • **Wednesday–Sunday 8–5** • **Free** • **W**
Fort Lancaster was garrisoned by companies of the 1st Infantry in 1855. Its purpose was to protect the Government Road from San Antonio to El Paso linking Forts Clark, Hudson, Lancaster, and Stockton. It quickly became an impressive installation with 25 permanent buildings and a complement of 72 men and four officers. With the onset of the Civil War, however, orders were issued to abandon the post. It was never regarrisoned. Visitors can view exhibits covering the post's archaeology and history, walk the short self-guided trail around the ruins, and even picnic at the old fort.

ACCOMMODATIONS

($ = Under $40, $$ = $40–$75, $$$ = $75–$100, $$$$ = Over $100)

CIRCLE BAR 76 MOTEL
Interstate 10 at Exit 372 (Taylor Box Rd.) • **392-2637** • **$$**
The Circle Bar 76 complex is a world unto itself. Situated six miles east of Ozona out in the middle of nowhere stands the motel, an RV park, a restaurant open round the clock, a convenience store, a gas station, and garage with mechanic. All rooms in the two-story motel are smoking units and come with cable TV (HBO) and phones (free local calls to Ozona). In addition to the solitary location, most visitors remember the indoor garden area which the rooms surround. Complete with its own pool, jacuzzi, and sauna, it's a pleasant change from most motels and a big surprise to most guests. Other pluses include complimentary coffee in the lobby, laundry facilities, and free parking. No pets. AAA, AARP, corporate, and military rates are available.

SAN ANGELO

TOM GREEN COUNTY SEAT ★ 84,474 ★ (915)

If San Antonio's Riverwalk is getting a bit too crowded for your tastes, head to San Angelo. Slowly and surely, this former frontier fort has become one of the state's most livable cities as well as a genuine tourist destination full of historical landmarks, beautiful botanical gardens, one-of-a-kind shops, and a landscaped, multi-use, four-mile River Walk.

The establishment of Fort Concho (1867) led to the development of modern San Angelo. This post, south of the confluence of the North and Main Concho rivers, gave rise to Santa Angela on the river's north bank. By the late 1880s, Santa Angela had become San Angelo, the Comanches were no longer a menace, and the railroad had arrived. Uncle Sam abandoned Fort Concho, but the city of 2,500 had developed strong roots in the Concho Valley as an agricultural hub and commercial center. Plenty of cattle graze on area ranches, but wool and mohair is big business. The weekly Producer's Livestock Auction is America's largest sheep auction and the second biggest cattle market in Texas (after Amarillo). Local craftsmen cater to these trades by producing some of the best known saddles, boots, and accessories in the state. Others work with the Concho Pearl. Produced by freshwater mussels in the streams and lakes that surround San Angelo, this pink or purple pearl has been prized for centuries. Like San Angelo, it's a rare find.

TOURIST SERVICES

SAN ANGELO CONVENTION & VISITORS BUREAU

500 Rio Concho Drive • 76903 • 653-1206 or 800-375-1206
Monday–Friday 8:30–5

The Visitors Bureau has put together several informative brochures to the San Angelo area that make a stop or a call worth the extra effort. Pick up the *Visitors Guide,* which describes the city itself, and the *Historical Walking Tour of Downtown San Angelo,* which details the oldest portion of town (not including Fort Concho).

SAN ANGELO

MUSEUMS

CHILDREN'S ART MUSEUM

36 Twohig on the first floor of the Cactus Hotel • 659-4391
Tuesday–Friday 1–6 • Saturday 10–5 • Sunday 1–5
Admission $2 • Gift shop • W+

The newest museum in San Angelo is actually an arm of the well-established **Museum of Fine Arts** (see below). Housed in the historic Cactus Hotel, the Children's Art Museum features rotating exhibits that offer kids an imaginative and interactive learning experience. Adults are also welcome.

FORT CONCHO NATIONAL HISTORIC LANDMARK

213 E. Avenue D • 657-4441 or 657-4444 • Tuesday–Saturday
10–5 • Sunday 1–5 • Adults $1.50, students $1.25

Founded in late 1867, the fort was the focus of the region for almost a quarter of a century. At its height, it quartered eight companies, i.e., roughly 400 men and 50 officers. After the west was won, the Army deactivated the post (1889), but the fort lived on as civilian housing and through a variety of commercial uses.

Beginning in the late 1920s, efforts to preserve the fort began. The City of San Angelo now holds title to Fort Concho, which was designated a National Historic Landmark in 1961. Among its innovative uses is as a public school and as a meeting place for groups, special events, and even conventions. The post hospital building not only houses the Robert Wood Johnson Museum of Frontier Medicine but also the Fort Concho Elementary School library. Across the yard, fourth graders sit beneath portraits of Grant, Lincoln, and Washington and learn lessons from primers used over a century ago. The Fort Concho Museum emphasizes the frontier Indian Wars and the heritage of Tom Green County with photos, maps, sabers, personal effects, cannon, even military wagons and mule teams. Each building houses a different exhibit, and loyal San Angeloans get gussied up as infantrymen, cavalry soldiers, laundresses, and officers' wives to make the fort come alive.

SAN ANGELO MUSEUM OF FINE ARTS

Quartermaster Storehouse • Fort Concho National Historic
Landmark • 658-4084 • Tuesday–Saturday 10–4 • Sunday
1–4 • Admission • W+

Located in the second oldest building in San Angelo and adjacent to the Headquarters Building at Fort Concho, the museum displays changing exhibits ranging from local and area history to photography, painting, drawing, ceramics, and textiles.

DANNER MUSEUM OF TELEPHONY
Officers' Quarters #4 at Fort Concho • 653-0756
Tuesday–Saturday 10–5 • Sunday 1–5
Hundreds of antique phones and switchboards are displayed in four rooms of this renovated Fort Concho Officers' Quarters. Many date back to the nineteenth century including one of Alexander Graham Bell's original telephones and a Kellogg single-position manual magneto switchboard.

ROBERT WOOD JOHNSON MUSEUM OF FRONTIER MEDICINE
Post Hospital at Fort Concho • 657-4444
Tuesday–Saturday 10–5 • Sunday 1–5 • W
Housed in the old Post Hospital, the museum surveys nineteenth century medicine by exhibiting the surgical tools and equipment of frontier surgeons and physicians.

MISS HATTIE'S PARLOR AND MUSEUM
18 E. Concho Street • 658-3735
Monday–Saturday • Admission $2
This renovated bordello was a thriving San Angelo enterprise until its demise in 1946. One of the better anecdotes about Miss Hattie's was the tunnel that linked the San Angelo National Bank with her thriving enterprise. Used by the more circumspect clients, it was a banking service rarely mentioned in the annals of high finance. Miss Hattie's also had an elaborate network of escape routes, warning bells, and flashing lights for the inevitable raids by Texas Rangers, sheriff's deputies, and other wet rags. Complete with original furnishings, Miss Hattie's is a delightful stop in the middle of historic downtown San Angelo. Tours are offered twice daily, in the morning and in the afternoon. **Miss Hattie's Parlor,** specializing in lingerie, bath accessories, and other unique gifts, occupies the first floor of the building and serves as headquarters for tickets and tours.

HISTORIC PLACES

CONCHO STREET
Once upon a time, San Angelo was known as Santa Angela and Concho was Santa Angela's first street. Much of the charm and

stylish design is evident in the nineteenth-century buildings that line Block One and are full of antiques, collectibles, fashions, gifts, saddles, and spurs. Some, like Miss Hattie's (see above) are preserved intact. Pick up a copy of *A Historical Walking Tour of Downtown San Angelo* at the San Angelo Convention & Visitors Bureau for thumbnail sketches of over thirty buildings including many on Concho Street.

OTHER POINTS OF INTEREST

RIVER WALK

Downtown along the banks of the Concho River

Much as it brought settlers to San Angelo over a century ago, the Concho River draws locals and tourists to its banks. The city has taken to heart the preservation of this important artery and through the River Beautification Project has revitalized over four miles in and around the downtown district. The most recent addition enhances the Celebration Bridge area: a beautiful bronze mermaid, *Pearl of the Conchos*. Scores of improvements like fountains, benches, picnic tables, seesaws, and swings are all within walking distance of downtown, as is Santa Fe Park and Golf course. For a quick look at the River Walk, drive along winding West River Drive. The jogging-walking trail readily accommodates strolls of any length. Once summer comes round, people flock to events on or near the River Walk and River Plaza including the River Raft Races and Fiesta del Concho in June and the popular Fourth of July concert by the San Angelo Symphony.

CIVIC LEAGUE PARK

Bounded by Pecos, Beauregard, and Park streets

Both the Municipal Rose Garden and the International Water Lily Collection are worth visiting in themselves. Together they form an unforgettable oasis just west of downtown San Angelo on the far bank of the Concho River. Terraced gardens and gurgling fountains are surrounded by acres of prime picnicking, historic turn-of-the-century houses, and St. Paul Presbyterian Church. Another reason to visit: Where else can you mingle with Cary Grant, Judy Garland, Queen Elizabeth, Princess Margaret, and hundreds of other famous and not-so-famous roses? Visit from March through September to view the water lily collection which features day and night blooming varietals.

ANGELO STATE UNIVERSITY PLANETARIUM
Nursing-Physical Science Building • 942-2188 or 942-2136
Programs Thursday at 8 p.m. and Saturday at 2 p.m.
Adults $3, students/seniors/military $1.50 • W+

One of the largest in Texas and one of the most advanced in America, this planetarium utilizes laser discs to dazzle visitors with its multi-image capability. The combination of fantastic sights and stereo sounds makes travel to far-off galaxies or membership on an Apollo or Voyager mission an essential part of any visit to San Angelo. Open to the public during the school year, portions of the planetarium can be leased for private functions.

PRODUCER'S LIVESTOCK AUCTION
Auction Barn • 1131 N. Bell • 653-3371

Site of the nation's largest sheep auction each Tuesday. The cattle auction is held Thursdays and is among the largest in Texas.

GOODFELLOW AIR FORCE BASE
Fort McKavett Road • 657-3876 (Public Affairs)

San Angelo's largest employer. Intelligence training for all four branches of the armed services is provided at Goodfellow. A recent addition is the fire training facility which came on line in 1993. The Public Affairs Office handles tours.

LAKE NASWORTHY
Six miles from town on Knickerbocker Road (FM 584)
944-3812

Bounded by residences and lake houses, located within the city proper, and owned by the city, Nasworthy is the oldest of San Angelo's reservoirs. Sunny summer days, weekends, and holidays are busiest with ski boats, ski doos, and bass boats crowding the lake. Nasworthy's level stays constant by regulating water flow from Twin Buttes Reservoir. On shore, the **San Angelo Nature Center** (942-0121) offers natural science programs and a natural history museum featuring a library, a xeriscape garden, and special events.

LAKE E.V. SPENCE
40 miles north of San Angelo via Highways 208 and 158

The first reservoir along the lengthy Colorado River, fishermen prefer out-of-the-way E.V. Spence because of better pickings and smaller crowds.

LAKE O.H. IVIE
40 miles east of San Angelo via FM 765 and FM 2134
Slightly larger than Lake E.V. Spence, this more distant lake is also owned by the Colorado River Municipal Water District and is at the confluence of the Colorado and Concho rivers. Marinas and recreational facilities are under construction.

O.C. FISHER RESERVOIR
Three miles northwest of town via Mercedes Street • **949-4757**
O.C. Fisher dams the North Concho River and prevents any future floods by a river that has twice ravaged the city. In addition to good fishing, facilities for camping, boating, swimming, horseback riding, bicycling, jogging, and hiking are available.

TWIN BUTTES RESERVOIR
Five miles west of town via US Highway 67 • **944-3812**
Whereas O.C. Fisher dams the North Concho, Twin Buttes dams the Middle and South forks of the Concho. The reservoir is actually two lakes connected by an equalization channel. Most activities—fishing, swimming, and camping—take place around the easier to reach north body of water.

SPORTS AND ACTIVITIES

Amusement Parks

NEFF'S AMUSEMENT PARK
River Park Mall • **653-3014**
Open during the summer only after 6:30 p.m. on weekdays and 1:30 p.m. on weekends • **Admission**
Located right along the Concho River in front of Celebration Bridge, Neff's has fun-filled rides and a mint condition merry-go-round that dates back several generations.

Fishing
There is more fishing around San Angelo than anywhere else in West Texas. Some of these lakes are even within the city limits (see **OTHER POINTS OF INTEREST** above). Choose **Nasworthy** for largemouth and white bass, channel, blue, and flathead catfish, white crappie, freshwater red drum, and redfish. Head to **O.C. Fisher** for largemouth bass, white crappie, white bass, channel, blue, and flathead catfish, and walleye. **Twin Buttes** offers

largemouth and smallmouth bass, white bass, crappie, channel, blue, and flathead catfish. Drive out to **E.V. Spence** for largemouth, smallmouth, striped, and white bass, crappie, channel, blue, and Flathead catfish. **O.H. Ivie** has largemouth and white bass, crappie, channel, blue, and flathead catfish, and walleye.

Golf

LAKESIDE GOLF COURSE
Mathis Field • 949-2069
Nine-hole course • Weekdays and weekends: $3.25

RIVERSIDE GOLF COURSE
900 W. 29th • 653-6130
Eighteen-hole course • Weekdays: $9 • Weekends: $12

SANTA FE GOLF COURSE
Santa Fe Park • 657-4485
Nine-hole course • Weekdays: $6 • Weekends: $7.50

Hunting

Tom Green County offers excellent white-tailed deer, pronghorn antelope, javelina, turkey, and quail hunting. The turkey hunting is some of the best in the state. Contact the visitor bureau at 800-375-1206 for details on hunting leases and outfitters.

COLLEGES AND UNIVERSITIES

ANGELO STATE UNIVERSITY
2601 W. Avenue N. • 942-2211
Recognized as one of the top ten "Up and Coming" regional universities in America as well as one of the top three state-supported regional universities in Texas (*U.S. News and World Report*), ASU joins with three other institutions to form the Texas State University System: Sam Houston (Huntsville), Stephen F. Austin (Nacogdoches), and Sul Ross (Alpine). With an enrollment of slightly more than six thousand, Angelo State offers 44 baccalaureate and 19 master degree programs. Situated north of Red Arroyo and close to the Concho River, new buildings and recent renovations dot the attractive campus, which is ideal for strolls, constitutionals, and jogs of any length. A distinctive aspect to the ASU experience is the Carr Academic Scholarship Program,

whose grants make high quality education more affordable for nearly 900 undergraduates and graduate students. On-campus activities include the University Planetarium (see **OTHER POINTS OF INTEREST**) and the home stands of numerous ASU Ram teams. Women's volleyball produces consistent Lone Star Conference champions while the ASU football team boasts the winningest record among Texas senior colleges during the 1980s (73-35-1) and a NAIA national championship (1978). Now a NCAA Division II member, the Rams have earned a spot in the top twenty rankings each year since the mid-1980s.

PERFORMING ARTS

The San Angelo Cultural Affairs Council sponsors a 24-hour telephone hotline featuring updates on the arts: 653-6793.

RIVER STAGE

By the Celebration Bridge • 657-4451 (Rec Dept.)

What seems like all of San Angelo can often be found along the banks of the Concho for a concert, melodrama, or musical at the River Stage. This outdoor facility showcases San Angelo's River Walk, and stands before open seats on blankets and occasionally under the stars.

SAN ANGELO CITY AUDITORIUM

West College Avenue at City Hall • 653-9577

The site of performances by the San Angelo Symphony and by the San Angelo Civic Ballet including an annual *The Nutcracker*.

SAN ANGELO COLISEUM

43rd and Coliseum Dr. • 653-9577 • W+ but not all areas

Home of the annual San Angelo Stock Show and Rodeo, the Coliseum is also a popular venue for events like the San Angelo Symphony Pops Concert and performances by entertainers like George Strait, Reba McEntire, T. Graham Brown, and Garth Brooks.

SAN ANGELO SYMPHONY

111 W. Twohig Avenue • 658-5877

Performances by the symphony are frequently in conjunction with the Ballet and the Chorale. The symphony also presents the prestigious Hemphill-Wells Sorantin Competition.

SHOPPING

BART MANN JEWELERS
105 S. Irving • 653-2902
Monday–Saturday 9:30 a.m. to 5:15 p.m.
The true home of the Concho Pearl is the lakes and streams around San Angelo, but this downtown shop has the best selection of native pearls in San Angelo. From pink to purple, in earrings, necklaces, rings, and studs, these freshwater pearls are elegantly set in tasteful designs. Many other jewelry items are also available.

CHICKEN FARM ART CENTER
2505 Martin Luther King Blvd. • 653-4936
Tuesday–Saturday 10–5 • W variable
You don't have to shop to enjoy this converted chicken farm. The art center now houses studios for local artists and artisans and also has a gallery, a bronze casting foundry, and learning facilities. Media include blacksmithing, metalsmithing, woodwork, fine and folk art, stained glass, pottery, weaving, sculpture, and painting. The gallery is open to the public, and much of the creative process (including the foundry) can be viewed.

R.E. DONAHO SADDLE SHOP
8 East Concho • 655-3270
Founded in the same location over a century ago, Donaho's was originally established as the Concho Saddle Shop in 1890. The operation is renowned for crafting the legendary Concho Saddle. Rector Story, son-in-law of the late Bob Donaho, has been behind the counter since 1938. If your mount doesn't need a new saddle, consider a Donaho belt, billfold, purse, or notebook.

EGGEMEYER'S GENERAL STORE
35 East Concho • 655-1166
Monday–Saturday 10–5:30 • Closed Sunday
Many patrons remember the old location next to Miss Hattie's, and the recent move across the street has only improved the cozy atmosphere, the delicious smells, and the many gift items. Designers like James Avery and Jeep Collins are featured next to spiral-sliced hams, Texas honey, jams, jellies, and gourmet coffees. Enjoy a nickel cup of coffee as you browse among the many children's items: games, toys, dolls, soldiers, and books. Eggemeyer's almost bursts with seasonal items around Easter, Halloween, Thanksgiving, and Christmas.

RUSTY FRANKLIN HANDMADE BOOT CO.

3725 Arden Road • 653-2668
Monday–Friday 8:30–5 (later if you call)
Rusty Franklin hails from the great bootmaking tradition of M.L. Leddy (his grandfather). A good portion of his 40-plus years have been spent working at a Leddy shop and, since 1986, at his own. Working cowboys, ranchers, and others looking for a rugged, comfortable boot buy Rusty's either off the shelf (prices start at $350) or custom made (prices start at $425). Allow 60 to 120 days for delivery on a custom pair. John Connally did. So did Henry Kissinger, Marcel Marceau, and Tommy Lee Jones (three times). On a local note, prosecutors linked all three defendants in the Agscam case—Mort Mertz, Wally McGowan, and Mo Morrow—by their Rusty Franklin boots. If you can't stop by, call for a brochure.

J. WILDE'S

15 E. Concho • 655-0878 • Monday–Saturday 10:30–5:30
You may already know the J. Wilde label from clothes and accessories at the Apparel and Gift Markets in Dallas. This downtown San Angelo store is the home of those creative designs and a colorful stop on any trip. Clothes, furnishings, decorator fabrics, and accessories are piled on floors and furniture throughout this wonderful shop right in the heart of Concho Street. Retail isn't the only trade; the J. Wilde touch has brightened homes and offices across Texas.

SIDE TRIPS

PAINT ROCK PICTOGRAPHS

30 miles east of San Angelo on RR 380 and one mile northwest of the town of Paint Rock on U.S. 83 • **732-4376 or 732-4418**
Call for an appointment • Admission: Adults $6, children $3
Freshwater springs and abundant game made this area a perennial camp for generations of native Americans. Comanche, Apache, Jumano, and Tonkawa decorated this one-eighth of a mile stretch of limestone cliffs with images of their enemies, their gods, their council meetings, and early Spanish missions at this nationally renowned site. Guides offer insightful explanations to the pictographs (rock paintings) whenever possible and also discuss painting techniques, Indian and settler history, and the commitment of the Sims and Campbell families to preserving this American treasure. Budget roughly two hours per tour unless

you take the longer barge trip up the Concho River on summer weekends. All tours are guided and need to be scheduled through Paint Rock Excursions. Groups meet and depart from the Paint Rock Excursions office on US 83 in the town of Paint Rock. If you arrive early, have a look at the handsome Concho County Courthouse (1886), which was partially constructed with limestone from the cliff location. Paint Rock is prime wool and mohair country, and **Ingrid's Custom Hand-Woven Rugs (800-752-8004)** offers an excellent selection of inexpensively priced items. On your way back to San Angelo, consider stopping in at the **Lowake Steak House** (see **RESTAURANTS**).

US 67 WEST

From the Red River to the Río Grande, US 67 meanders over 700 miles from the Arkansas state line clear to Chihuahua. Though sparsely populated, the 160-mile portion west of San Angelo to Fort Stockton covers some of the most historic sites in Texas history.

Twenty-four miles west of San Angelo, **Mertzon** is the county seat of Irion County. Generations of Kickapoo, Comanche, and Apache hunted these rolling hills and gurgling streams. Over a century has passed since a five-hour battle with Kickapoo tribesmen left 22 Confederates and Texans dead and 19 wounded at nearby Dove Creek (1865). Slow down to go antique shopping at the Treasure Chest (directly across from the C&W convenience store on the right as you come into town), to buy native plants from Steve and Valerie Lewis (up the block from the First National Bank of Mertzon on your left), or to stock your larder at Nicholson's Meat Company on US 67 with teriyaki, *jalapeño*, or regular beef jerky and beef sticks. Irion County's first courthouse (1899) and cemetery are a pleasant two-mile detour to **Sherwood,** a mile back toward San Angelo and another mile west on RR 72.

Seventy miles west of San Angelo stands the largest dry lake in Texas, 1½ miles south of **Big Lake.** Less ironically and more importantly, **Santa Rita No. 1** lies 13 miles farther west (83 miles From San Angelo) surrounded by acres of pump jacks and scores of No Trespassing signs. This discovery well rivals Spindletop and Daisy Bradford No. 3 in Texas lore. Plenty of signs and historical markers highlight the hallowed ground that brought in the Big Lake Field, led to the development of the Permian Basin (the world's largest inland petrochemical complex), and made the University of Texas and the Texas A&M systems among the nation's wealthiest. Long ago the original rig was dismantled and reassembled in Austin at the corner of Trinity and Martin Luther King, Jr.

McCamey is almost 120 miles west of San Angelo; **Girvin** is a dozen miles farther. Zane Grey aficionados know this country by heart: **Castle Gap** and the ford at **Horsehead Crossing,** milestones in American history, are local landmarks. For thousands of nineteenth century pioneers, Castle Gap was the Western equivalent of Daniel Boone's Wilderness Road through the Cumberland Gap. Forty-niners, the Butterfield Overland Mail, and trail driver Charles Goodnight are a few of the many who followed this native American trail through the distinctive mesa formation and down to the Pecos River, site of Horsehead Crossing. This ford across the treacherous Pecos was littered with the skulls and skeletons of hundreds of horses (and cattle) stolen in Mexico by Comanche raiders, herded across miles of dry desert only to die at the river's edge, too parched to stop drinking. Learn more about both sites and obtain specific directions to Horsehead Crossing (Castle Gap is on private property) at the **Mendoza Trail Museum** in McCamey at Santa Fe Park, Tuesday through Friday from 1:00 to 5:30 p.m. Also available at Santa Fe Park are free RV parking, picnicking, and camping courtesy of the McCamey Chamber of Commerce.

ANNUAL EVENTS

April

SABERS, SADDLES, & SPURS

Fort Concho National Historic Landmark • 657-4441

Beginning with the opening ceremony, which is led by living history riders from Fort Concho, this event is an equine enthusiast's dream. Riding demonstrations and special drills are staged by the San Angelo Saddle Club and the Tom Green County Sheriff's Posse. Some of the events that fill the rest of the day include period drills by the Fort Concho Cavalry, cowboy polo, skill riding, and sidesaddle riding. The American Horse and Cavalry Review ends with a grand closing ceremony featuring show jumpers, Tennessee Walkers, and Paso Finos.

POLO IN THE PARK

Hoolihan Acres • *One mile east of Mertzon on US 67*
949-4837 • Last Sunday of the month • Admission • W

Journey out to Mertzon for an afternoon fundraiser to benefit Sonrisas, a therapeutic riding program. Polo matches feature local, professional, and celebrity polo players. An awards ceremony, auction, and party follow.

June

FIESTA DEL CONCHO

Fort Concho and along the Concho River • 657-4441
Third weekend of the month • Admission varies • W

Concho River activities include river barge rides and the river parade Saturday night. In and around San Angelo enjoy western dances, arts and crafts, plenty of music, and Frontier Day at Fort Concho (an event in itself).

December

CHRISTMAS AT OLD FORT CONCHO

Fort Concho National Historic Landmark
First weekend of the month • Admission

Lasting all weekend, this event features more than just hundreds of booths and tasty concessions. Fort Concho serves as the backdrop while entertainers and volunteers perform traditional holiday stories and reenact nineteenth-century military and civilian life. Different buildings host different themes like Victorian House, Czech Christmas House, German House, and Mexican/Southwest House. Cowboy poets, campfires, cavalry demonstrations, and wagon rides run all week long during this unique San Angelo tradition. A shuttle bus runs from the San Angelo Convention Center parking lot for Fort Concho every 20 minutes Friday, Saturday, and Sunday.

RESTAURANTS

($ = Under $7.50, $$ = Under $15, $$$ = $15+ plus tax & tip)

No mention of dining in San Angelo is complete without paying homage to John Zentner (1899-1994). The son of a German immigrant, he was raised near Rowena and went on to found restaurants as far south as Del Rio and north to Abilene. Without peer in West Texas, his signature was superb cuts of beef served in Texas-sized portions. His legacy is a string of renowned steak houses including two of the state's best known—the Lowake Inn and the Lowake Steak House. Even well into his nineties, he was a part of the daily operation of Zentner's Daughter Steak House on Knickerbocker Road.

CHINA GARDEN

4217 College Hills Blvd. at Loop 306 • 949-2838
Daily • **Lunch and dinner** • **$–$$** • **Cr** • **W+**

Ask any San Angeloan about China Garden and he'll mention Favorites like Willow Beef, the shrimp plates, and the Pu Pu Platter. By far the most popular choice for lunch is the buffet during the week ($) and on Sunday ($$). From the bar, consider a Suffering Bastard but beware of the Tiki Punch. It's as potent as it is easy to down. Bar.

CONCHO PEARL and RAPHAEL TUCK & SONS OLD ENGLISH PUB

2400 College Hills Blvd. (Park 2400 Shopping Center)
949-5161 • **Lunch daily except Sunday** • **Dinner Thursday, Friday, and Saturday** • **$–$$** • **Cr** • **W+**

Given San Angelo's reputation for sheep production, it's a surprise that few restaurants serve lamb. A notable exception is the Concho Pearl, whose rack of lamb and lamb chops are in a class by themselves. The extensive wine list, featuring mature Bordeaux and Cabernets, complements any entrée selection. Next door, Raphael Tuck & Sons Old English Pub serves Guinness Stout and other fine imports in a sophisticated setting replete with Tuck family mementos dating back to the nineteenth century. Stop by Saturdays for Pint Night featuring specials on beer by the pint. Bar.

DUN BAR EAST RESTAURANT

1728 Pulliam • **655-8780**
Daily • **Breakfast, lunch, and dinner** • **$–$$** • **AE D MC V** • **W**

Staffed by hard-charging waitresses serving generous portions hot from the kitchen, the Dun Bar East is nothing fancy and that's probably why it's packed from dawn to dusk. High marks for the T-Bone and the filet. Sandwiches and burgers for the kids. Onion rings and/or an order of hot rolls is mandatory. Beer and wine.

LOWAKE STEAK HOUSE

Take Highway 67 (the Ballinger Highway) 27 miles north through Miles • *Just before Rowena, turn right on FM 381 and go 6 miles* • **Lowake** • **442-2301** • **Tuesday–Sunday lunch and dinner** • **$–$$** • **MC V**

Seafood, chicken, and sandwiches are listed on the menu but most patrons skip the small talk and order beef: T-Bones, ribeyes, filets, clubs, and K.C. for 7 ($87.50). Pass on the french fries and order a baked potato. Even better, get the onion rings. All entrées come with a trip to the salad bar and plenty of Texas toast. Beer and wine coolers.

MEJOR QUE NADA

1911 S. Bryant Blvd. • **655-3553** • **Monday–Saturday**
Lunch and dinner • **$–$$** • **AE D MC V** • **W**
   What began as breakfast *burritos* several years ago has turned
into San Angelo's most popular Mexican restaurant with all the
style, presentation, and service one expects in San Antonio but
not the high prices. Savor the *fajitas*, the steak *á la mexicana*, and
any of the delicious *enchiladas*—beef, cheese, chicken, or shrimp.
Mejor Que Nada is worth a visit just for their house *margarita*,
made with Gran Marnier and Cuervo Gold. Bar.

THE SPAGHETTI WESTERN ITALIAN GRILL

26 E. Concho • **653-1300**
Lunch 11–2 • **Dinner 5–9** • **Happy hour 4–7**
   Located in the old San Angelo National Bank Building. Generations of San Angeloans have ventured this way for good times
(there used to be an underground passageway from the old bank
to Miss Hattie's). Cold beer, live entertainment, and 1,800 margaritas keep the crowds coming—college kids, yuppies, rednecks,
even an occasional cowgirl or two. Plenty of space for dining. The
Italian kitchen serves it up chicken-fried, Italian-fried, or scampi-
style (with a marinara sauce). Bar.

TASTE OF ITALY

3520 Knickerbocker Rd. • **944-3290**
Daily except Sunday • **Lunch and dinner** • **$–$$** • **AE D
MC V**
   Contrary to popular opinion, good Italian cooking can be
found in the Concho Valley. At Taste of Italy, veal and chicken are
the forte. The *parmigiana*, the *piccata*, and the *marsala* are equally
popular. Skip your normal bar order and consider the extensive
wine cellar stocked with chardonnays, merlots, cabernets, and
Italian varietals. Bar.

ZENTNER'S DAUGHTER STEAK HOUSE

1901 Knickerbocker Rd. • **949-2821**
Daily • **Lunch and dinner** • **$–$$** • **AE D DC MC V** • **W**
   With locations in San Angelo (right across from Bobcat Stadium) and Abilene, Zentner's Daughter Steak Houses are testimo-
ny to the Zentner tradition. The K.C. Steak for Two easily feeds
four ($$$). Two tenderloins are required to serve an order of Ten-
ders ($$), the tenderloin on the eye of the T-Bone. And the one-
pound burgers ($) are ground from trimmings off the loins
butchered by the restaurant's staff. Bar.

ZENTNER'S STEAK HOUSE
2715 Sherwood Way • 942-8631
Daily • Lunch and dinner • $–$$ • Cr
Open the door to Zentner's and you're greeted by autographed photos of Garth Brooks, Randy Travis, Alan Jackson, the Judds, and Reba McEntire. Founded by one of the many Zentners in the restaurant industry locally, Zentner's features excellent cuts of beef and an award-winning chicken-fried steak. Bar.

CLUBS AND BARS

MAXX 2000
3520 Knickerbocker Rd. • 949-6766 or 942-9456 (Event Line)
Monday–Saturday till 2 a.m.
College students and the just-out-of-school crowd pack this popular club. Daily drink specials, buffets, and occasional cash prizes or gift certificates combine with plenty of top 40, rock & roll, techno, and progressive selections to keep the dance floor full and waitresses hopping. Tough on underage drinkers.

ACCOMMODATIONS

($ = Under $40, $$ = $40–$75, $$$ = $75–$100, $$$$ = Over $100)
Room Tax 13%

LA QUINTA INN
2307 Loop 306 • 949-0515 or 800-531-5900 • $$
This two-story inn located a mile west of Angelo State University has 170 units, including suites and non-smoking rooms, with cable TV (Showtime) and room phones (free local calls). Amenities include complimentary continental breakfast from 6:30 to 10 a.m., free coffee in the lobby, and an adjacent Cafe La Quinta which also provides room service. Right off Loop 306 at the Knickerbocker exit, half a dozen different restaurants are within a couple of miles. On the premises are an outdoor unheated pool and hot tub, a laundry room, a 24-hour courtesy shuttle to and from Mathis Airport, and free parking. Smaller pets, under 25 pounds, welcome. AAA, AARP, government and military rates available.

OLE COACH MOTOR INN
4205 S. Bryant • 653-6966 • $
This two-story property has 82 smoking and non-smoking units. Rooms include cable TV (HBO) and phones with no charge

for local calls. Amenities include complimentary coffee in the lobby, the Coachmen Club, an outdoor unheated pool, and free parking. Pets under 20 pounds OK. AAA, AARP, corporate, government, military rates available.

RAMADA INN

2502 Loop 306 • 944-2578 or 800-272-6232 • $$

This two-story red brick Ramada sits off Loop 306 at the Knickerbocker exit. The 101 rooms, including suites and non-smoking rooms, have cable TV and room phones (free local calls). Amenities include the Little River Cafe and Club, an outdoor heated pool and hot tub, an exercise room, courtesy van to Mathis Airport (limited hours), and free parking. No pets.

SONORA

SUTTON COUNTY SEAT ★ 3,320 ★ (915)

A prosperous town at the western edge of the Edwards Plateau, Sonora serves as a hub for wool and mohair producers and for natural gas exploration and production. Established near plentiful Indian springs in the late nineteenth century, Sutton County is also the site of one of America's best caving experiences and draws visitors from around the globe to tour the Caverns of Sonora.

TOURIST SERVICES

SONORA CHAMBER OF COMMERCE

706 Southwest Crockett • Sonora • 76950 • 387-2880

Besides plenty of information and assistance, the chamber is your best contact for white-tailed deer hunting in this area.

HISTORIC PLACES

SUTTON COUNTY COURTHOUSE

Water Avenue and Oak Street • 387-2711 • W

Noted Texas architect Oscar Ruffini designed the Sutton County Courthouse which was completed in 1891. The heart of the Sutton County is still courthouse square. As you park on its south side, note the markers recognizing families who pioneered this wilderness in the late 1800s and early 1900s. Information on a self-guided walking tour is available in the courthouse and includes the restored Santa Fe Depot, the Miers Home Museum (1889), and a marker for the Frisco Trailway, a one-of-a-kind right-of-way owned by the Fort Worth and Rio Grande Railroad that extended *100 miles* from Sonora to Brady. This right-of-way, 250 feet wide, was the world's longest fenced cattle trail until trucking became more economical.

SHOPPING

OL' SONORA TRADING COMPANY
Exit 400 off I-10 • South one block
387-5507 or 800-852-2784

Sutton County is located in the heart of the largest mohair producing area in America. Stretching from San Antonio to Fort Stockton, this belt accounts for 92% of America's mohair—the fine, silky fiber sheared from Angora goats. Ol' Sonora Trading Company stocks an assortment of attractive mohair sweaters, jackets, throws, blankets, even socks featuring this lightweight, durable fiber—warmer than wool at a third of the weight.

SIDE TRIPS

CAVERNS OF SONORA
Exit 392 off I-10 seven miles west of Sonora and follow the signs along FM 1989 south approximately eight miles
387-6507 • Open daily except Christmas • Admission varies per tour • Snack Bar • Picnic Area • Gift shop

The best description of this geological landmark comes from Bill Stephenson, a former president of the American Speleogical Society, who says, "This is the most indescribably beautiful cavern in the world. Its beauty can't possibly be exaggerated—even by Texans." What makes the Caverns of Sonora so remarkable is the number and quality of helictites. More have been identified at the Caverns of Sonora than in all caverns worldwide. Helictites emerge from cave walls to form loops, horseshoes, and elk's horns, and the most distinct form is the butterfly formation. Several tours are offered. The Crystal Palace Tour is a 45-minute walk, the Horseshoe Lake Tour takes about an hour and fifteen minutes, and both are combined in the Adventure Package which runs 2½ hours. Special photographic and geological tours are available by reservation only. The temperature in the Caverns is a steady 71 degrees, and the humidity is 98 percent. Members of your party can also follow the above-ground Nature Trail that traces the subterranean tours on paths hundreds of feet above the caverns.

RESTAURANTS

($ = Under $7.50, $$ = Under $15, $$$ = $15+ plus tax & tip)

COMMERCIAL CAFE

167 SW Plum • 387-9928 • Monday–Saturday
Lunch and dinner • $ • Out-of-town checks with driver's license • BYOB

For three generations and nearly three-quarters of a century, the Commercial Cafe has been a Sonora landmark. Lemuel Lopez, the cafe's proprietor and mayor of Sonora, maintains that the cheese *enchiladas* are as good today as when his grandparents served them. One reason why is because the red sauce is still made without chile powder. Though Mexican plates are the specialty, the chicken-fried steak is a treat. Located in the heart of town away from the interstate, take the Highway 277 exit (#400) to the first stop light, then a right onto Main Street, the first left (Glasscock), and go two blocks to Plum. If you're planning on enjoying a cold one with your meal, stop at one of the convenience stores on your way there. No alcohol is served.

SUTTON COUNTY STEAKHOUSE

I-10 Exit 400 • 387-3833
Monday–Saturday breakfast, lunch, and dinner
Sunday breakfast and lunch • $–$$ • AE MC V • W

Service is prompt, portions are large, prices are reasonable. Try the steak bits. Cubed and then cooked to order, they're delicious. Most entrées come with a monstrous baked potato, soup or salad bar. Bar.

ACCOMMODATIONS

($ = Under $40, $$ = $40–$75, $$$ = $75–$100, $$$$ = Over $100)

DEVIL'S RIVER INN
I-10 Exit 400 • 387-3516 • $$
This two-story motel sits right beside I-10 and right next to the Sutton County Steakhouse. With 99 rooms including non-smoking ones, it has cable TV (HBO) and free local calls. Amenities include free coffee, an outdoor unheated pool, and laundry. Pets OK. AAA and AARP discounts available.

You can judge a visit to West Texas by many criteria: sights seen, vistas viewed, miles logged, empties on the floorboard. Consider your trip a success if you take home even an inkling of why this land and its inhabitants—past and present—epitomize what people worldwide imagine exists when the word "Texas" is mentioned.

Index